Homemaking in the Russian-speaking Diaspora

Russian Language and Society Series

Series Editor: Lara Ryazanova-Clarke, University of Edinburgh
This series of academic monographs and edited volumes consists of important scholarly accounts of interrelationships between Russian language and society, and aims to foster an opinion-shaping 'linguistic turn' in the international scholarly debate within Russian Studies, and to develop new sociolinguistic and linguo-cultural perspectives on Russian. The series embraces a broad scope of approaches including those advanced in sociolinguistics, rhetoric, critical linguistics, (critical) discourse analysis, linguistic anthropology, politics of language, language policy, and related and interdisciplinary areas.

Series Editor
Lara Ryazanova-Clarke is Professor of Russian and Sociolinguistics at the University of Edinburgh.

Editorial Board
Professor Lenore Grenoble (University of Chicago)
Professor John Joseph (University of Edinburgh)
Professor Aneta Pavlenko (University of Oslo)
Professor Vladimir Plungian (Institute of Russian Language/Institute of Linguistics, Russian Academy of Sciences)
Professor Patrick Seriot (Université de Lausanne)
Dr Alexei Yurchak (University of California, Berkeley)

Titles available in the series
The Russian Language Outside the Nation, ed. Lara Ryazanova-Clarke
Discourses of Regulation and Resistance: Censoring Translation in the Stalin and Khrushchev Era Soviet Union, Samantha Sherry
French and Russian in Imperial Russia: Language Use among the Russian Elite, ed. Derek Offord, Lara Ryazanova-Clarke, Vladislav Rjéoutski and Gesine Argent
French and Russian in Imperial Russia: Language Attitudes and Identity, ed. Derek Offord, Lara Ryazanova-Clarke, Vladislav Rjéoutski and Gesine Argent
Russian Speakers in Post-Soviet Latvia, Ammon Cheskin
Public Debate in Russia: Matters of (Dis)order, Nikolai Vakhtin and Boris Firsov
Language on Display: Writers, Fiction and Linguistic Culture in Post-Soviet Russia, Ingunn Lunde
Politics of the Russian Language Beyond Russia, ed. Christian Noack
Homemaking in the Russian-speaking Diaspora: Material Culture, Language and Identity, ed. Maria Yelenevskaya and Ekaterina Protassova

Visit the Russian Language and Society website at
www.edinburghuniversitypress.com/series/RLAS

Homemaking in the Russian-speaking Diaspora
Material Culture, Language and Identity

Edited by Maria Yelenevskaya and Ekaterina Protassova

Edinburgh University Press is one of the leading university presses in the UK. We publish academic books and journals in our selected subject areas across the humanities and social sciences, combining cutting-edge scholarship with high editorial and production values to produce academic works of lasting importance. For more information visit our website: edinburghuniversitypress.com

© editorial matter and organisation Maria Yelenevskaya and Ekaterina Protassova, 2023, 2024
© the chapters their several authors, 2023, 2024

Edinburgh University Press Ltd
13 Infirmary Street
Edinburgh EH1 1LT

First published in hardback by Edinburgh University Press 2023

Typeset in 11/13pt Monotype Ehrhardt
by Cheshire Typesetting Ltd, Cuddington, Cheshire

A CIP record for this book is available from the British Library

ISBN 978-1-4744-9449-6 (hardback)
ISBN 978-1-4744-9450-2 (paperback)
ISBN 978-1-4744-9451-9 (webready PDF)
ISBN 978-1-4744-9452-6 (epub)

The right of Maria Yelenevskaya and Ekaterina Protassova to be identified as the editors of this work has been asserted in accordance with the Copyright, Designs and Patents Act 1988, and the Copyright and Related Rights Regulations 2003 (SI No. 2498).

Contents

List of Figures and Tables vii
List of Contributors xi
Acknowledgements xv

    Introduction: Images of Home away from Home   1
    Maria Yelenevskaya and Ekaterina Protassova

1. Constructing Home away from Home: The Case of the Interwar Russian Refugees and the Post-Soviet Migrants in Greece   20
   Kira Kaurinkoski

2. Russian Objects and Russian Homes: A Sociological Reflection on Homes and Migration   43
   Anna Pechurina

3. 'Material Stories' and Cross-referencing: Experiences of Home and Migration among Women from Russia Living in Japan   63
   Ksenia Golovina

4. The Role of Material Objects in the Home Interiors of Russian Speakers in Finland   78
   Ekaterina Protassova and Kirill Reznik

5. The Role of Possessions in Adaptation to a New Life   97
   Marika Kalyuga

6. The Hollywood *Kazwup*: Historic Russian Restaurants in Los Angeles, 1918–1989   119
   Sasha Razor

7. Language as a Home Tradition: Linguistic Practices of the Russian Community in San Javier, Uruguay   140
Gleb Pilipenko

8. The Russian-Israeli Home: A Blend of Cultures   164
Maria Yelenevskaya

9. Russian-speaking Immigrant Women in Turkey: Histories of Moving 'Homes' and 'Homelands'   187
Liaisan Şahin

10. A Journey to a New Home: Language, Identity and Material Culture   209
Larissa Aronin

Index   230

Figures and Tables

FIGURES

Figure 1.1 Queen Olga of Greece after the church service at the Holy Trinity Church in Athens. © https://bigolive.wordpress.com/2015/12/17/the-russian-church-of-athens/ — 25

Figure 1.2 Exterior view of the Church of the Holy Trinity in Athens, also known as the Church of the Saviouress of Lykodemos or simply the 'Russian Church'. © https://bigolive.wordpress.com/2015/12/17/the-russian-church-of-athens/ — 26

Figure 1.3 Ahead of the municipal elections in 2004, Pontic Greek 'return' migrants who arrived in Greece in the 1960s visit a house of more recent 'return' migrants, who have come to Greece in the early 1990s. Tea is served from cups that have been made in the Soviet Union. Menidi, Greater Athens, 2004. © Kira Kaurinkoski — 32

Figure 1.4 Soviet Greek 'return' migrants in Menidi: a moment of female sociability. Menidi, Greater Athens, 2002. © Kira Kaurinkoski — 32

Figure 1.5 Mother's Day concert at the Embassy of Ukraine, organised by the Ukrainian community in Athens. The participants, mostly independent female labour migrants, listen attentively to the choir, the speeches and the testimonies of Ukrainian women who have worked as volunteers in Eastern Ukraine. Athens, 2015. © Kira Kaurinkoski — 35

Figures 2.1 and 2.2 My grandmother's arithmometer photographed in my current home in Sweden © Anna Pechurina — 47

Figure 2.3 My diasporic object: an old matryoshka doll which I bought in one of the charity shops in the UK after eleven years of living there. © Anna Pechurina — 52

Figure 3.1 Tonya's kettle. © Ksenia Golovina — 65

Figure 3.2 A deserted *danchi* building nearby Natalia's apartment in Tokyo. © Ksenia Golovina — 73

Figure 4.1 Icons and old books in the homes of the 'Old Russians' in Finland. © Kirill Reznik — 80

Figure 4.2 Balalaika, realistic paintings and photographs in the homes of the 'Old Russians'. © Kirill Reznik — 82

Figure 4.3 Gzhel and Khokhloma ware, dictionaries and books, portraits of Sergei Yesenin and Alexander Pushkin. Photographs by the owners of the objects. — 83

Figure 4.4 Souvenirs from Russia and bookshelves. Photographs by the owners of the objects. — 84

Figure 4.5 A decorated Christmas tree, Old New Year tree decorations and an old suitcase. © Valentina Kurikka and Ekaterina Protassova — 91

Figure 5.1 Madonna china sets. — 102

Figure 5.2 A fur coat (*shuba*). — 105

Figure 5.3 A dish for jellied meat. — 108

Figure 5.4 A garlic press. — 108

Figure 5.5 Tea towels. — 109

Figure 5.6 A travel iron. — 109

Figure 5.7 A landscape. — 113

Figure 5.8 A landscape. — 114

Figure 6.1 Ivan Lebedeff and Norma Boleslavsky with an artefact from the collection of Dr Armand Hammer, on exhibition at Bullock's Wilshire, Los Angeles, 1932. — 120

Figure 6.2 De Bluhmental-Russian Tea House. Slavic Handicraft Center, 135 North Euclid Avenue, Pasadena, 1920. — 121

Figure 6.3 Poster for *The Midnight Sun* (1926). — 125

Figure 6.4 Poster for *Stenka Razin, Life of Brigands from the Lower Reaches* (1908). — 126

Figure 6.5 Postcard image of the Ship Cafe, Venice, California (c. 1920s). — 126

Figure 6.6 Katinka Russian Restaurant on Beverly Boulevard (c. 1939). — 128

Figure 6.7 Prince Michael Romanoff, popular Hollywood pretender to Russian royal blood, Los Angeles, 1934. — 129

Figure 6.8 Postcard of Bublichki Russian Café (c. 1940s). — 131

Figure 6.9 Commercial advertisements for Kavkaz and

Mischa's restaurants in Los Angeles Russian press, from the mid-1960s to the mid-1980s. 133

Figure 6.10 Scene from *Anastasia* (1956), directed by Anatole Litvak. Commercial advertisement for Violet's restaurant in *Soglasie* magazine, 1986. 136

Figure 7.1 Fields of sunflowers in the vicinity of San Javier. © Gleb Pilipenko 142

Figure 7.2 The Pobieda ('Victory') cinema in San Javier. © Gleb Pilipenko 144

Figure 7.3 A banner in four languages at the entrance to San Javier. © Gleb Pilipenko 145

Figure 7.4 Ivan Voronin's passport. © Gleb Pilipenko 158

Figure 7.5 Embroidered towel in the house of P.M. © Gleb Pilipenko 159

Figure 8.1 In some homes painted wooden spoons and Khokhloma dishes, Gzhel cups and Palekh boxes are on display as decorative objects, but in others they are dismissed as part of the past and hidden away in cupboards. 169

Figure 8.2 A legendary tin opener. 174

Figure 8.3 Calendars, notes, photographs of memorable events, children's drawings and telephones of 'husbands for an hour' turn refrigerators into communicative spaces *par excellence*. 181

Figure 8.4 Multilingualism in Russian-speaking Israeli homes starts early. Parents and grandparents read Russian books to the children. Pre-schoolers learn to read in Hebrew, and in the first to fourth grade of the elementary school English is also added to the mix. Most likely, when playing with this *Ivanushka* doll, its owner resorts to translanguaging, imitating everyday communication in the family. 182

Figure 9.1 Ethnic items used in kitchens for practical and decorative purposes. 202

Figure 9.2 Some cultural artefacts are used purely for decoration (amber panel pictures, painted trays, etc.). Some are used as visual aids in teaching Russian or Tatar languages (matryoshkas, souvenir dolls and other ethnic items). A photograph of the owner's home village is an object endowed with an emotional meaning. 203

Figure 9.3 Items displayed in the workplace and at home for the purpose of ethnic representation: flags, albums, books, magazines, paintings, photographs, decorative dishes, ethnic handicrafts and tea sets. 204

Figures 10.1a and 10.1b Language-defined objects with

various languages maintained in one home. Image courtesy of
Ekaterina Protassova. 217
Figure 10.2 The traditional Russian *vatrushka* pastry. Image
courtesy of Maria Yelenevskaya. 218
Figure 10.3 Keyboard used to write in Hebrew, English and
Russian. 223

TABLES

Table 1.1 Immigrant population from the FSU in Greece
according to the 1991 and 2001 censuses, 1997 legalisation
programme, and valid resident permit data as of 15 January
2006 and 27 May 2014. Statistically relevant nationalities. 23

Table 1.2 Immigrant population from the FSU in Greece
according to valid resident permit data as of 27 May 2014. 30

Table 5.1 Demographic information on participants. 100

Contributors

Larissa Aronin is an associate professor at the Oranim Academic College of Education, Israel. She was a Visiting Scholar in the Department of Linguistics and Philosophy in the School of Humanities, Arts, and Social Sciences at the Massachusetts Institute of Technology (MIT), USA, Visiting Research Fellow at Trinity College, Dublin, Ireland, and a KIVA guest professor at Technical Universität Darmstadt, Germany. She served two terms as a secretary of the International Association of Multilingualism and is an editorial board member of a number of international peer-reviewed journals. Professor Aronin has published in a range of international journals on a wide array of topics connected with multilingualism and has authored and co-authored several books on multilingualism.

Ksenia Golovina is an associate professor in the Department of Global Diversity Studies at Toyo University, Japan. Her research interest is in material studies in connection to migration, community, gender, home-making, creativity and the life cycle. She has published articles in, among others, *Antropologicheskij Forum*, *Asian Anthropology* and *the Japanese Review of Cultural Anthropology* and is the author of *Russian Women in Japan: Migration, Marriage, and Life Crafting* (Akashi Shoten, 2017, in Japanese).

Dr Marika Kalyuga is an associate professor and course authority (Russian Studies) in the Faculty of Arts at Macquarie University, Sydney, Australia. Her main research interests are in the areas of cognitive linguistics, language teaching and Russian culture. She has published many articles and book chapters on these topics, as well as the book *Russian Prepositional Phrases: A Cognitive Linguistic Approach* (Springer, 2020).

Kira Kaurinkoski is a research associate at Aix-Marseille University (UMR 7307 Institut d'ethnologie méditerranéenne européenne et comparative). Her research focuses on Russian and post-Soviet Greek and Ukrainian diaspora and migration, and on mobility and minorities in the Aegean region. Among her recent publications are the articles 'La migration de retour des Grecs d'ex-Union-Soviétique en Grèce. Réflexions sur les logiques diasporiques d'exclusion et d'appartenance' (*Revue européenne des migrations internationales*, 2021), 'From labour migrants to a diaspora community? The case of Ukrainian migrants in Greece' (*Balkanologie*, 2021), and the monograph *Le 'Retour' des Grecs de Russie. Identités, mémoires, trajectoires* (École française d'Athènes, 2018).

Dr Anna Pechurina is an associate professor in Sociology at Karlstad University, Sweden. She was born and studied sociology in Russia. She then moved to the UK where she conducted her PhD research on Russian migrants' homemaking. Her research interests include home and homemaking practices, belonging, culture, migration and qualitative methods, and, more recently, migration and ageing. In relation to home and migration, her work particularly engages with qualitative, ethnographic and autobiographical methods used to uncover relationships between the meaning and use of material objects, homemaking practices, and migrants' shifting sense of identity. She has published in a number of journals including *Current Sociology* and *Sociological Research Online*. She is the author of *Material Cultures, Migrations, and Identities* (Palgrave, 2015).

Dr Gleb Pilipenko works in Moscow at the Institute of Slavic Studies of the Russian Academy of Sciences, where he received his PhD in Philology in 2011. His scholarly interests include contact linguistics, Slavic dialectology and ethnolinguistics. He investigates the language and identity of Slavic minority groups and the language situation of Hungarians living among Slavic peoples. Gleb Pilipenko has also conducted field studies in Europe and South America. Gleb Pilipenko is author of the papers 'The Ukrainian language in Argentina and Paraguay as an identity marker' (*Slověne. International Journal of Slavic Studies*, 7:1 (2018), 281–307) and 'Hungarian-Slavic bilingualism in Transcarpathia, Vojvodina and Prekmurje', *Yearbook of Finno-Ugric Studies*, 10:1 (2016), 20–30).

Ekaterina Protassova holds a PhD in Philology and Hab. in Pedagogy and is Associate Professor in Russian Language at the University of Helsinki. She has authored and co-authored over 400 monographs, articles and book chapters, headed and participated in various international and national projects investigating language pedagogies, child and adult bilingualism, and the role of language and culture in immigrant integration. Her service to the profession includes editorial work for various journals and publishers and the organisation of seminars and conference panels.

Sasha Razor is a lecturer in the Film and Media Studies Department at the University of California, Santa Barbara. She specialises in Russophone and East-Central European cinemas. She earned her PhD in Slavic Languages and Literatures from UCLA in 2020, with a dissertation focused on Soviet screenwriting in the 1920s and 1930s. She is co-founder of the Russophone Los Angeles Research Collective, which promotes the study of Russophone migration to Southern California. Her research interests span from diasporic and film studies to Belarusian and Ukrainian literature and culture, and visual arts.

Kirill Reznik works as a freelance researcher in Finland. His life and research interests include structural linguistics, social and visual anthropology, and mathematical methods in the humanities.

Liaisan Şahin is a lecturer at the Institute of Turkic Studies, Marmara University, Turkey. She is Kazan Tatar, born in the Republic of Tatarstan of the Russian Federation. She holds a PhD in International Relations from Marmara University, Turkey. Her main research interests are dynamics of Russian–Kazan Tatar relations, Kazan Tatar identity and historical imagination, post-Soviet history writing in Russia, history school textbooks in Tatarstan, the Russian-speaking diaspora and the Kazan Tatar diaspora in Turkey. She has published several articles on these topics in Tatar, Turkish, Russian and English and translated scholarly works between these languages. She has also presented the results of her research at a number of international conferences and organised conferences on topics related to Tatar history. Since 2019 she has been participating in the international collaborative research project *Modern Japan, Turkey, and the Turkic World: An Interregional History in Eurasia* started by Boğaziçi University Asian Studies Centre and the Japanese Studies Association.

Dr Maria Yelenevskaya is affiliated with the Department of Humanities and Arts at the Technion-Israel Institute of Technology. Her academic publications primarily deal with the use of language in multilingual and multicultural settings. She investigates lingua-cultural features of computer-mediated communication, socio-cultural aspects of immigration and linguo-anthropological aspects of humour. She has authored and co-authored over eighty peer-refereed articles and book chapters and three scholarly monographs. She has co-edited three special issues in international academic journals and an academic monograph. Yelenevskaya has presented the results of her research at more than a hundred international conferences, and she sits on the editorial boards of two international journals as well as of the Israel Association for the Study of Language and Society.

Acknowledgements

We would like to thank anonymous reviewers for their constructive comments on the previous versions of the chapters in this volume. We are deeply grateful to the head of the series *Russian Language and Society*, Professor Lara Ryazanova-Clarke, for her interest in our project, insightful comments on the manuscript, and her support which inspired us in our editorial work. We are thankful to Laura Quinn for her expert and patient advice on all the stages of revisions, and to Sam Johnson who supervised the production process.

Our thanks also go to the authors of the chapters who were enthusiastic about the idea to investigate the role of home and homemaking in the life of Russian speakers who have emigrated but retained ties with Russian language and culture. Last but not least, we are thankful to all the interviewees who shared their stories and contributed to our understanding of the multicoloured mosaics of Russian culture away from Russia.

This volume was submitted for publication in 2020. Working on their chapters the authors could not imagine that a devastating war would break out in Ukraine, shattering a diasporic perception of the home country. This book shows what the world of the Russian-speaking diaspora was like before the war.

INTRODUCTION

Images of Home away from Home

Maria Yelenevskaya and Ekaterina Protassova

The sun at home warms better than the sun elsewhere.
                                        (Albanian proverb)

Who loves to roam may lose his home.
                                        (Italian proverb)

Better free in a foreign land than a serf at home.
                                        (German proverb)

Ищи счастье на стороне, а дом люби по старине.
(Look for your happiness overseas but love your home like your forefathers did.)
                                        (Russian proverb)

HOME IN THE FRAMEWORK OF THEORY

Explorations of diasporic homes in this volume rely on an integrative theoretical framework. Like many other researchers of material culture (see, e.g., Berger 2014; Buchli 2020; Dant 1999; Knapett 2011), we advocate investigating human–object relations from a multidisciplinary vantage point, applying theories tested in the fields as diverse as anthropology and sociology, consumer and market research, sociolinguistics and semiotics. Applying a number of theories which could serve as perspectives focusing the researchers' attention on the connections between home and society with its wide repertoire of discourses and practices seems to be an appropriate approach to gain different perspectives and thus gain a richer and more critical vision of home, homemakers and artefacts with which they interact (Berger 2014: 13–27; Durham and Kellner 2012: 3–4). The suitability of the chosen theories is determined by their effectiveness in providing modes of explanation and interpretation of sociocultural practices and structures related to home. And here we agree with Durham and Kellner (2012) who write that cultural and social theories are descriptive and interpretive; they highlight specific topics, make connections, contextualise, provide interpretations and offer explanations. We are aware that 'descriptive' and 'interpretive' are often used as pejorative terms in evaluating research projects as devoid of scientific vigour, yet in issues related to human life and values we deal with subjectivities which are not amenable to quantification or modelling, and thorough descriptions and reflective interpretations may thus prove to be the most revealing.

In theorising culture in general, and material culture in particular, researchers are often confronted with the question of how knowledge of culture is acquired and whether it is inseparably connected to language. Influential work by Bloch (1991 and 2018) challenges the leading role of the language. He postulates that much cultural knowledge is nonlinear and non-sentential but purpose-dedicated, formed through the extensive practice of closely related activities. Fairchild also defines culture as communication of behavioural patterns that are transmitted by symbols, and does not even mention language (Fairchild 1966: 80). Bourdieu, on the other hand, suggests that consumption of art, which is also part of material culture, is a stage in a process of communication, that is, an act of deciphering and decoding, which presupposes practical or explicit mastery of the necessary cipher or code. Therefore, a work of art, and an artefact, for that matter, has meaning only for someone who possesses the cultural competence, that is, the code, into which it is encoded (Bourdieu 1984: 2). Clearly, this is true, because, just as our contemporaries would not be able to explain the meaning and use of some of the house utensils of our ancestors, so would our ancestors be baffled by the electronic devices that have become an integral part of our homes (see the narratives about the role of electronic devices connecting diasporans with their home country in the chapters by Golovina, Şahin and Aronin).

For the contributors of this volume it is important to explore the representation of material culture of the diasporans' homes as it appears in the discourses, and also to interpret the meaning of the artefacts for their owners through their function and symbolism. This task is carried out through the application of the theoretical framework proposed by Berger. He suggests that artefacts can be understood on three levels:

- what the artefact does
- aspects of the artefact's functionality of which we may be aware

- unrecognised symbolic meanings connected to the artefacts (Berger 2014: 33).

This framework helps us to analyse how functional and symbolic aspects of various objects in immigrants' homes interact and change over time. It also makes us investigate how aware their owners are of these changes and whether their symbolic meanings remain unrecognised, or whether interviews encourage immigrants to reflect on histories of their possessions and their impact on life in a new country.

By studying culture lived through objects we can better understand social structures and such dimensions of the social system as inequality and social difference, as well as human action, gendered roles and emotions. Discourses related to artefacts show how the meanings of the objects are established and negotiated, sometimes following social structures and conventions and sometimes challenging them (cf. Woodward 2007: 4).

These negotiations of meaning confirm that culture is inseparable from communication, and artefacts embody and concretise various cultural values and achievements. An important initial assumption made by scholars of material culture is that belief, idea and intention are important to action and practice. It follows, then, that the conceptual has some impact on the patterning of the material, and the ideational component of material patterning is not opposed to but integrated with its material functioning. It is possible therefore to infer both utilitarian and conceptual meaning from the patterning of material evidence (Hodder 2012: 181).

An essential element of material culture theory is the relationship between mind and matter, and between agent and artefact (Knappett 2011). Transformations of people and objects are closely interconnected, and, as Kopytoff proposed, just as we study biographies of people, we can study biographies of things. Investigating objects from this perspective we can pose a set of questions that does not differ much from an inquiry into a person's biography. For example, where does the thing come from and who made it? What are the recognised periods in its 'life'? What sort of 'career' has it had? What is the status of this class of things in the culture and period being studied and how have these possibilities been realised? Virtually all contributions in this book contain narratives telling biographies of the objects connecting their owners with their pre-emigration life in Russia or the Soviet Union (see, e.g., the chapters by Pechurina and by Protassova and Reznik). Moreover, it turns out that the more significant the artefact, the more emotional is its biography as told by the interviewees. Biographies of things can make salient what might otherwise remain obscure and hidden from analysts. For the chapters in this volume, it is important that, in situations of cultural contact, they can show that what is significant about the adoption of alien objects is not the fact that they were adopted, but the way they are culturally redefined and put to use (Kopytoff 1988: 66–7). So, throughout their existence, objects accumulate history. As Hoskins posits, when things, which may be even the simplest household objects, are entangled in the events of a person's life they may acquire extraordinary significance and become a vehicle for a sense of selfhood. The stories about such objects turn them into 'biographic objects' and provide a form of introspection. Hence we witness the transgression of boundaries between persons and objects and see how far those highly valued possessions come to be perceived as surrogate selves (Hoskins 1998). And it is the objects that accompany their owners on the journey through time and move with them to other places that form a symbiosis with people.

In doing ethnographic work for their projects and analysing fieldwork material, most contributors to this volume rely on social semiotics which focuses on the people who participate in the semiotic activity, interacting in different ways in concrete social contexts. Unlike mainstream structural semiotics, which cuts off semiosis from society and emphasises structures and codes, social semiotics attributes meaning to power (Hodge and Kress 1988: 1–2). It locates the origin of meaning within the process of context-bound and conflict-laden interpersonal interaction. So, meaning emerges out of the concerted intercourse of humans, each differing in their outlook, motives and goals (Vannini 2007). Notably, social semiotics is neither 'pure' theory nor a self-contained field. As van Leeuwen aptly notes, 'It only comes into its own when it is applied to specific instances and specific problems, and it always requires immersing oneself not just in semiotic concepts and methods as such but also in some other field' (2005: 1).

The result of the evolving types of multimodality of communication is that neither linguistics nor sociolinguistics is any longer sufficient as the theoretical enterprise to account fully and plausibly for central aspects of representation and communication (Kress 2001: 67). All the chapters in this volume contain both text and photographs. The role of images is important because what the interviewees say about their homes may deviate from or clash with what the researchers document in their photographs. So, analysing both in parallel stimulates repeated and critical analysis of the verbal material collected during fieldwork.

METHODOLOGY IN THE STUDIES OF HOME

Most chapters in this book are based on empirical data obtained by means of interviews and group discussions, monitoring of social media, and participant observation. The recorded data includes audio and visual documents and in some chapters statistical data as well. Methods of analysis range from thematic and critical discourse analysis, from ethnography of communication to pragmalinguistic analysis. Thematic analysis makes researchers single out salient themes, which present patterns of meanings related to the core theme of the interviews and thus revealing to the analyst how individuals make meaning of their experience. This method enables the researcher to see how the broader social context affects those meanings, while retaining focus on the analysed material (Braun and Clarke 2021). Critical discourse analysis is highly appropriate for this project because it brings a variety of theories into the research inquiry, especially social theories on the one hand and linguistic theories on the other, so that its theory is a shifting synthesis of other theories, although what it itself theorises in particular is the mediation between the social and the linguistic – the 'order of discourse', the social structuring of semiotic hybridity (interdiscursivity) (Chouliaraki and Fairclough 1999: 16). That is to say, the diverse and complex interrelations between discourse and society cannot be analysed adequately unless both linguistic and sociological approaches are combined (Weiss and Wodak 2003: 4).

Since fieldwork for the chapters was conducted with Russian speakers away from the metropolis, the data elicited is amenable to the study of linguo-cultural maintenance and change, translanguaging as a mode of multilinguals' communication, and hybridisation processes caused by language contact situations – all those phenomena that are the subject matter of the ethnography of communication (Saville-Troika 2003). While analysing interviews contributors do not limit themselves to the interview transcripts as a resulting product of their fieldwork, but also look at pragmalinguistic aspects of communication – that is, at the relationship of the speaker and the listener (both interviewers and interviewees alternate these roles), at their intentions, explicit and implicit, and at the realisation of potential meanings of utterances in specific socio-communicative contexts of the interview encounters (Watts 1981: 18). Finally, all the case studies included in this volume use observational techniques, noting genuine settings of the interviewees' home life. The authors apply focused observation, concentrating on well-defined everyday activities and roles (Angrosino and Mays de Perez 2000). Whether in-group or out-group members, they demonstrate the skill of capturing cultural meanings specific for the group they study and present them in a way that would be accessible to the readers coming from other linguo-cultural groups. The reader will see that the Russianness of the participants' identity and communication patterns is interlaced with elements from the contact cultures of their receiving societies, resulting in multifaceted hybrids. It is a fascinating task to single out those elements of Russian culture that are so robust that they do not disappear despite migrants' immersion into other cultures but are transferred to the next generations of diasporans, whether consciously or unconsciously. Since most of the chapters are based on in-depth interviews, the book will make the voices of migrants audible, turning them from guided 'informants' into research participants, with clear-cut agency. The volume is richly illustrated, giving a glimpse into the home life of Russian speakers outside Russia.

Borders have become porous, international travel more affordable, and electronic technologies allow migrants to be virtually present in the places they have left. Individual chapters, as well as the book as a whole, seek to answer questions relevant to numerous immigrant communities: How have the mobility and superdiversity of contemporary life affected imagery and representations of home in distant places? Do they contribute to migrants' feeling that they dwell in both places at once, and if they do, is it detrimental to the process of rooting in their new country? How are the proliferation of visuals created by individuals today and new modes of online communication changing the nature of narratives about distant home and homemaking practices? Do these new developments reinforce or challenge the myth of return, creating a new one about reconstructing the lost home away from home?

Home as a communicative space

Home is among the most value- and emotion-loaded concepts in the human mind and communication. It is linked to the development of our identities and relations with other people. It is in the centre of our experience of personalising space and turning it into a meaningful place; above all, it forms an indispensable part of our lifelong striving for the 'feeling of wholeness' (Marcus 1992). In fact, the evolution of the concept 'home' has turned it into such a rich conglomeration of meanings that it has become elusive and difficult to define (Mallet 2004). This fusion of meanings is particularly true when we deal with migrants. Trying to make a home, to find a safe and comfortable place for living, becomes especially challenging in the times of trouble, uncertainty and change (Aybek et al. 2015; Selwyn and Frost 2018).

Furthermore, the complexity of the concept of home is in its belonging to both the external world of buildings, furniture, gadgets, decoration and other objects, and also to the inner world of emotions and feelings. So, studies of home and homemaking should be approached as part of interlocking processes which are at once global and intimate, tangible and intangible, material and symbolic (Selwyn and Frost 2018: 11–13). Importantly, these pairs do not form oppositions; rather they interpenetrate and complement each other. Bartmiński (2012: 149–61; 2018) and scholars in his interdisciplinary project (Fiodorowa and Pazio-Wlazłowska 2015) consider the concept of the home cross-linguistically in different cultures. Jukushevich (2018) collected contexts of the use of the Russian word *dom* 'house and home'. The situation of migrants searching for and arranging available and affordable dwelling that is liveable is extremely vulnerable (Fialkova and Yelenevskaya 2007: 124–7; Nikolko and Carment 2017; Turaeva 2018). Moreover, sometimes when a new dwelling fails to meet immigrants' expectations and is too far from the idealised home of memories and dreams, a public place, such as a community centre, a restaurant or a sports club, where one can feel at ease and spend time with co-ethnics, turns into a substitute for home (Varshaver et al. 2017; Razor, this volume). Cities where immigrants settle also become more friendly and homelike to newcomers once signs and advertisements in their language appear. Streets that are 'readable' become more functional and welcoming. The number and variety of signs in immigrants' languages demonstrate the linguistic vitality of the immigrant community, its social status in the society, and its rootedness (Barni and Bagna 2010; Gorter 2006; Protassova 2013; Yelenevskaya and Fialkova 2017).

Immigrants also reflect on how, in the first stages of life in a new country, many things outside their dwellings look and sound alien, but gradually a town where they settle – and the entire host country – come to be perceived as home (Kaurinkoski, this volume). It usually takes time and effort and happens when newcomers get used to the climate, architecture, food habits, festive traditions, etiquette and the language. This new feeling of home is also associated with the ambivalence related to the country of origin: they feel nostalgic and wish to visit it, but, once they are there, they realise it is no longer their real home (see the chapters by Yelenevskaya and Şahin in this volume).

Developing proficiency in the dominant language is an essential part of integration. Although Russian still dominates in many immigrants' homes, it borrows numerous words and expressions from the dominant language(s) of the host country. Russian is developing as a pluricentric language (Mustajoki et al. 2019; Ryazanova-Clarke 2014), and its value is not only cultural but also economic (Muth 2017; Ryazantsev and Pismennaya 2017). Immigrants' linguistic repertoires change, but as Blommaert et al. state, the presence of immigrants in a place requires sociolinguistic and discursive reconfigurations of the host society as well. The local population is confronted with linguo-communicative processes previously unnecessary in everyday life, and various institutions have to deal with subjects who may lack sufficient linguistic resources and competences. This affects 'the sociolinguistic economy of place' (Blommaert et al. 2005: 201). The importance of maintaining the Russian language and the ways in which this can be done effectively are a frequent topic of on- and offline conversations. Clearly, using Russian as a home language is an essential but not sufficient condition for developing proficiency that allows one to use the language not only in the symbolic but also in the instrumental function (Pilipenko, this volume).

Home as a symbol

A person's home tells visitors about the owner's character and essence in the same way as her or his clothes, because it reflects individual and group identity (Kron 1983; see also <www.identityontheline.eu>). Both aspects are significant for migrants, since it is important for them to talk about losing their old home and acquiring a new one (Boccagni 2017; Boccagni et al. 2018). A lot of time, effort and money is spent on the interior of a house (from wall, floor and ceiling decoration to the furniture, window decoration, and paintings and ornaments on display), but householders in general rarely reflect on this. Home decoration is the application of a system of symbols adopted in a certain culture, where everything matters – shape and colour, volume and material, purpose and structure (Levin 2016; Wang Jie 2018). Migrants often mention how the decoration of their homes changed during their integration into a new culture, how they had to decipher everyday habits (e.g. learn to furnish an apartment, throw out or recycle rubbish, pay for utilities in a new context), thereby integrating into a formerly unknown environment. To live in a house, or to communicate with neighbours, you need to follow certain locally accepted rules, and it takes a lot of effort to maintain order.

Collecting is widespread in the diaspora. The collectors' culture of the past few centuries is a very useful resource for artists and designers, giving them an impetus for innovation (van Leeuwen 2005: 6). Moreover, they form a semiotic storehouse that gives sociologists, anthropologists and linguists many a useful clue for understanding the social life of the past. People may strive to acquire the same objects as a famous or rich person, copying that person, and embodying the same habits in everyday life, but blind imitation does not constitute belonging to the same group: you need to find a similarity, an analogue, making the style or taste your own, rather than a borrowed one (Fox 2016). In a foreign country the old role models do not always work, which can lead to confusion because it is unclear whom one should imitate.

A person's property is almost a part of him- or herself, an extension of the physical body (Marcus 1995). Property calms and gives a sense of stability and predictability. Some things are kept in wardrobes, hidden from view, while others are on display but not used in everyday life (Miller 2001). Some people can tell you why they have put something in a certain place or out of sight; others have given no thought to this at all. Some have a complex system of signs, talismans and secret charms, but are afraid to talk about them for fear of destroying their 'magic power'. It is difficult to keep personal items away from prying eyes when you are in close contact with the people you live with. Some people migrate when they are past their prime, which raises specific challenges for homemaking in the new place (Näre et al. 2017; Walsh and Näre 2016).

Making a home is a continuous process of making choices: which neighbourhood to select; where to put things; how to keep them in good condition; whether to buy or not to buy; to make new acquisitions visible only to oneself, to other members of the household or also to visitors; to draw attention to them or to cherish them by keeping them out of sight. Some evaluate the way other people live, and care about their own representation in the outer world. Photographic documentation of the home with its various details can provide precious insights into migrants' lives (Gomez and Vannini 2017). Moving to a big city and establishing new relationships with the workplace may require the restructuring of community ties (Wilkins 2019) and affects the private territory of migrants' homes.

It would of course be impossible to list all instances of the symbolism of home in scholarly literature and fiction (Yapo and Boccagni 2020), but it is worth mentioning that many books begin or end with a description of a house, and that one's soul – a key term in the Russian linguistic worldview – is often compared to the home. Loss of home due to war, fire, relocation, exile, prison, non-inheritance or emigration is often perceived as the loss of part of a person's identity. Morley (2000) believes that television and other media help migrants to compensate for the absence of their former homes. In search of a home, immigrants seek not only material but also spiritual comfort in order to feel confident, adapt to a new environment, and adapt it to themselves (Boccagni and Brighenti 2017).

People are in mutual exchange with their space: the architect, the designer and the owner communicate to create an appearance that suits them, and then the residents draw strength and comfort from this joint project, spending most of their time in the house (Rattner 2019). The house has physical and spiritual dimensions, where travels begin and end, culture is born, and synaesthetic associations are formed (Bykovskaya 2013). If a person's lifestyle changes, his or her home changes, and vice versa. By collecting objects – signs of events and decisions – inside and around the house, the storage space itself becomes a symbol. Some things can be moved to another place, and some cannot (Sutcliffe 2004). The home is a place of relaxation and strength, of past, present and future. The way people organise their homes not only affects the house's performance but also reflects the social norms of society, and in this sense, here, subjectivity and objectivity collide. The quality of his or her home life largely determines the success and stability of the individual (Rapport and Dawson 1998). It is not by chance that the metaphor determining the European policy of migrant reception is to 'make every immigrant feel at home' (Kadysheva et al. 2019). One of the reasons for this humane approach is the current change in the sovereignty and power of the state over its territory. Some components of sovereignty have been relocated to supranational entities. Moreover, intellectual technologies that allow governments to control their subjects, their territory and immigration flows have shifted to non-state institutions (Sassen 2000). As a result, many business initiatives involving immigrant labour have emerged, and various NGOs try to prevent overexploitation and unfair treatment of immigrants. In practice, however, people's minds change only slowly, and members of the host society often feel that their national home is being 'invaded' because their governments are too generous with their 'hospitality' (see Andrikopoulos 2017; Bell 2010).

Home in migration

People migrate in search of a better life, a secure future and a new home. Even in situations when going back is impossible, ties with the old home are seldom broken completely. They may be as concrete as remittances sent to families left behind, or they may be symbolic, devoid of material form and perpetuated in memories, stories and mental images. Nostalgia used to be an indispensable part of migrants' life and a fertile ground for creating diasporic myths (Cohen 2008). Idealising the past and reaffirming one's connections to it show up strongly in the context of migration as resistance to minorisation in the host society. It helps individuals feel part of a group, distinguishing themselves and their in-group members from others and in this way expressing distinctiveness. Notably, this desire may surface strongly when the group's culture mixes with the cultures of others (Extra and Kutlay 2004; Remennick 2013).

Despite a vast body of scholarly literature on migration, the theme of migrants' lifestyles and the interrelation of materiality with spiritual inner life seldom comes up in immigration studies (Davies and Fitchett 2006). And yet, we should take into account the paradox noted by Miller (2010: 4): '[T]he best way to understand, convey and appreciate our humanity is through attention to our fundamental materiality.' The artefacts surrounding us can be invisible in a familiar environment, but when this changes, do we pay more attention to them? Do they preserve the same meaning or acquire a new one? How can we explain that some of the most mundane household objects, such as children's toys or cooking utensils, dishes or towels, brought from the old home are imbued with a new importance in migrants' eyes? The shorter the lifecycle of objects, the more we value artefacts that survive from the past, in particular if they have been our own and our families' companions for a long time. Sometimes such objects continue being used for their intended purpose, but frequently they lose their functionality, turning into items of decoration and domestic display preserved as tokens of the past and an assertion of one's belonging (as happened with samovars, painted wooden cutlery and painted metal trays in many Russian immigrants' homes).

Ours is the age of consumerism, and together with Baudrillard we may wonder whether it is possible to classify and adequately describe the 'luxuriant growth of objects', a growth so fast that we constantly have to invent new words to name them (Baudrillard 2005: 1). Making a new home away from the old country requires adapting to the local climate, learning local traditions and codes of material culture, and also acquiring the relevant vocabulary in the language(s) of the receiving country. Our material life today is much more dependent on language than in the past. The food packaging and medications, the simplest household gadgets and complex electric appliances, the robotic children's toys and the various digital devices that fill our homes come with user instructions, warnings, recommendations and so on. So, when carrying out research projects on migrants' homes, we should observe the language of the books displayed on shelves and desks, which scripts appear on computer keyboards, and in what languages family members exchange notes and electronic messages. Answers to these and similar questions help us determine the Dominant Language Constellation (DLC) in immigrants' homes and also trace its changes over time (for the theory of DLC, see Aronin 2016 and 2019). As a result, by studying immigrants' homes we learn about changing immigrants' consumption patterns and also get a glimpse of evolving bi- and multilingualism, which gives us a better understanding of how cultures become blended and 'attached' to the languages in material things (Aronin 2018: 26).

This book seeks to show how people make choices when, either voluntarily or due to external pressures, they have to change their physical and social environment, and how they affirm their right to be what they are despite the imagined or real pressure of the societies where they live to become 'like us'. While most of the chapters focus on the material culture of Russian speakers outside the nation, not all of them are concerned with ethnic Russians. However, all put into focus emigrants from the former Soviet Union or descendants of those who used to live in close contact with the Russian language and culture.

Home as identity

Research into the lifestyles of Russian-speaking migrants abroad, their identities and multicultural practices is manifold: it explores everyday routines, consumption preferences, principles guiding household practices, and tastes in interior design (see, e.g., Akifieva 2017; Mole 2018; Willett 2007). Such investigations need to be combined with the study of migrants' reflections as to what makes a home either homely or alienating, which, in turn, leads to the discussion of the interdependence of the material and the spiritual.

When thinking about post-Soviet space and the Soviet legacy imported through migrants to other countries or transferred by them from one space to another during further migration, we need to analyse which basic individual values prove to be resilient and still influence people's everyday habits irrespective of changes in the environment. We should also study which factors of transition to other customs are discernible in migrants' behaviour. This volume includes micro- and macro studies of self-representation, revealing how migrants act as inhabitants of contemporary multicultural homes, and as proponents and interpreters of different styles of interior design, whether experienced and skilful, or awkward yet ambitious. The old and newly acquired tastes and values are mirrored in the collection of objects that fill migrants' houses (see the chapter by Kalyuga).

As Southerton (2012: 335) puts it, changing attitudes and values do not necessarily lead to a change in what people consume, or, more importantly with respect to sustainability, they do not change the resource-intensity of their consumption. The Soviet culture of managing shortages in consumer goods and admiration for Western products shaped the minds and behaviours of the first-generation immigrants who left their homeland in the 1970s–90s. Their children brought up as bicultural bilinguals are more flexible. They have learned to value consumption patterns prevalent in the host society and often view their parents' attitudes to objects and homemaking as anachronistic. Yet, as research conducted in different countries shows, immigrants of the 1.5 generation whose initial socialisation had started before their families left the former Soviet Union demonstrate significant cultural retention (Protassova and Reznik 2020; Remennick 2017; Stepanov 2017), which affects the way they organise their homes.

The cult of the 'bright' future that reigned in Soviet ideology called for constant innovation, and scanty resources presupposed minimalism in the use of consumer goods. Yet, in the post-war years, since the beginning of Brezhnev era in particular, members of the Soviet and post-Soviet public have displayed a strong interest in material wellbeing, and gradually evolved into mature and autonomous consumers (Chernyshova 2013). When it stopped being dangerous to do so, people also came to cherish the remnants of the imperial past. Re-conceptualised as the 'legacy of the people', the culture of the past was partially rehabilitated, which elevated the status of the literature and fine arts of the nineteenth century, tzarist palaces and manor houses of the gentry. Some family memorabilia were lost or destroyed during the 1917 Russian Revolution and the Civil War; others were sold in exchange for food in the periods of starvation; still others were 'expropriated' in the years following the revolution. The veneration of the pre-revolutionary past that had already started in the first Soviet decade went hand in hand with a fashion for artefacts that connected people with the past. Yet, Soviet consumption patterns, attitudes to the artefacts that fill people's homes, and aspirations to attain material wellbeing still linger (Gronow 2009; Vedery 1996). The mosaics of cultures and attitudes demonstrated in the chapters of this volume are characteristic of the simultaneous homogenisation and heterogenisation of today's globalised culture. Appadurai posits that, at least as rapidly as forces from various metropolises are brought into new societies, they tend to become indigenised in some way, be it through music or housing style, or even science and terrorism (2012: 588). These disjunctions are true not only of communities and nations but also of individuals, who often wish to be 'as unique as everybody else'.

Studies included in this volume detect the persistence of immigrants' old habits and attitudes as well as innovations in their lifestyles inspired by cultural contacts with the receiving societies. Discursive construction of the old and new homes in the narratives quoted in the chapters confirm Appadurai's views about the crucial role of the imagination in contemporary cultural processes: fantasy and imagining are no longer privilege of the elite but a widespread social practice (2012: 587). Indeed, we often see that people try to model their homes and lifestyles on what they remember from childhood and what is idealised, or emulate imaginary lifestyles popularised in the media and films. Another aspect common to the chapters in the book is that immigrants' narratives share biographies of their most treasured objects, objects that connect them to memories of people and events. Whether joyful or sad, these memories are highly emotional and self-reflective.

* * *

The editors see the main contribution of this volume as advancing the theory of multilingualism and multiculturalism by providing a multifaceted and empirically based analysis of the material culture of Russian-speaking migrants. The themes of interdependence of materiality and emotions, of materiality and language use, have been investigated by Western scholars in theoretical treatises and empirical studies. Some of these are devoted to migrant communities, but there is a dearth of scholarship elucidating these research questions as regards Russian-speaking migrants.

Some chapters in this volume analyse the material culture of the people who left imperial Russia; others are devoted to the homes of ex-Soviets, while still others deal with those who left their homeland in the post-Soviet period. Scholars engaged in immigration studies see specific features distinguishing immigrants of different waves. Emigration from Russia started as early as the seventeenth century when Old Believers fled to escape persecution and preserve their religious practices. In various periods compact settlements of Russophones formed in North America, China, Germany, Slovakia, Palestine and some other countries. The emigration processes intensified at the end of the nineteenth century. People were leaving the country for religious, political or economic reasons, seeking employment. Yet, at the state level, emigration was not considered a positive phenomenon for the country and was hampered in every possible way. Suffice it to say that, until 1906, the promotion of emigration in the country was prohibited by law, and punishment awaited those who moved to another country without permission and stayed for long periods of time (Aghamirzayev 2021). While different countries that had massive flows of newcomers from Russia have their own classification of Russian immigration waves, in Russia researchers in the field of immigration studies agree that the country has experienced five massive multi-vector emigration waves. The first wave triggered by the upheaval of the revolution is dated 1917–21 and was mainly political. The second wave occurred in 1940–45 and included people who for various reasons found themselves outside the Soviet Union and chose not to return to the homeland despite the threat of forced repatriation. The third wave, which was particularly intensive in the period from 1970 to 1990, was primarily ethnic but also included dissidents and prominent members of the intelligentsia. The fourth wave (1991–8) was caused by the stressful situation of the first post-Soviet decade. The fifth wave is still in full swing (see Ryazantsev et al. 2018; Budnitskiy and Ryazantsev 2019). This volume shows that, although the motives behind migration were different for those who left their homeland with different waves, they still share many of the homemaking traditions of their or their ancestors' homeland.

We view the study of home as a multidimensional endeavour bringing together theoretical knowledge derived from sociology, social and environmental psychology, urban anthropology, the anthropology of space, and sociolinguistics. Authors of the chapters explore discursive practices in which migrants' homes are framed, negotiated and constructed, revealing the complexity and ambivalence of home as a concept and as a phenomenon of social life.

There is nothing special in the idea of making a home somewhere else than in the country of birth, yet it is perceived as a crucial change in one's life. Combined with the linguistic characteristics of narratives about one's 'own' and the 'other's', migrants' reflections about moving home tell us about various stages in the process of linguistic and cultural adaptation and integration. They reveal the challenge of simultaneously adhering to the traditions of the old and the new country, which are sometimes different and even incompatible.

The material included in this book targets scholars in various fields, including Russian studies, Russian language and culture, sociolinguistics, cultural anthropology and migration studies. It may also be of interest to ethnolinguists, urbanists, and scholars of Soviet and post-Soviet cultural policies. There is a scarcity of publications in English about the transnational lifestyles of post-Soviet migrants, their affinities with the culture of their home country, and the growing hybridity of their identities and language use. The editors are convinced that the book will make these topics available to a much wider audience than before.

Some of the contributions included in the volume have been presented in scholarly conferences, and discussions emerging after presentations indicate that the problems under study have both theoretical and applied value. While the book is primarily addressed to academics and students, we can foresee that practitioners in the fields of immigrant integration, education, social work and urban planning will also benefit from it.

REFERENCES

Aghamirzayev, A. Ch. (2021), 'Historical and cultural formation, evolution and ideological direction of Russian emigration literature', *Technium Social Sciences Journal*, 23, pp. 755–62.

Akifyeva, R. N. (2017), '"The main task is to preserve Russian": language transmission in migrant and mixed families in Madrid'. *Working Papers of Centre for German and European Studies* 9.

Andrikopoulos, A. (2017), 'Hospitality and immigration in a Greek unban neighborhood: an ethnography of mimesis', *City & Society*, 29:2, 281–304.

Angrosino, M. V. and K. A. Mays de Pérez (2000), 'Rethinking observation: from method to context', in N. K. Denzin and Y. S. Lincoln (eds), *Handbook of Qualitative Research*, 2nd edn, Thousand Oaks: Sage, pp. 673–702.

Appadurai, A. (2012), 'Disjuncture and difference in the global cultural economy', in M. G. Durham and D. M. Kellner (eds), *Media and Cultural Studies: KeyWorks*, 2nd edn, Oxford: Blackwell Publishing, pp. 584–603.

Aronin, L. (2016), 'Multicompretence and dominant language constellation', in V. Cook and L. Wei (eds), *The Cambridge Handbook of Linguistic Competence*, Cambridge: Cambridge University Press, pp. 142–63.

Aronin, L. (2018), 'Theoretical underpinnings of the material culture of multilingualism', in L. Aronin, M. Hornsby and G. Kiliańska-Przybyło (eds), *The Material Culture of Multilingualism*, Dordrecht: Springer, pp. 21–45.

Aronin, L. (2019), 'What is multilingualism?', in D. Singleton and L. Aronin (eds), *Twelve Lectures on Multilingualism*, Bristol: Multilingual Matters, pp. 3–34.

Aybek, C. M., J. Huinink and R. Muttarak (eds) (2015), *Spatial Mobility, Migration, and Living Arrangements*, Heidelberg: Springer.

Barni, M. and C. Bagna (2010), 'Linguistic landscape and language vitality', in E. Ben-Rafael, E. Shohamy and M. Barni (eds), *Linguistic Landscape in the City*, Clevedon: Multilingual Matters, pp. 3–18.

Bartmiński, J. (2012), *Aspects of Cognitive Ethnolinguistics*, Sheffield: Equinox.

Bartmiński, J. (2018), *Language in the Context of Culture: The Metaphor of 'Europe as Home' in this Day and Age*, Katowice: Stowarzyszenie Inicjatyw Wydawniczych.

Baudrillard, J. (2005), *The System of Objects*, London: Verso.

Bell, A. (2010), 'Being "at home" in the nation: hospitality and sovereignty in talk about immigration', *Ethnicities*, 10:2, 236–56.

Berger, A. A. (2014), *What Objects Mean: An Introduction to Material Culture*, 2nd edn, London: Routledge.

Bloch, M. (1991), 'Language, anthropology and cognitive science', *Man*, n.s., 26, 183–98.

Bloch, M. (2018), *How We Think They Think: Anthropological Approaches to Cognition, Memory and Literacy*, New York: Routledge.

Blommaert, J., J. Collins and S. Slembrouck (2005), 'Spaces of multilingualism', *Language and Communication*, 25, 197–216.

Boccagni, P. (2017), *Migration and the Search for Home: Mapping Domestic Space in Migrants' Everyday Lives*, New York: Palgrave Macmillan.

Boccagni, P., S. Bonfanti, A. Miranda and A. Massa (2018), *Home and Migration: A Bibliography*, HOMInG Working paper no. 2, Trento: HOMInG.

Boccagni, P. and A. M. Brighenti (2017), 'Immigrants and home in the making: thresholds of domesticity, commonality and publicness', *Journal of Housing and the Built Environment*, 32, 1–11.

Bourdieu, P. (1984), *Distinction: A Social Critique of the Judgment of Taste*, Cambridge: Harvard University Press.
Braun, V. and V. Clarke (2021), *Thematic Analysis: A Practical Guide*, London: Sage.
Buchli, V. (ed.) (2020), *The Material Culture Reader*, London: Routledge.
Budnitskiy, O. V. and S. V. Ryazantsev (2019), 'Emigratsia', in S. L. Kravets (ed.), *Bol'shaia Rossiiskaia Entsiklopedia*, available at: https://bigenc.ru/text/5733358 (last accessed 16 November 2022).
Bykovskaya, T. V. (2013), 'Poetics of home: icons of internal space of the person', *Modern Problems of Science and Education*, 4, 402–10.
Chernyshova, N. (2013), *Soviet Consumer Culture in the Brezhnev Era*, London: Routledge.
Chouliaraki, L. and N. Fairclough (1999), *Discourse in Late Modernity*, Edinburgh: Edinburgh University Press.
Cohen, R. (2008), *Global Diasporas: An Introduction*, 2nd edn, New York: Routledge.
Dant, T. (1999), *Material Culture in the Social World*, Buckingham: Open University Press.
Davies, A. and J. A. Fitchett (2006), '"Crossing culture": a multi-method enquiry into consumer behaviour and the experience of cultural transition', *Journal of Consumer Behaviour*, 3:4, 315–30.
Durham, M. G. and D. M. Kellner (2012), 'Adventures in media and cultural studies. Introducing the key works', in M. G. Durham and D. M. Kellner (eds), *Media and Cultural Studies. KeyWorks*, 2nd edn, Malden, MA: Blackwell, pp. 1–26.
Extra, G. and K. Yagmur (eds) (2004), *Urban Multilingualism in Europe: Immigrant Minority Languages at Home and School*, Clevedon: Multilingual Matters.
Fairchild, H. P. (1966), *Dictionary of Sociology and Related Sciences*, Totowa, NJ: Littlefield, Adams & Co.
Fialkova, L. and M. Yelenevskaya (2007), *Ex-Soviets in Israel: From Personal Narratives to a Collective Portrait*, Detroit: Wayne State University Press.
Fiodorowa, L. L. and D. Pazio-Wlazłowska (2015), 'Rosyjski językowo-kulturowy obraz domu', *LA-SiS*, 1, 149–75.
Fox, M. A. (2016), *Home: A Very Short Introduction*, Oxford: Oxford University Press.
Gomez, R. and S. Vannini (2017), 'Notions of home and sense of belonging in the context of migration in a journey through participatory photography', *The Electronic Journal of Information Systems in Developing Countries*, 78:1, 1–46.
Gorter, D. (2006), 'Introduction: the study of linguistic landscape as a new approach to multilingualism', in D. Gorter (ed.), *Linguistic Landscape: A New Approach in Multilingualism*, Clevedon: Multilingual Matters, pp. 1–6.
Gronow, J. (2009), 'Fads, fashions and the "real!" innovations: novelties and the social change', in E. Shove, F. Trentmann and R. Wilk (eds), *Time, Consumption and Everyday Life: Practice, Materiality and Culture*, Oxford: Berg, pp. 129–42.
Hodder, I. (2012), 'The interpretation of documents and material culture', in J. Goodwin (ed.), *Sage Biographical Research. Vol. 1, Biographical Research: Starting Points, Debates and Approaches*, Los Angeles: Sage, pp. 171–88.
Hodge, R. and G. Kress (1988), *Social Semiotics*, Cambridge: Polity Press.
Hoskins, J. (1998), *Biographical Objects: How Things Tell the Stories of People's Lives*, New York: Routledge.
Jakushevich, I. V. (2018), *Simvol 'dom' v russkom jazyke i poeticheskom tekste*, Vladimir: Tranzit-Iks.
Kadysheva, O., P. Taran, P. Wickramasekara, L. Fondello, D. Gnes and S. Pfohman

(2019), *Common Home: Migration and Development in Europe and Beyond*, Brussels: Caritas Europa.
Knappett, C. (2011), *Thinking through Material Culture: An Interdisciplinary Perspective*, Philadelphia: The University of Pennsylvania Press
Kopytoff, I. (1986), 'The cultural biography of things: commoditization as process', in A. Appadurai (ed.), *The Social Life of Things: Commodities in Cultural Perspective*, Cambridge: Cambridge University Press, pp. 64–92.
Kress, G. (2001), 'Sociolinguistics and social semiotics', in P. Cobley (ed.), *The Routledge Companion to Semiotics and Linguistics*, London: Routledge, pp. 66–82.
Kron, J. (1983), *Home-Psych: The Social Psychology of Home and Decoration*, New York: Potter.
Levin, I. (2016), *Migration, Settlement, and the Concepts of House and Home*, London: Routledge.
Mallet, S. (2004), 'Understanding home: a critical review of the literature', *The Sociological Review*, 52:1, 62–89.
Marcus, C. C. (1997), *House as a Mirror of Self: Exploring the Deeper Meaning of Home*, Berkeley, CA: Conary Press.
Miller, D. (ed.) (2001), *Home Possessions. Material Culture behind Closed Doors*, Oxford: Berg.
Mole, R. C. M. (2018), 'Identity, belonging and solidarity among Russian-speaking queer migrants in Berlin', *Slavic Review*, 77:1, 77–98.
Morley, D. (2000), *Home Territories: Media, Mobility and Identity*, London: Routledge.
Mustajoki, A., E. Protassova and M. Yelenevskaya (eds) (2019), *The Soft Power of the Russian Language: Pluricentricity, Politics and Policies*, London: Routledge.
Muth, S. (2017), 'Russian language abroad: viewing language through the lens of commodification, *Russian Journal of Linguistics*, 21:3, 463–92.
Näre, L., K. Walsh and L. Baldassar (2017), 'Ageing in transnational contexts: transforming everyday practices and identities in later life', *Identities*, 24:5, 515–23.
Nikolko, M. and D. Carment (eds) (2017), *Post-Soviet Migration and Diasporas: From Global Perspectives to Everyday Practices*, London: Palgrave Macmillan.
Protassova, E. (2013), 'Russkij jazyk v turisticheskom landshafte zarubezh'ja', *Russkij jazyk za rubezhom*, 5, 53–61.
Protassova, E. and K. Reznik (2020), 'Russkii iazyk v Finljandii: dom kak simvol doma', *Sibirskii filologicheskii forum*, 3, 89–101.
Rapport, N. and A. Dawson (eds) (1998), *Migrants of Identity: Perceptions of Home in a World of Movement*, Oxford: Berg.
Rattner, D. M. (2019), *My Creative Space: How to Design Your Home to Stimulate Ideas and Spark Innovation*, New York: Skyhorse.
Remennick, L. (2013), 'Transnational lifestyles among Russian Israelis: a follow-up study', *Global Networks*, 13:4, 478–97.
Remennick, L. (2017), 'Generation 1.5 of Russian-speaking immigrants in Israel and in Germany: an overview of recent research and a German pilot study', in L. Isurin and C. M. Riehl (eds), *Integration, Identity and Language Maintenance in Young Immigrants. Russian Germans or German Russians*, Amsterdam: Benjamins, pp. 69–98.
Ryazanova-Clarke, L. (ed.) (2014), *The Russian Language Outside the Nation: Speakers and Identities (Russian Language and Society)*, Edinburgh: Edinburgh University Press.
Ryazantsev, S. and E. Pismennaya (2017), '"Russian-speaking economy abroad" as an instrument for adaptation of migrants', *International Trends*, 15:4, 115–32.
Ryazantsev, S., E. Pismennaya, A. Lukyanets, S. Sivoplyasova and M. Khramova (2018),

'Modern emigration from Russia and formation of Russian-speaking communities abroad', *Mirovaia ekonomika i mezhdunarodnye otnosheniia*, 62:6, 93–107.

Sassen, S. (2000), 'Regulating immigration in a global age: a new policy landscape', *ANNALS, AAPSS*, 570, 65–77.

Saville-Troike, M. (2003), *The Ethnography of Communication*, 3rd edn, Oxford: Blackwell.

Selwyn, T. and N. Frost (2018), 'Introduction: home and homemaking in a time of crisis', in N. Frost and T. Selwyn (eds), *Travelling towards Home: Mobilities and Homemaking*, Oxford: Berghahn Books, pp. 1–14.

Southerton, D. (2012), 'Habits, routines and temporalities of consumption: from individual behaviours to the reproduction of everyday practices', *Time & Society*, 22:3, 335–55.

Stepanov, A. M. (2017), 'Analiz transnatsional'nykh praktik emigrantov iz byvshego SSSR v N'iu-Yorke i Los-Andzhelese: Russkie v Amerike ili amerikantsy iz Rossii?', *Monitoring of Public Opinion: Economic and Social Changes*, 1, 196–208.

Sutcliffe, T. (2004), *Reminders of Home: A Semiotic Survey of the Signs Related to Human Dwelling Places*, Dominguez Hills: California State University.

Turaeva, R. (2018), 'Imagined mosque communities in Russia: Central Asian migrants in Moscow', *Asian Ethnicity*, 20:2, 131–47.

van Leeuwen, T. (2005), *Introducing Social Semiotics*, London: Routledge.

Vannini, P. (2007), 'Social semiotics and fieldwork', *Qualitative Inquiry*, 13:1, 113–40.

Varshaver, E. A., A. L. Rocheva and N. S. Ivanova (2017), 'Integration of the second generation migrants aged 18–30 in Moscow: first results of the research project', *Monitoring of Public Opinion: Economic and Social Changes*, 6, 63–81.

Vedery, K. (1996), *What was Socialism, and What Comes Next?* Princeton: Princeton University Press.

Wang, J. (2018), *Applied Research on Semiotics in Interior Design*, Pecs: University of Pecs.

Walsh, K. and L. Näre (eds) (2016), *Transnational Migration and Home in Older Age*, London: Routledge.

Watts, von R. J. (1981), *The Pragmalinguistic Analysis of Narrative Texts: Narrative Cooperation in Charles Dickens's 'Hard Times'*, Tübingen: Narr.

Weiss, G. and R. Wodak (2003), 'Introduction: theory, interdisciplinarity and critical discourse analysis', in G. Weiss and R. Wodak (eds), *Critical Discourse Analysis: Theory and Interdisciplinarity*, New York: Palgrave Macmillan, 1–33.

Wilkins, A. (2019), *Migration, Work and Home-Making in the City: Dwelling and Belonging among Vietnamese Communities in London*, Abingdon: Routledge.

Willett, G. A. (2007), 'Crises of self and other: Russian-speaking migrants in the Netherlands and European Union', PhD thesis, University of Iowa.

Woodward, I. (2007), *Understanding Material Culture*, Thousand Oaks: Sage.

Yapo, S. and P. Boccagni (2020), *On the Uses, Functions and Meanings of Homing in the Literature. An Interdisciplinary Analysis over Time*, Trento: University of Trento.

Yelenevskaya, M. and L. Fialkova (2017), 'Linguistic landscape and what it tells us about the integration of the Russian language into Israeli economy', *Russian Journal of Linguistics*, 21:3, 557–86.

CHAPTER I

Constructing Home away from Home: The Case of the Interwar Russian Refugees and the Post-Soviet Migrants in Greece[*]

Kira Kaurinkoski

INTRODUCTION

Home, displacement and nostalgia

Home *like* roots – terms which are often assumed to imply spatial fixity can also be mobile. Mobility often implies a return, lack of movement or a fixed belonging, even in the process of movement. Across time, space and peoples, this idea of movement changes, generating fixity and continuity irrespective of the changes. A key element in understanding the relation between place, location, movement and people is what stays the same as change occurs. Often this is something social – for example the form of kinship in which people engage – or something conceptual – for example a cosmology or cultural approach towards belonging and movement (Green 2016).

Social and political revolutions, armed conflicts and wars typically trigger massive movement affecting the ability of people to move, as well as the meaning and relevance of that movement. What changes and what stays the same in such situations is not always self-evident. Here, we must also consider the difference between 'locality' and 'location'. Appadurai describes locality as being 'primarily relational and contextual rather than [. . .] scalar or spatial' (1995: 178). But the change of location, in the spatial sense, can be equally significant (Green 2016).

Homeland can mean a place or a region, but also territory and landscape, to which the migrant relates emotionally rather than politically

---

[*] I wish to thank Maria Yelenevskaya and Ekaterina Protassova for their constructive comments on earlier drafts of this chapter, and Martin Baldwin-Edwards for his expert advice on statistics relevant to the immigrant population from the FSU in Greece.

or geographically (Medved 2000). It can also be linked to the concept of fatherland (or motherland), an idea or a territory. With the emergence of the modern nation state, we see the congruence between land and people and a strong relationship between blood and soil (Runblom 2000). For diaspora, blood and soil do not always coincide (Just 1989). Moreover, not all diasporans share a homing desire through a wish to return to a place of 'origin' (Brah 1996: 192). Brah further makes a distinction between 'feeling at home' and declaring a place as home. It is quite possible to feel at home in a place, and yet the experience of social exclusion may inhibit public proclamations of the place as home. 'The concept of diaspora places the discourse of "home" and "dispersion" in creative tension, inscribing a homing desire while simultaneously critiquing discourses on fixed origins' (Brah 1996: 197). Hobsbawm also underlines this distinction between home and homeland. Home is primarily private. But in a wider sense, home is public, a collective definition, and, as such, a social construction (Hobsbawm 1991).

Nostalgia that often characterises displaced groups can be a consequence of cultural exclusion in the new host society, but also a question of different values. Davis distinguishes between plain, reflexive and interpretative nostalgia. The first is an idealisation of the past; the second, a critical analysis of the past. Just as collective memory, nostalgia also has a consolidating function as far as group identity is concerned. Contrary to social memory, nostalgia is not the same as knowledge of the past, but rather an emotional experience of the past and linked to collective memory. Collective nostalgia can be defined as a reaction to cultural transition, for example when large numbers of people are confronted with solitude and alienation. Nostalgia then becomes an element in the quest of collective identity, which looks backward towards tradition, rather than forward to new experiences, and sets as goal the need to define oneself rather than the openness to new horizons (Davis 1979).

This chapter examines how the interwar Russian refugees and the post-Soviet migrants in Greece have addressed the question of homemaking in the context of migration and exile. How can one break with the past and at the same time ensure continuity? Home is a complex concept which is much more than a point on the map or a physical structure in which people live surrounded by objects. It is a place with meaning, shaped by people's activities and feelings. The meaning of home is different for different people, and for everyone it changes over time reflecting evolution of identities. The chapter is based on intermittent field research and interviews conducted by the author in Greater Athens between 2001 and 2016, as well as on secondary sources. Research on the interwar Russian refugees in Greece is based on secondary sources.

Ethnic Greek return migration from Russia and the former Soviet Union

Ethnic Greek return migration from Russia and the former Soviet Union to Greece in the twentieth century can be divided into four waves. The first wave refers to those who 'returned' to Greece in the wake of the Russian Revolution and Civil War (1917–23), and the second to those who 'returned' in the context of the Stalinist purges in the 1930s (Zapantis 1982). Thereafter, 'return' migration to Greece resumed in 1965 and continued in the 1970s and 1980s. The limited number of ethnic Greeks who 'returned' to Greece during this period constitute the third wave. Most were political refugees of the Greek Civil War (1946–9) and held Greek passports (Lampropoulos 2014). The fourth wave, which is the most heterogeneous and numerous, started in the late 1980s and can be stretched to 2010[1] (Christopoulos 2012; Kaurinkoski 2018; Notaras 1998; Voutira 2011).

The Greek context

In the aftermath of the Russian Revolution, approximately 50,000 expatriate and ethnic Greeks, as well as a smaller number of up to 10,000 Russians and Ukrainians fleeing their sovietised homelands, temporarily settled in Greece (Zapantis 1982). In addition, between November 1920 and October 1921, some 50,000 Don and Kuban Cossacks were temporarily camped on the Greek island of Lemnos by the French authorities, waiting for a host country to be found. Among them, some 2,500 eventually settled in Greece (Bruni 2009). According to the 1928 Greek population census, there were 3,329 Russians in Greece. The great majority lived in Athens, a smaller number in Thessaloniki (Divani 1994: 64, 67).

The interwar Russian refugees in Greece were an ethnically, socially and politically heterogeneous group, but considered themselves as Russians. There were military officers and soldiers of the White Army of General Wrangel, politicians, scientists, artists, musicians, members of the aristocracy, and priests – some of whom had formerly officiated at the Russian Embassy church in Athens – as well as clerks, traders, servicepeople and so on (Zhalnina-Vasilkioti 2015).

Greece's participation in the Allies' efforts to overthrow the Bolsheviks in Southern Russia on the side of the White Army created a moral obligation to extend hospitality not only to returning Greeks but also to a certain number of Russian refugees (Divani 1994: 52–3).[2] Greece then had a population of 4.5 million and was at war with various Balkan states and, later, Turkey. After the arrival of some 1.5 million Greek Orthodox refugees from Asia Minor in the early 1920s, following the population exchange established by the Treaty of Lausanne in 1923 (Hirschon 1998 and 2003), Russian refugees were no longer welcome in Greece (Divani 1994: 65–6).

Perestroika and the break-up of the Soviet Union provoked even larger flows. Between 1987 and 2000 Greece welcomed some 200,000–300,000 migrants from the former Soviet Union (FSU), of whom 150,000–200,000 were ethnic Greeks.[3] Most were Pontic Greeks but there were also Mariupol Greeks (Kaurinkoski 2003 and 2018; Voutira 1991 and 2011). Among migrants of non-Greek ethnic origin, Georgians, Ukrainians, Russians, Moldovans and Armenians were the largest groups. In 2001 Greece's population stood at 10.9 million, of which foreigners numbered 762,191 accounting for 7 per cent of the total population (Table 1.1) (Baldwin-Edwards 2004 and 2008).

In Greece the preservation and promotion of a unified national identity and culture have been a concern for successive Greek governments

Table 1.1 Immigrant population from the FSU in Greece according to the 1991 and 2001 censuses,* 1997 legalisation programme, and valid resident permit data as of 15 January 2006 and 27 May 2014. Statistically relevant nationalities.

Country	1991	1997	2001	2006	2014
Armenia	–	2,734	7,742	5,145	5,586
Belarus	–	100	350	1,111	1,230
Georgia	–	7,548	22,875	13,496	15,653
Kazakhstan	–	297	2,256	1,135	1,221
Moldova	–	4,396	5,716	10,561	8,676
Russia	–	3,139	17,535	10,084	12,697
Ukraine	61	9,821	13,616	20,283	17,298
Uzbekistan	–	156	802	895	958
Total foreign immigrant population**	167,276	371,641	762,191	586,474	457,774

Sources: Baldwin-Edwards 2008: 2; Ministry of Public Order, Greek Statistical Service; Ministry of the Interior, Greece.

Notes:
* It is not clear whether ethnic Greeks or *homogeneis* were counted as Greek nationals or foreigners in the 2001 census (Baldwin-Edwards 2008: 2). However, the significant diminution of Russian and Georgian nationals in Greece between 2001 and 2006 suggests that the 2001 figures included ethnic Greeks from these countries who by 2006 had received Greek citizenship. The increase in the number of Ukrainians between 2001 and 2006 can probably be explained by the fact that an increased number had regularised their legal stay in the country, as well as family reunification.
** Total foreign population refers to the 1991 and 2001 census figures.

since the country's inception as a state in 1832. Both citizens of the homeland and their *homogeneis* (persons of the same ethnic origin) in other countries are presumed to belong to the same community, sharing a collective identity independently of any actual collective experience. In the terms of Benedict Anderson (1983), they belong to the 'imagined community' that make up the nation (Voutira 2011). In Greece the *homogeneis* have privileged access to Greek citizenship, eventually also to other benefits. Migrants of non-Greek ethnic origin are labelled as *allogeneis*. The Greek government thus creates migrants, and the desirability or undesirability of mobility, by defining who counts as a potential citizen (Anderson 2013).

An ethnic or a national group's strength is partially the status it can derive from its old homeland and from its earlier presence in the host country. For historical reasons the representations of Russia in Greece have been rather positive. Both are largely Orthodox countries; moreover, Russia supported Greece against the Ottomans in the Greek War of Independence (1821–32) (Kitromilidis 1989).

Between the eighteenth and early twentieth centuries large numbers of Greeks from the northern shores of the Black Sea coast in current Turkey, mainland Greece, and the Greek islands settled in Russia where many found a good life and even prosperity. Some came to occupy important civic positions in Russian and later Soviet society (Chassiotis 1997; Kaurinkoski 2018).

Moreover, the Greek royal family had close relations with the Russian imperial family, and among its members counted several Romanovs, most prominently Queen Olga (1851–1926; Figure 1.1), spouse of King George I of the Hellenes (1867–1913) and regent of Greece in 1920.[4] King George I himself was brother of the Russian empress Maria Feodorovna (1847–1928).[5] Another prominent personality who actively engaged in social and charity work in Greece during the Balkan Wars and in the aftermath of the Russian Revolution was Grand Duchess Elena Vladimirovna (1882–1957) (Zhalnina-Vasilkioti 2015).[6]

THE INTERWAR RUSSIAN REFUGEES IN GREECE

A group portrait: the Russian Orthodox Church as the centre of social and spiritual life

The Russian refugees who settled in Greece in the aftermath of the Russian Revolution had fled war, hunger, social change and even terror. In Greece many of them developed and retained the memory of old

Figure 1.1 Queen Olga of Greece after the church service at the Holy Trinity Church in Athens © <https://bigolive.wordpress.com/2015/12/17/the-russian-church-of-athens/>

Russia and the story of exile because of the historical changes and potential danger for their lives. Many also retained a Russian identity and gave a Russian education to their children who were brought up in the belief that they would eventually return to Russia. With time, many came to realise that return to Russia was impossible. In emigration, life continued and was closely related with the Russian Orthodox Church, the émigré community, and its numerous charitable, educational, cultural, religious, scientific and political organisations.

As a result of earlier Greek–Russian relations and Russian presence in Greece, a Russian Orthodox church already existed in Athens. Dedicated to the Holy Trinity, this church, also known as the Church of the Saviouress of Lykodemos, is located in one of the oldest medieval buildings in Athens, dating to 1031 (Figure 1.2).[7] In 1847 Tsar Nicholas

Figure 1.2 Exterior view of the Church of the Holy Trinity in Athens, also known as the Church of the Saviouress of Lycodemos or simply the 'Russian Church'.
© <https://bigolive.wordpress.com/2015/12/17/the-russian-church-of-athens/>

I (reigned 1825–55) proposed to acquire the church to provide religious services to the Russian community in Athens. The Greek government agreed on condition that the existing church would be reconstructed in its original form (Bouras 2004). In 1850 the church was renovated by the tsar with the help of the Russian community in Athens. The latter actively engaged in charity work in Greece providing theological training for the Greek clergy and renovating churches and monasteries. These activities served the interests of the Russian government. Queen Olga, particularly, played an important role in the development of the Russian community in Athens and in the establishment of the Russian church as a place for religious, artistic, cultural and musical encounters. She also founded the Russian Orthodox marine cemetery in Piraeus.[8]

In exile, many intellectuals, indifferent until then, found a mental shelter and relief from nostalgia in church. Like elsewhere in Europe, the local churches often became the centre of the refugees' social life and acted as symbolic collective homes (Baschmakoff and Leinonen 2001; Divani 1994; Kaurinkoski 1998; Laggoune 2014; Struve 1996; Zhalnina-Vasilkioti 2015).

The financial survival of the church was thus of outmost importance. In the early days the Serbian Embassy in Athens took care of this. The community's registry office was established in Yugoslavia where births, deaths and weddings were registered (Divani 1994: 64–5). Since 1924 the church has been under the jurisdiction of the Archbishop of Athens, the Primate of the Church of Greece.

The last ambassador of Tsar Nicholas II (reigned 1894–1917) in Athens, Prince Elim Demidov (1868–1943) and his spouse, Princess Sofia Demidova (1870–1953), are buried in the courtyard of this church. After the revolution Prince Demidov remained in Greece as an elected leader (*starosta*) of the Russian Orthodox Church. Sofia Demidova, born Vorontsova-Dashkova, who outlived her husband by ten years, dedicated her remaining life to the Russian community, selling most of her artworks and property. In the end she even dismissed her chauffeur and sold her car to help needy refugees (Zhalnina-Vasilkioti 2015).

Émigré associations and life in exile

The first charity organisation, the Aid to Russians in Greece Union (*Soyuz pomoshchi russkim v Gretsii*), was established in 1919 to help the arriving Russian refugees. The Union of Russian Émigrés (*Soyuz russkih emigrantov*), established in 1927, had a semi-official status and issued identity certificates for its members (Divani 1994). The Society of Russian Monarchists in Greece (*Obshchestvo russkih monarhistov v Gretsii*) was divided between those supporting Grand Duke Kirill Vladimirovich (1876–1938) and those supporting Grand Duke Nikolai Nikolaevich (1856–1929) as successor to the throne. After Nikolai Nikolaievich passed away in 1929, relations between the two fractions slowly eased (Zhalnina-Vasilkioti 2015). The Cossacks and the Greeks from Russia had their own organisations. In the case of the latter, the Society of the Greeks from Russia (Σωματείο των εκ την Ρωσία Ελλήνων) was the most prominent (Pavlides 1953).

There was a Russian hospital in Piraeus, a Russian school in Athens (until 1935), and a Russian magazine (*Russkaia gazeta*). Great efforts were made to keep the Russian school operating. To this end, money was raised by organising balls and other charity activities; American organisations also helped in this endeavour. Some sent their children to foreign private schools for them to learn foreign languages, deemed to be important if individuals were to play a role in society (Zhalnina-Vasilkioti 2015).

In relation to the political situation in Greece in the period 1910–22, known as the Greek National Schism,[9] the refugees were also divided:

some sympathised with King Constantine I who favoured close ties with Germany; others supported Eleftherios Venizelos who acted in the interests of the Allies.

The establishment of diplomatic relations between Greece and the Soviet Union in 1924 made the situation of the Russian refugees even more difficult (Kondis 1985). In that same year the Second Greek Republic was proclaimed, and the Crown was abolished for eleven years. Properties of the royal family, as well as former Russian hospitals and other private institutions, were nationalised (Divani 1994; Zhalnina-Vasilkioti 2015).

Some Russian refugees found work as private teachers, drivers, pianists, artists, silent film actors, or caregivers for the elderly and the sick (Zhalnina-Vasilkioti 2015). Engineers and doctors managed to integrate well. Some artists distinguished themselves by making miniatures at the Benaki Museum or as painters in the pottery workshops of the Kerameikos district in Athens (Divani 1994). The Kauffmann bookshop in Stadiou Street in central Athens, which later specialised in French and educational books, was founded by a Russian refugee in the mid-1920s. The pastry shops Petrograd and Rossikon in the same street were also run by Russians. In the seaside neighbourhood of Faliro there were Russian restaurants (Divani 1994: 67). It has been estimated that 80 per cent of the soldiers and officers of General Wrangel's White Army worked in mines, factories, agriculture and viticulture. Many endured famine, exploitation and harsh conditions. After the arrival of refugees from Asia Minor, finding manual jobs became difficult (Zhalnina-Vasilkioti 2015).

Considering the difficult situation in Greece, and understanding that return to Russia was not possible, by the mid-1920s many émigrés, especially the young and the healthy, continued their journey to France and the United States. Some settled in Serbia. Among those who stayed in Greece, many had scarce resources. After World War II, obtaining Greek citizenship became easier (Divani 1994: 67). Nevertheless, like elsewhere in Europe, some lived and died with a Nansen passport without taking up the citizenship of their host country, even when such a possibility existed. Naturalisation was perceived as denaturalisation and was a delicate subject (Kaurinkoski 1998).[10]

The Nansen passport for stateless persons, named after the Norwegian diplomat and humanitarian Fridtjof Nansen,[11] was a certificate that allowed refugees to cross borders legally and which at various times was recognised by more than 50 governments. Although the passport was created initially for refugees from Russia, it was later extended to other groups, for example the Greek and Armenian refugees from the Ottoman Empire (Voutira 1997).

As far as the Russian refugees in Greece were concerned, in many fields, interaction with, and integration into, the host society was obvious and self-evident. At the same time, the collection of memoirs, published by Irina Zhalnina-Vasilkioti in 2015, suggests that the interwar Russian émigré community in Greece was also largely self-sufficient. They created and lived in their own 'Russian World'.[12] Because prominent community members had access to well-placed people in Greek society, and took an active part in social and charitable activities, many Russian refugees were able to find jobs, housing, medical aid, schooling and food. Intra-group solidarity, informed by collective consciousness, was 'primordial', a concept developed by Durkheim to explain how unique individuals are bound together into collective units like social groups and societies. Collective consciousness thus refers to the set of shared beliefs, ideas, attitudes and knowledge that are common to a social group or society.[13] Partially, the relative self-sufficiency of the interwar Russian community in Greece can be explained by educational factors and shared experiences. They valued the companionship of their compatriots with whom they shared a common past, preoccupations and a certain worldview.[14] Many had relatives in other European countries with whom relations were maintained. The aristocracy was cosmopolitan, in the Greek, classical sense of the word; they were an elite[15] group who felt they were citizens of the world. *Cosmos* in Greek refers to worldwide humanity, and *polis*, to a local community or a city (Darieva 2016).

Towards the end of their lives many émigrés emphasised how much they felt at ease in Greece, as the general atmosphere towards the Russian refugees was welcoming. They came from a grand and previously friendly country. They also enjoyed the moral, and at times also the practical, support of the Greek royal family with whom some members of the Russian community maintained close relations (Zhalnina-Vasilkioti 2015).

POST-SOVIET MIGRANTS IN GREECE

Ethnic Greeks and others

The points of departure, the reasons for coming to Greece, the initial expectations, and the situations of the vast and nationally, ethnically, culturally and linguistically heterogeneous group of post-Soviet migrants were different. The global conjuncture had also changed. In the case of the Pontic Greek migrants, who make up the great majority of migrants from the FSU between 1990 and 1993, the migration was sudden, massive

Table 1.2 Immigrant population from the FSU in Greece according to valid resident permit data as of 27 May 2014.

Country	Work	Other	Family reunification	Studies	Total
Armenia	571	1,534	3,342	139	5,586
Azerbaijan	11	1	55	4	71
Belarus	255	168	784	23	1,230
Georgia	2,776	4,294	8,404	179	15,653
Kazakhstan	52	123	1,038	8	1,221
Kyrgyzstan	-	11	71	3	85
Moldova	1,270	2,753	4,535	118	8,676
Russia	1,177	1,688	9,612	220	12,697
Tajikistan	-	-	-	1	1
Turkmenistan	-	1	14	2	17
Ukraine	2,483	5,222	9,348	245	17,298
Uzbekistan	88	99	752	19	958
USSR	-	-	1	-	1
Total FSU	8,683	15,894	37,956	961	63,494
Total foreign migrant population	67,985	175,660	208,234	5,895	457,774

Source: Ministry of the Interior, Greece.

and collective (Pratsinakis 2013). Although few had any ties to Greece, many still considered it an 'eternal homeland' (Grigorakis and Kataiftsis 2019). This led to a large-scale family migration and finally to complete relocation of kinship or locality based networks (Voutira 1991). Voutira argues that their repatriation should be construed as 'affinal repatriation' meaning 'return to each other', rather than 'return to a place' (Voutira 2011 and 2020). In the case of the Mariupol Greeks, the Ukrainians, the Georgians and the Moldovans, the main incentive was economic. Later migration from the post-Soviet states is largely explained by family reunification (Baldwin-Edwards 2004 and 2008; Nikolova and Maroufof 2016) (Table 1.2).

In Greece some post-Soviet and mainly Pontic Greek migrants have settled in enclaves inhabited by their compatriots, giving rise to a 'reverse diaspora' – a frequent phenomenon in the case of ethnic Greek, German, Jewish and Finnish populations from the FSU who live in their ancestral homelands or other diaspora centres (Hess 2014; Kaurinkoski 2018; Trier 1996; Voutira 2011). What characterises these diaspora groups is often a disillusion, which can be explained by their early, negative or unexpected experiences in the ancestral homeland or another country of settlement, and the subsequent sentiment of rootlessness which often results from the endured or perceived hostility of the host population.

These groups often develop a hybrid group consciousness characterised by solidarity with former compatriots, and the development of relations which can result in circular migration, as well as temporary or permanent return to the country of origin (Hess 2014).

In Greater Athens, ethnic Greeks from the former Soviet Union are numerous in the outskirts of the city, in the municipalities of Kallithea, Acharnon[16] and Aspropyrgo. In Acharnon many Pontic Greeks live in houses they themselves have constructed. The material culture of these houses bears the imprint of the homeland left behind. Teacups, crystal glasses, kitchenware and furniture have been brought from the Soviet Union. Russian is the main language of communication in their domestic circle, and Russian television is watched.

According to my interviewees, in Greece a good number of Pontic Greeks from the FSU mainly socialise with other Pontic Greeks, and with other Russian speakers from the former Soviet Union (Figures 1.3 and 1.4). Many emphasise the positive aspects of the education system in the Soviet Union, the richness of Russian culture, and their belonging to the Russian-speaking world (Kaurinkoski 2018). In this context, the enclave of co-ethnics, or compatriots, perceived as like-minded people, acts to create a link between a location and a people, a concept of 'rootedness' which underlines the concept of the nation state (Malkki 1992).

During the first years after their arrival, many Ukrainians, as well as other migrants from Eastern Europe, typically lived in the old city centre of Athens where rent was affordable (Kaurinkoski 2018 and 2021). In their case, the forms of solidarity observed were not so much 'durable and reproductible', but discursively constructed 'networks of exchange' and 'performances of community' which were fluid and virtual and emerged in the moments of enactment and interaction (Ryazanova-Clarke 2014: 11). While other languages and dialects (Ukrainian, Georgian, Greek, Turkic) are also spoken by these groups, Russian often serves as a lingua franca.

The demand and production of Russian-language cultural products

The demand for Russian cultural products led to the establishment of the first Russian-language newspapers and bookshops in Athens and Thessaloniki in the early 1990s. The first Russian-language weekly newspaper, *Omonia* (Unity), started appearing in 1993. It was founded by Aris Papanthimos (1955–99), a member of the Greek Communist Party who had studied in Moscow. Papanthimos was also the founder of the first Athens-based Russian-language bookshop. *Afinskii Kur'er* (Athens

Figure 1.3 Ahead of the municipal elections in 2004, Pontic Greek 'return' migrants who arrived in Greece in the 1960s visit a house of more recent 'return' migrants, who have come to Greece in the early 1990s. Tea is served from cups that have been made in the Soviet Union. Menidi, Greater Athens, 2004. © Kira Kaurinkoski

Figure 1.4 Soviet Greek 'return' migrants in Menidi: a moment of female sociability. Menidi, Greater Athens, 2002. © Kira Kaurinkoski

Courrier), founded in 1999, and *Afiny & Ellas* (Athens & Hellas), which was founded by Ilona Talantseva in 2004 and published until 2014, were other Russian-language weeklies with a similar profile. Some of these newspapers also gave space to articles in Ukrainian. Some Pontic Greek and Ukrainian associations had their own newsletters (Kaurinkoski 2018 and 2021). In 2022 *Omonia*, renamed *Mir i Omonia*,[17] and *Afinskii Kur'er* still exist. Both are international Russian-language newspapers published in cooperation with their Moscow editors. They are distributed in Greece and Cyprus.

Some migrants of Greek origin have written prose in which they discuss life in the FSU and their first years in Greece (Budakidu 2008; Prokopidi 2016; Prokopidou 2012; Talantseva 2004; Talantseva and Arabadzhi 2006). Some of these books are written in Russian, others in Greek, while some have been published in both languages. The Soviet past is usually discussed and depicted with warmth and nostalgia, and the difficulties encountered in Greece, with a sense of humour, as tribulations of life. The decision to come to and remain in Greece, and the wish to integrate into Greek society, are presented as the right choices, particularly in the case of protagonists of ethnic Greek origin (Kaurinkoski 2010 and 2018). The most prolific of the post-Soviet writers in Greece is Sofia Prokopidou, a Thessaloniki-based journalist of Pontic Greek origin from Kazakhstan who came to Greece in 1990. Her collection of short stories, Μια βαλίτσα μαύρη χαβιάρη και άλλες ιστόριες της Αντιγόνας (A Suitcase with Black Caviar and Other Stories by Antigone), published in Greek in 2012, and in Russian in 2016, is a hymn to life, full of light and hope (Kaurinkoski 2018).

There are also exceptions – books in which nostalgia and melancholy are pivotal (Budakidu 2008; Kaurinkoski 2010). As Fialkova writes referring to the Russian-language prose of migrants in Germany, 'the artificial and utopian concept of the "Soviet people" has left a nostalgic trace on many histories of migration' (Fialkova 2013: 196). This tendency is also visible in Greece. Migration literature, as the lived experiences of migrants, is located 'in between' cultures and characterised by hybridity (Bhabha 1996: 58).

The 'accidental diaspora' and reinvention of identities

In our postmodern, uprooted, mobile and deterritorialised world, identity is an ongoing process that is in a constant state of flux. The disintegration of the Soviet Union produced a post-multinational type of Russian-speaking community, an 'accidental diaspora' (Brubaker 2000).[18] The migration process has further altered the migrants' views of their own identities, in part responding to the expectations of the host society. Ethnic Greeks frequently reconstruct their social identities in ways that emphasise their Greek roots and their allegiances to the Greek nation. In Greece some Ukrainian migrants who previously considered themselves as 'Soviet people' have constructed a Ukrainian identity (Kaurinkoski 2018 and 2021).

On a collective level, various advisory, social, cultural and educational associations have been established by the post-Soviet migrants in Greece. The more established Pontic Greek associations frequently work towards the recognition of the Pontic Greek genocide (1916–23) by the wider international community[19] and organise secular pilgrimages to the Pontos region in current-day northern Turkey (Bruneau 1998). In the early days they also provided help with acquisition of Greek citizenship and with other practical and legal issues (Kaurinkoski 2018).

The Ukrainian associations in Greece take an active position on matters relevant to Ukrainian foreign policy. After the illegal annexation of Crimea by Russia in 2014, and the start of the war in Eastern Ukraine, they have organised demonstrations in front of the Greek Parliament in favour of the territorial unity of Ukraine. In cooperation with the Ukrainian Embassy, they have also organised art exhibitions and concerts addressing the war in Eastern Ukraine (Figure 1.5) (Kaurinkoski 2018 and 2021).[20] The war between Russia and Georgia in 2008 triggered a similar reaction from Georgians living in Greece.[21]

Here, I would like to draw attention to the Union of Russian Émigrés named after Princess Sofia I. Demidova, mentioned above. Established in 1927, it carried out its charity activities until 1984, when its last president died. In 2010 it was reactivated by the new wave of migrants from the FSU with the support of descendants of White Russian emigrants living in Greece. Countess Xenia Sheremeteva-Sfiri (b. 1942) was nominated honorary president.[22] The current members come from different parts of the FSU and represent various nationalities and professions. What unites them is their love for Russia, its history and culture, and a feeling of belonging to the 'Russian World'.[23] The association organises excursions, exhibitions and voluntary activities (Kaurinkoski 2018). In this instance, we see a beautiful example of continuity between the different waves of migrants. Moreover, we see that movement and change do not diminish the pull of places, which often retain a powerful significance in people's lives.

Any nostalgia present in the groups studied is multifaceted. In the early days following migration and settlement in the new host country, we can speak of what Bourdieu (1977) calls 'hysteresis of habitus', or a

Figure 1.5 Mother's Day concert at the Embassy of Ukraine, organised by the Ukrainian community in Athens. The participants, mostly independent female labour migrants, listen attentively to the choir, the speeches and the testimonies of Ukrainian women who have worked as volunteers in Eastern Ukraine. Athens, 2015.
© Kira Kaurinkoski

lack of fit between one's internalised dispositions and the new rules of the game – in other words, lack of agency and control. Some are nostalgic because of the memories of the material culture and their earlier private lives, and, in the case of the post-Soviet migrants, because of the 'habitus of socialism', thus enabling them to share a discourse on cultural belonging. However, nostalgia for the relics of an era does not necessarily mean nostalgia for its political ideology. Often, it is a cultural and spiritual vacuum that migrants experience far away from home (Nadkarni and Shevchenko 2015).

For some migrants, the church and the parish community provide an anchorage through which they find faith and hope. In the Russian Orthodox church of Athens, mentioned earlier, today's parish members are mainly migrants from the FSU, but there are also members and descendants of earlier waves of migration and embassy representatives, as well as local Greeks. The celebration of Divine Liturgy takes place in Slavonic and Greek.[24] The church also runs a Sunday school for children, and organises excursions and pilgrimages to churches, monasteries and holy sites. It is a place where newly arrived migrants meet and receive spiritual and practical support. The church thus facilitates integration and at the same time distinguishes the migrants in their host society. It is also a place where 'cultural intimacy' (Herzfeld 2005)[25] is recreated. In Athens there are also other churches where the service is celebrated in Slavonic, as well as Ukrainian churches, both Uniate and Christian Orthodox. Some practise their faith in a Greek Orthodox church of their choice. There are also adepts of the Adventist Church and sects. Others have no contact with religious institutions or formally established migrant institutions (Kaurinkoski 2018).

For some it is sufficient to adjust to the demands of the moment, acquire the necessary skills to deal with practical issues in the new host society, and to reconstruct their identities with the view of a 'new life' in Greece. There are also differences according to gender lines. However, this does not mean that Greece is necessarily the final stop for all post-Soviet migrants who have arrived there after perestroika. Migration tends to generate new mobilities. A certain number of ethnic Greeks have resettled – temporarily or permanently – in Cyprus or Germany. Some others circulate between their former homelands, Greece and/or Cyprus (Kaurinkoski 2018).

In the case of some migrants, regular visits to the old home country started soon after arrival and settlement in Greece. Return migration to Russia and Ukraine has also been observed. Yet many migrants have no plan to return to their former countries of settlement (Kaurinkoski 2018; Nikolova and Maroufof 2016). Instead, they are in the process of transforming their former homes into a cultural site, a talisman, a place that provides material reality for ideals and a sense of belonging, which helps to keep them oriented in their new places elsewhere (Green 2016). Some migrants are citizens of several states – and, in fact, trans-migrants with multiple, often hybrid, identities and relations. In their case, we can speak of new forms of cosmopolitanism which include non-elite forms of openness to cultural differences and the willingness to engage with 'the other' (Darieva 2016). Others who are less active, dynamic or lucky tend to reproduce limited, local or parochial attachments as a reply to their cultural and social exclusion (Kaurinkoski 2018).

CONCLUSION

The interwar Russian refugees who arrived in Greece in the aftermath of the 1917 Revolution were an elite group and their migration political, a result of forced migration. Many longed for a return and later realised that return was not possible. They carried their roots with them calling themselves, not 'immigrants', but 'emigrants' or 'refugees'. Identity maintenance and integration were complementary processes.

The migration that happened after perestroika and the end of the Soviet Union was mostly economic and voluntary, a mass migration. The post-Soviet migrants, notwithstanding their ethnic origins, did not call themselves emigrants and did not speak of emigration. For many, these terms had retained the stigma of the Soviet era when emigration was understood as treason against the fatherland (Yelenevskaya and Fialkova 2002). Over the years a shift and differentiation have been observed in the ethnic and national identities and loyalties in the context of migration. Russia, as successor state of the Soviet Union, is no longer the (only) point of reference for everybody. The incipient Ukrainian and Georgian diaspora in Greece are good examples. Although Russian is widely spoken and serves as a lingua franca among different migrants, it is not the only language in their repertoire and for many it is not their first language. The Ukrainian community is largely from Western Ukraine and their language is Ukrainian. Pontic and Mariupol Greek dialects, the different Turkic dialects of these groups, Georgian and, last but not least, modern Greek, are also widely spoken.

Constructing home is often the result of family reunification, sustainable living conditions and personal accomplishments. Engaging in community life, the exchange of information, mutual aid, the maintenance of culinary traditions and the celebration of holidays that were important in the old home country, as well as remembering the past, also contribute to the feeling of being at home (Čapo 2015; Kaurinkoski 2018). For some the local Russian or Ukrainian church is an important reference point, a place where social and cultural intimacy is recreated. For others the 'true nation' can only be imagined as a 'moral community' (Malkki 1992: 35) – as a community of shared values (Kaurinkoski 2018).

In the case of the post-Soviet migrants, who are free to travel, visit and even return to their old home countries, some are deliberately reconstructing the relation between their new locations and the places where they were born or grew up, redefining what it means to be from there. Russia, Ukraine, Georgia and other former Soviet republics, depending on the migrants' places of origin or earlier settlement, have thus become 'pilgrim sites', or special places to be visited to renew themselves, to remind themselves of their own values and principles, and of their commitment to certain notions of belonging and identification.

In the end, what remains are social relations, particularly kinship ties, which can be seen as the key to a sense of belonging: often, people belong where their kin ties are located. Culture and cultural belonging, which in some cases is informed by nostalgia, also matter. Their culture is continually recreated through their social interaction, rather than having it imposed on them (Cohen 1985). In the end, 'to have it all' is possible only where the present triumphs over the past (Nadkarni and Shevchenko 2015: 88–9).

NOTES

1. Between 1987 and 2010 acquisition of Greek citizenship by ethnic Greeks from the former Soviet Union was regulated by specific laws. After 2010 they were covered by the general law that applies to ethnic Greeks from third countries (Christopoulos 2012; Kaurinkoski 2018).
2. To ensure British and French support for his forthcoming campaign in Eastern Thrace and Asia Minor, Greece's prime minister, Eleftherios Venizelos, had declared himself willing to send an expeditionary force to Ukraine in January 1919 (Kontis 1985; Petsalis-Diomidis 1972).
3. Between 1987 and 2000 155,319 ethnic Greeks arrived in Greece: 97,133 arrived with a 'repatriate visa' and 58,156 with a 'tourist visa'. By 2004 approximately 180,000 had received Greek citizenship. Later, Greek citizenship was revoked from some of those who had received it on false grounds (Christopoulos 2012; Kaurinkoski 2018).
4. Grand Duchess Olga Konstantinovna, granddaughter of Tsar Nicholas I.
5. The eldest son of Queen Olga and King George I, Constantine I, was King of Greece 1913–17 and 1920–22.
6. Granddaughter of Tsar Alexander II, the third child of Queen Olga and King George I, and spouse of Prince Nicholas.
7. Until 1701 it was the main church of a Roman catholic monastery, later a parish church of the Greek Orthodox monastery of Kaisariani. The 1705 earthquake and the Greek War of Independence damaged the building severely.
8. Originally, Russian marines were buried at this cemetery. More latterly Russian immigrants have also been buried there.
9. The National Schism was a series of disagreements between King Constantine I and Prime Minister Eleftherios Venizelos regarding the foreign policy of Greece in the period 1910–22 and culminated around the question whether Greece should enter World War I. Venizelos was in support of the Allies and wanted Greece to join the war on their side, while the king wanted Greece to remain neutral, which would favour the plans of the Central Powers (Koliopoulos and Veremis 2002).
10. Information on the number of those, if any, who took up Soviet citizenship and returned to the Soviet Union after World War II is missing.
11. Fridtjof Nansen (1861–1930) was a Norwegian explorer, oceanographer, diplomat and humanitarian. In the final decade of his life he devoted himself to the League of Nations as High Commissioner for Refugees working on behalf of the displaced victims of World War I and related conflicts. His main achievement was the resettlement of the Russian refugees displaced by the upheavals of the Russian Revolution. In 1922 Nansen was awarded the Nobel Peace Prize for his work. From 1925 onwards Nansen spent much time trying to help Armenian refugees, victims of the Armenian Genocide.
12. See below, note 24.
13. <https://www.thoughtco.com/collective-consciousness-definition-3026118> (last accessed 7 April 2021).
14. Testimony from a first-wave Russian emigrant at the international scientific-practical

seminar, *Russian Emigration: History and Modernity*, Russian Centre of Science and Culture in Athens, 11 May 2018.
15 The term 'elite' is here used as defined by Frédérique Leferme-Falguières and Vanessa van Renterghem 2000.
16 Pontic Greeks from the former Soviet Union started settling in Acharnon (Menidi) in the 1960s. Today they constitute 25 to 30 per cent of the total population in the municipality.
17 The word *mir* in Russian has a double meaning, both 'peace' and 'world'.
18 According to Brubaker, 'accidental diasporas' are constituted by the movement of borders across people; they crystallise suddenly following a dramatic – and often traumatic – reconfiguration of political space; they come into being without the participation, and often against the will, of their members; they are more concentrated and territorially rooted than labour migrant diasporas; they consist of citizens of the countries in which they live; and they are shaped to some extent by migration (Brubaker 2000: 2).
19 The Pontic Greek genocide was recognised by the Greek parliament in 1994, and 19 May was established as a day of commemoration of the genocide of the Pontic Greeks. There is no international consensus on the use of the term 'genocide' to characterise the acts of violence committed by the Young Turks in the years 1914–22.
20 Ukrainians began to organise in 1995, when a Ukrainian page was launched in the Russian-language weekly *Omonia* (Unity). In November 1997 a separate Ukrainian newspaper, *Visnyk-Ageliaforos* (Herald), began to appear. The first Ukrainian cultural association in Greece, The Land of Storks (*Žuravlinyi krai*), was created in 1998. A Ukrainian school composed of ten classes and registered with the Ministry of Education in Ukraine was opened in Athens in 1999. In 2020 six Ukrainian cultural associations were registered in Athens (Kaurinkoski 2021).
21 Personal observation by the author, Athens, autumn 2008.
22 Daughter of Princess Irina Sheremeteva and Count Nikolai Sheremetev, and granddaughter of Prince Felix Felixovich Yusupov and Princess Irina Alexandrovna Romanova.
23 The idea of the 'Russian World' can be traced to the early nineteenth century but has acquired a new meaning after the dissolution of the Soviet Union and mass emigration. Its theoreticians view it as a multi-ethnic supranational phenomenon based on shared language, culture and memories. They include in this imagined community not only those who live in Russia and migrants of different waves and their descendants, but also everyone who has affinities with Russia and its culture. Moreover, they believe that the perception of host societies of migrants from the FSU as homogeneous groups of Russians and their real or perceived discrimination contribute to the feeling of belonging to the Russian World. However, they do admit that migrants' attitudes to the state and its history can be ambivalent (Yelenevskaya and Protassova 2015: 141; Tishkov 2008).
24 Greek was introduced as liturgical language in the 1960s when the descendants of the first wave started to lose their Russian and the parish members became increasingly Greek speaking (Divani 1994).
25 Herzfeld explains cultural intimacy as aspects of cultural identity that provide insiders with their assurance of common sociality, in opposition to outsiders. It has become a crucial element in current debates on inclusion and exclusion.

REFERENCES

Anderson, B. (1983), *Reflections on the Origin and Spread of Nationalism*, London: Verso.
Anderson, B. (2013), *Us and them? The Dangerous Politics of Immigration Control*, Oxford: Oxford University Press.
Appadurai, A. (1996), *Modernity at Large: Cultural Dimensions of Globalization*, Minneapolis: University of Minneapolis Press.
Bagni, B. (2009), 'Lemnos, l'île aux Cosaques', *Cahiers du Monde russe*, 50:1, 187–230.
Baldwin-Edwards, M. (2004), *Statistical Data on Immigrants in Greece: An Analytic Study of Available Data and Recommendations for Conformity with European Standards*, Athens: Panteion University.
Baldwin-Edwards, M. (2008), Immigrants in Greece: characteristics and issues of regional distribution', Mediterranean Migration Observatory, MMO Working Paper, 10.
Baschmakoff, N. and Leinonen, M. (2001), *Russian Life in Finland 1917–1939: A Local and Oral History*, Helsinki: Institute for Russian and East European Studies.
Bhabha, H. (1996), 'Culture's in-between', in S. Hall and P. du Gay (eds), *Questions of Cultural Identity*, London: Sage, pp. 53–60.
Bouras, Ch. (2004), 'The Soteira Lykodemou at Athens. Architecture', *Δελτίον της Χριστιανικής Αρχαιολογικής Εταιρείας*, 25, 11–24.
Bourdieu, P. (1977), *Outline of a Theory of Practice*, Cambridge: Cambridge University Press.
Brah, A. (1996), *Cartographies of Diaspora: Contesting Identities*, London: Routledge.
Brubaker, R. (2000), *Accidental Diasporas and External Homelands*, Vienna: Institute for Advanced Studies.
Bruneau, M. (ed.) (1998), *Les Grecs pontiques. Diaspora, identité, territoires*, Paris: CNRS.
Budakidu, V. (2008), *Grechanka, russkaia dushoj*, Saint Petersburg: Aleteia.
Čapo, J. (2015), '"Durable solutions," transnationalism, and homemaking among Croatian and Bosnian former refugees', *Refuge*, 31:1, 19–29.
Chassiotis, I. (ed.) (1997), *Οι Έλληνες της Ρωσίας και της Σοβιετικής Ένωσης. Μετοικεσίες και εκτοπισμοί. Οργάνωση και Ιδεολογία*, Thessaloniki: University Studio Press.
Christopoulos, D. (2012), *Ποιος είναι Έλληνας πολίτης; Το καθεστώς ιθαγένειας από την ίδρυση του ελληνικού κράτους ως τις αρχές του 21^{ου} αιώνα*, Athens: Vivliorama.
Cohen, A. (1985), *The Symbolic Construction of Community*, London and New York: Tavistock Publications.
Darieva T. (2016), 'Global cosmopolitanism and cosmopolitans', in J. Stone, R. M. Dennis, P. S. Rizova, A.D. Smith and X. Hou (eds), *The Wiley Blackwell Encyclopedia of Race, Ethnicity, and Nationalism*, Malden, MA: John Wiley & Sons.
Davis, F. (1979), *Yearning for Yesterday: A Sociology of Nostalgia*, New York: Free Press.
Divani, L. (1994), 'The Russian refugees in Greece: a first attempt to register', *Balkan Studies*, 35:1, 47–69.
Fialkova, L. (2013), 'Immigrant literature about the fourth wave of Russian emigration: the case of Germany', in L. Fialkova and M. Yelenevskaya (eds), *In Search of the Self: Reconciling the Past and the Present in Immigrants' Experience*, Tartu: ELM Scholarly Press, pp. 185–214.
Gatrell, P. (1999), *A Whole Empire Walking: Refugees in Russia during World War I*, Bloomington: Indiana University Press.
Green, S. (2016), 'Epilogue: moving places – relations, return and belonging', in

N. Gregorič and J. Repič (eds), *Moving Places: Relations, Return and Belonging*, Oxford: Berghahn Books, pp. 211–21.
Grigorakis, A. and Kataitftsis, D. (2019), 'From open markets to Russian products stores to "big business": economics and ethics in Pontic Greek communities of Thessaloniki after the Soviet experience', *SEESOX Diaspora Working Paper Series* 5.
Hess, C. (2014), 'What are "reverse diasporas" and how are we to understand them?', *Diaspora*, 17:3, 288–315.
Herzfeld, M. (2005), *Cultural Identity: Social Poetics in the Nation State*, 2nd edn, New York: Routledge.
Hirschon, R. (1998), *Heirs of the Greek Catastrophe: The Lives of Asia Minor Refugees in Piraeus*, 2nd edn, New York: Berghahn Books.
Hirschon, R. (ed.) (2003), *Crossing the Aegean: An Appraisal of the 1923 Compulsory Population Exchange between Greece and Turkey*, New York: Berghahn Books.
Hobsbawm, T. (1991), 'Introduction', *Social Research*, 58:1, 65–8.
Just, R. (1989), 'Triumph of the ethnos', in E. Tonkin, M. McDonald and M. Chapman (eds), *History and Ethnicity*, London: Routledge, 71–88.
Kaurinkoski, K. (1998), 'Les communautés russe et italienne de Nice dans l'entre-deux-guerres: similitudes et différences', *Cahiers de la Méditerranée*, 58, 133–55.
Kaurinkoski, K. (2003), 'Les Grecs de Mariupol. Réflexions sur une identité en diaspora (Ukraine)', *Revue européenne des migrations internationales*, 19:1, 125–46.
Kaurinkoski, K. (2010), 'Homeland in the fiction and written narratives of ethnic Greeks from the former Soviet Union (FSU) in Greece', *Balkanologie*, 12:1, at <https://journals.openedition.org/balkanologie/2141>, last accessed 20 February 2021.
Kaurinkoski, K. (2018), *Le 'Retour' des Grecs de Russie. Identités, mémoires, trajectoires*, Athens: École française d'Athènes.
Kaurinkoski, K. (2021), 'From labour migrants to a diaspora community? The case of Ukrainian migrants in Greece', *Balkanologie*, 16:1, at <https://journals.openedition.org/balkanologie/2750>, last accessed 20 February 2022.
Kitromilidis, P. (1989), 'Από την ορθόδοξη κοινοπολιτεία στις εθνικές κοινότητες: Ελληνο-Ρωσσικές πνευματικές σχέσεις', *Τα Ιστορικά*, 10:6, 29–46.
Koliopoulos, J. and Veremis, T. (2002), *Greece: The Modern Sequel from 1831 to the Present*, New York: New York University Press.
Kontis, B. (1985), 'The re-establishment of Greek-Soviet relations in 1924', *Balkan Studies*, 26, 151–7.
Laggoune, A. (2014), 'Les Russes de Cannes (1879–1939)', Master's thesis 2, Université de Nice Sophia Antipolis, UFR LASH.
Lampropoulos, E. M. (2014), *Belonging to Greece and the Soviet Union: Greeks of Tashkent 1949–1974*, Toronto: York University.
Leferme-Falguières, F. and van Renterghem, V. (2000), 'Le concept d'élites. Approches historiographiques et méthodologiques', *Hypothèses*, 1, 57–67.
Malkki, L. (1992), 'National Geographic: the rooting of peoples and the territorialization of national identity among scholars and refugees', *Cultural Anthropology*, 7:1, 24–44.
Medved, F. (2000), 'The Concept of Homeland', in H. Runblom (ed.), *Migrants and the Homeland. Images, Symbols and Realities*, Uppsala: Uppsala University, pp. 74–99.
Nadkarni, M. and Shevchenko, O. (2015), 'The politics of nostalgia in the aftermath of socialism's collapse', in O. Angé and D. Berliner (eds), *Anthropology and Nostalgia*, New York: Berghahn Books, pp. 61–95.
Nikolova, M. and Maroufof, M. (2016), 'Ukrainian migration to Greece: from irregular work to settlement, family reunification and return', in O. Fedyuk and M. Kindler

(eds), *Ukrainian Migration to the European Union: Lessons from Migration Studies*, Springer Open, Centre of Migration Research, IMISCOE Research Series, pp. 151–62.
Notaras, G. (1998), 'État et société helléniques face au problème pontique', in M. Bruneau (ed.), *Les Grecs pontiques. Diaspora, identité, territoires*, Paris: CNRS, pp. 229–39.
Pavlides, E. (1953), *Ο Ελληνισμός της Ρωσίας και τα 33 χρόνια του εν Αθήναις Σωματείου των εκ Ρωσίας Ελλήνων*, Athens: Somateio ton ek Rosias Ellinon.
Peeling, S. (2014), 'Emigration (Russian Empire)', in U. Daniel, P. Gatrell, O. Janz, H. Jones, J. Keene, A. Kramer and B. Nasson (eds), 1914–1918-online, *International Encyclopedia of the First World War*, Berlin: Freie Universität Berlin.
Petsalis-Diomidis, N. (1972), 'Hellenism in Southern Russia and the Ukrainian Campaign: their effect on the Pontos Question (1919)', *Balkan Studies*, 13:2, 221–63.
Pratsinakis, M. (2013), 'Contesting national belonging: an established-outsider figuration on the margins of Thessaloniki, Greece', PhD thesis, University of Amsterdam.
Prokopidi, S. (2016), *Babka Lemona uhodit v raj i drugie rasskazy Antigony*, Moscow: Nonparel'.
Prokopidou, S. (2012), *Μια βαλίτσα μαύρη χαβιάρη και άλλες ιστορίες της Αντιγόνας*, Thessaloniki: Adelfoi Kyriakidi.
Runblom, H. (2000), 'Introduction: homeland as imagination and reality', in H. Runblom (ed.), *Migrants and the Homeland: Images, Symbols and Realities*, Uppsala: Uppsala University, pp. 9–30.
Ryazanova-Clarke, L. (2014), 'Introduction: the Russian language, challenged by globalisation', in L. Ryazanova-Clarke (ed.), *The Russian Language Outside the Nation*, Edinburgh: Edinburgh University Press, pp. 1–30.
Talantseva, I. (2004), *Ispoved' mil'onera*, Athens.
Talantseva, I. and Arabadzhi, K. (2006), *Maska. Istorii emigrantov v Gretsii*, Athens: Afiny-Ellas.
Tishkov, V. (2008), *The Russian World: Changing Meanings and Strategies*, Washington, DC: Carnegie Endowment for International Peace.
Trier, T. (1996), 'Reversed diaspora: Russian Jewry, the transition in Russia and the migration to Israel', *Anthropology of East Europe Review*, 14:1, 34–42.
Voutira, E. (1991), 'Pontic Greeks today: migrants or refugees?', *Journal of Refugee Studies*, 4:4, 400–20.
Voutira, E. (1997), 'Population transfer and resettlement policies in interwar Europe: the case of Asia Minor refugees in Macedonia from an international and national perspective', in P. Mackridge and E. Yannaki (eds), *Ourselves and Others: The Development of a Greek Macedonian Cultural Identity since 1912*, Oxford: Berg.
Voutira, E. (2011), *The 'Right to Return' and the Meaning of 'Home': A Post-Soviet Greek Diaspora Becoming European*, Berlin: Lit.
Voutira, E. (2020), 'Genealogies across the Cold War divide: the case of the Pontic Greeks from the former Soviet Union and their "affinal repatriation"', *Ethnography*, 21:3, 355–72.
Yelenevskaya, M. and Fialkova, L. (2002), 'When time and space are no longer the same: stories about immigration', *Studia Mythologica Slavica*, 5, 207–30.
Yelenevskaya, M. and Protassova, E. (2015), 'Global Russian: between decline and revitalization', *Russian Journal of Communication*, 7:2, 139–49.
Zapantis, A. (1982), *Greek–Soviet Relations, 1917–1941*, New York: Columbia University Press.
Zhalnina-Vasilkioti, I. (2015), *Russkaia emigratsiia v Gretsii. Sud'by. XX vek*, Moscow: Staraia Basmannaia.

CHAPTER 2

Russian Objects and Russian Homes: A Sociological Reflection on Homes and Migration

Anna Pechurina

INTRODUCTION

In this chapter the materiality of the migrant/diasporic home and its significance for understanding cultural identity and sense of belonging will be discussed by using the study of Russian migrants' homes in the UK. The chapter will evaluate the role of material objects in the process of migrant/diasporic homemaking and how far particular objects contribute to a sense of home or non-home. In this sense, the chapter aims to show the ambivalent and complex nature of home in the context of migration and the related sense of being at home – one which material objects may help (re)construct or take away.

The chapter is located at the intersection of research into home and migration, the subfield of social sciences that has been gaining importance in recent years (Ahmed et al. 2003; Boccagni 2017; Boccagni and Kusenbach 2020; Fog Olwig 2007; Hondagneu-Sotelo 2017; Wiles 2008). Recent scholarship has shown that the notion of home, whether imagined, remembered or experienced, is closely interconnected with the experience of migration (Boccagni 2017) and thus reveals important insights into everyday life, identity and culture. Within this framework, home is defined as a multidimensional and multifaceted concept, one which combines notions of homeland (imagined, remembered or 'real') and dwelling, or 'lived experiences, social relations and emotional geographies of home' (Blunt 2005: 506). Researchers also emphasise the ambivalent character of migrant homemaking. For example, Ahmed et al. (2003) use the concept of uprootings/regroundings to describe an experience of migration during which one simultaneously uproots oneself from familiar contexts and regrounds with new ones.

Furthermore, some scholarly work on diasporic identities puts particular emphasis on the defining role of home within the process of identity construction (Ehrkamp 2005; Story and Walker 2016). Ehrkamp (2005) describes the connection between home and diasporic identity as negotiated, or (re)constructed in relation to 'multiple societies and places' (348), while for Silva (2009) diasporic identities are constituted through a continuous search for Home, where Home is an elusive construct linked to sensory experiences (Silva 2009: 694). Following Giogi and Fasulo, migrant homemaking can be described as a 'work in progress that accompanies changes and different versions of identity through time' (Giogi and Fasulo 2013: 113).

Material cultures, including domestic objects and products of the soil, occupy an important part within migrant and diasporic homemaking and thus offer a resourceful way of approaching broader topics of identity and belonging. As Rosales posits, material cultures and practices of consumption form 'both a powerful resource to address the subject's narratives regarding their migration experiences and, more importantly, a constituent of those same experiences' (2010: 509). In other words, objects that migrants keep, acquire, leave or bring can express and produce identities and relationships with new cultural contexts (Giorgi and Fasulo 2013; Savas 2014) and reveal valuable connections between sense of home and belonging (Walsh 2006) as well as establish boundaries (Frykman 2009). For example, items such as furniture, souvenirs and traditional objects as well as everyday objects not only create particular aesthetics of the home but also produce shared spaces of belonging and channel ongoing experiences of migration and resettlement, simultaneously creating closeness and a reminder of distance (Pechurina 2020).

In a similar way, studies of ethnic food and food from home have demonstrated their powerful potential for revealing and bringing back memories, and the ability to (re)connect migrants with significant people and places in an affective and emotional way (Christou and Janta 2019; Raman 2011; Rosales 2009). The mobility of food, as well as practices of making and consuming it, are important in immigration. Food manifests its presence within homes, through tastes, smells, photographs and pictures displayed on walls, through cooking and eating, through memories and stories of the past and hopes for the future, and in this way represents 'the thread of connectivity between past, present and future' (Christou and Janta 2019: 16). Within deterritorialised or transnational contexts, the meaning of food reveals the constantly changing notions of identities and cultures that produce it (Chapman and Beagan 2013) when new experiences and tastes get incorporated into traditional notions of what constitutes the food from home. In this respect, constantly changing or 'hybridised foodways' (Abbots 2016) reflect the earlier-mentioned arguments about the dynamic and expanding nature of diasporic identity (Appadurai 1996; Remennik 2002).

The study of Russian migrants' homes presented in this chapter follows the outlined approach and considers domestic objects and products of the soil as meaningful indicators of Russian migrants' sense of home and cultural identity. The original research conducted in 2006–10[1] aimed to explore the meaning of home and homemaking among Russian immigrants in the UK using the material cultures of homes as a gateway to trace the practices and experiences of migration and the ways in which both Russian identity and the feeling of belonging to a homeland were created and maintained. To do so, the study used qualitative home-based interviews with Russian speakers from mixed social and generational backgrounds, who identified themselves as Russian and who had resided in the UK over a span of five to forty years at the moment of the interview. A major part of the interview was devoted to the discussion of participants' material possessions, but other questions relating to everyday activities, social circles, language and religion were also discussed. On some occasions, photographs of some of the possessions and interior details were taken either by myself or the participants.

While several studies of Russian-speaking migrants in the UK have explored issues related to identity (Byford 2009 and 2014; Kopnina 2005), the role of language (Kliuchnikova 2015 and 2016), and political mobilisation (Byford 2012; Morgunova and Byford 2018), less attention has been given to the meaning of home and homemaking practices, particularly compared to migrants from other Central and Eastern European countries (Burrell 2009; Forero and Smith 2010; Rabikowska 2010; White 2011). In this respect, this study offers an original empirical case study of Russian migrants' homemaking that explores the meanings and use of material objects in close relation to biographical stories of migration.

A word of caution, however, is necessary when positioning this study in relation to broader research on Russian migration and identity. First, the study deployed a constructivist approach to identity (Hall 1990) and relied on participants' self-identification with Russian culture. 'Russian' in this context was understood as a cultural identity, which is constructed in the course of everyday life: it presumes diversity and is subject to change. Thus, the study aimed to explore how this 'Russian' identity is constructed in immigration from the perspective of the participants themselves, acknowledging the changing and diverse character of said identity and thus recognising that there was no one particular way of being Russian. Consequently, the strategies of 'Russian' homemaking which were revealed in my research did not constitute the ultimate list of Russian practices and cultural repertoires and were not fixed in time and space – whether my participants still keep their objects or maintain the same interiors is unclear and, in fact, constituted one of the conclusions of the study which was that Russianness (the ways and meanings of being Russian) and home are complex and elusive phenomena that involve constantly changing social relationships, meanings and practices.[2]

Second, it is necessary to acknowledge that other factors, including age, socio-economic status, circumstances of arrival, and migration status, certainly impacted domestic practices and objects presented at home and thus added an additional layer to the meanings of the particular types of objects – whether it was food, souvenirs or elements of decor such as visual art and interior details.[3] The essential aspect of this study was not only the focus on what the objects showed but also on how those objects were used in the context of the home. Thus, the value of the study is not in the description of what Russian people had in their homes but in revealing how people used their objects to either feel at home in a new country or less estranged from it and whether this feeling of home or non-home was connected to their ethnicity and culture.

Finally, the study also acknowledges positionality and the role of the researcher – home is lived and made as well as (re)presented, and in this sense my interpretation of the objects and their meanings also revealed my own biography and migration stages. At the same time, while acknowledging the fact that my gaze could have been focused more at times on certain things that resonated with my background, I aimed to maintain sensitivity towards and respect for my participants and tried not to speak over their voices. The use of autobiographical reflections alongside my analysis is there to show that home and migration as well as the way of researching it are in constant interplay, reshaping each other through time and space.

The chapter is structured around several themes that emerged from the study. I will start with a discussion of the notion of Russian objects and Russian homes, followed by a description of groups of objects that I refer to as 'sticky' and 'diasporic'. I will then proceed to the discussion of language and the ways it can be seen within the migrants' homes.

RUSSIAN OBJECTS AND RUSSIAN HOMES

Several years ago, while living in the UK, I visited the home of my friend 'V.' – a Kazakhstan-born Russian speaker in her late thirties who grew up in Germany before coming to the UK with her family. I remember coming into the living room and quickly noticing the interior details as well as some familiar objects – a matryoshka doll on the coffee table, a Kazakh hat, some books in Russian in the bookcase . . . I was particularly struck, however, by a very recognisable object: on one of the shelves was a Soviet-style arithmometer (digital mechanical calculator; see Figures 2.1 and 2.2), the same one as I had in my own home which I had transported

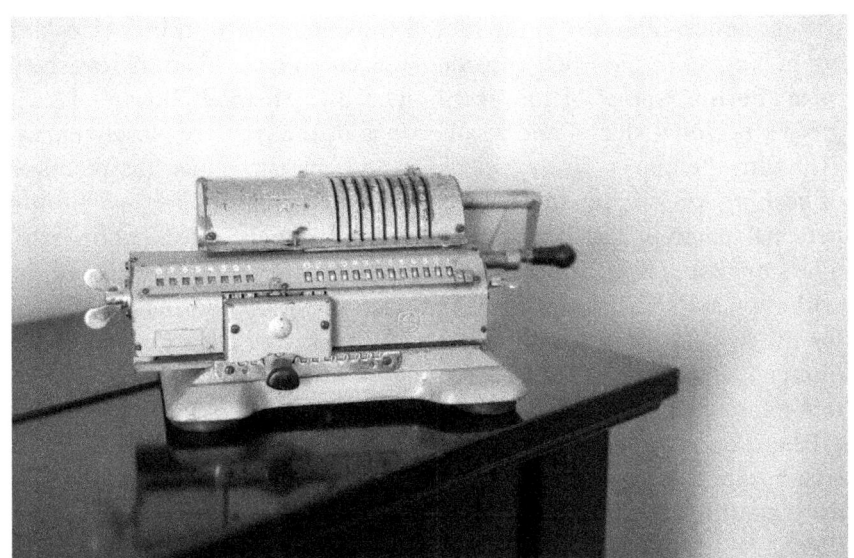

Figures 2.1 and 2.2 My grandmother's arithmometer photographed in my current home in Sweden.

from my grandmother's home in Siberia, first to Moscow and then to the UK. 'I have exactly the same arithmometer!' I said to my friend, excitedly thinking about this amazing coincidence. 'Ah, this one,' responded V., 'we actually brought from Sweden. It's not a Soviet but a Swedish machine.' I moved closer and clearly saw the label on top of the machine.

I chose this example as I think it nicely illustrates several common themes related to the study of domestic objects and their meanings within homes. The first is the idea of the biography of things (Hoskins 2006; Kopytoff 1986) that considers objects to have biographies which form the life stories of the people who own them. Following Hecht (2001), personal stories and recollections of the past are closely entangled with the objects individuals keep and cherish. Thus, the practices of keeping, preserving and talking about such objects offer insight into personal histories as well as a 'collective sense of past' (Hecht 2001: 144). The story about my arithmometer (or rather a story about myself and the arithmometer that I carried with me across various borders) unfolded for me when I noticed a similar object. Following Smart's idea of the interconnectiveness of personal life (Smart 2007), it can be argued that at that moment the memory also brought forward the cultural and historical contexts it was embedded in. Thus, stories about objects reveal their significance to people's personal biographies, but they are also sociologically significant as they are shared and recognised by many others (Smart 2007).

As my study showed, the objects appeared in people's homes by different routes and in various circumstances – samovars were carried on plane flights; books were bought in second-hand shops or on trips 'home'. There were friends' and relatives' gifts and presents as well as spontaneous purchases made on the go. As some interviews showed, the journey that objects undertook to get to their homes was part of their value and significance for the owner. N. was a married woman in her late twenties, and her story of her samovar is one such example. Having received it from her parents in Russia as a present, N. had to take it as hand luggage with her on a flight to the UK:

1. **N. (married woman in her late twenties)**: It was packed in a box and I dragged it along; it was horrible, with the tray as well, all those things. It felt like it was made of cast iron. When I was transporting it last spring I felt I would go crazy.[4]

Despite this experience, the samovar would be one of the items she would take with her if there were a housefire. As she put it: 'There are things one gets "stuck" to . . . I would have to haul it around with me.'[5]

Then, there was M. (a single man in his thirties) who talked about his nineteenth-century Orthodox icon, particularly emphasising the difficulties of bringing objects of this kind across the border and the risk of them being confiscated. Of course, it should be pointed out that not all objects were brought straight away; many were accumulated gradually over time and reflected other life events, such as changing jobs, relationships or location. All these processes connected to possessions were part of their owners' biographies and contributed to the migrants' relationships with the places they lived in.

My next point is about the 'visibility' of objects, some of which stand out for the visitor/researcher more than others. The souvenirs and so-called 'ethnic' objects (Olesen 2010) on display are the ones that are more likely noticeable to a visitor, especially in the context of a study on homes and migration. The presence of specific objects such as folk souvenirs, photographs, pieces of art and craft that picture or refer to a specific country contribute to the overall perception of the home interior not only in terms of its connection to national culture but also in terms of class and related aesthetics.[6] Furthermore, sometimes objects could be noticed or recognised by a researcher/visitor because their qualities (shape, colour, texture) conjured memories and associations that made those objects more 'visible'. Noticing the arithmometer was one of those occasions when the physical qualities of the object attracted my attention as well as revealed my own memories, attachments and emotions.

Similarly, during my research interviews, I took notice of objects that referred to Russia (matryoshka dolls, Orthodox icons, folk souvenirs, glass cabinets, faceted drinking glasses), and sometimes I 'saw' objects that reminded me of my own previous homes or the homes of relatives, including porcelain cups and a particular type of wallpaper (Pechurina 2016). It is important to note, however, that the connection between the (presumed) visibility of some objects and their significance to the owner is not straightforward and can reveal complex and ambivalent meanings. Thus, while some items may visibly carry national or traditional symbolism, their actual significance to the owner can be a lot more complex and multi-layered – a point that I will come back to later in this chapter. My suggestion, however, is that, regardless of whether the objects are on display or hidden, they are embedded in the personal lives of their owners and thus, their significance should be studied in close connection to people's lives (Smart 2007).

The final point is that the meanings of objects are not static; they continuously change, revealing the fluidity and relationality of home-making practices and experiences that happen in the course of migration (Boccagni 2017). Georgi and Fasulo develop the concept of the 'transformative' home, considering it as a continuous set of experiences and practices through which a sense of home and 'different versions of identity' (2013: 113) evolve as time goes on. Objects are accumulated, sorted out, rearranged, hidden or given away; they are packed and unpacked, finding a new place in the new home. My arithmometer that I brought from Russia to the UK is now in our new home in Sweden where I am still unpacking boxes after our recent move. As 'the search for home' (Boccagni 2017) continues, the objects (both present and absent) help with filling it with meanings and stories.

'STICKY' OBJECTS AND DIASPORIC OBJECTS

In the previous section I discussed how objects can get 'stuck' to their owners who may feel a special connection to them because of the experience of carrying the objects with them during their migration and then keeping them in their new home. Marcoux (2001) developed the idea of 'mnemonic objects' that acquire a special significance over time, especially after a move during which people often sort things out and in doing so reflect on the importance of their possessions in connection with self-identity, memories and family history. As Marcoux posits, in the process of moving, such objects act as the main instrument that links people, places, and memory together (Marcoux 2001). In my study, many souvenirs or so-called 'ethnic' items were kept precisely as reminders of the people who gave them or as a symbol of the home country – some were put on display, while others were hidden away.[7] Sometimes during the interviews participants had a moment of discovery and remembered some of those items (for example an old card or a religious icon given by a relative).[8] On other occasions it could be me pointing at something on display in a bookcase or cabinet. Furthermore, while some participants arranged items as part of the planned home decor, others admitted that they just wanted to put the items somewhere where there was space available, not necessarily remembering how an object got to where it was. This could happen with souvenirs or gifts from relatives that people did not think they needed but which at the same time they could not bring themselves to throw away – they 'did not have the courage' to do so, as some said.[9] Following Woodward (2015), these objects can be described as dormant objects, or the ordinary things that can be stored away for years, sometimes forgotten, but still vital to people's lives and relationships. Even if the only function of the objects on display was a term of reference, they were retained by their owners and thus were kept alive or at least had a potential for life.

While some objects were kept as reminders of joyful memories, there were also objects that revealed ambivalent or difficult feelings. These objects can be compared with 'inherited' objects (Finch and Mason 2000), which people sometimes feel uncomfortable possessing, but familial obligation prevents them from throwing these things away. In this sense, some 'Russian' objects can be thought of as something 'inherited'. People cannot escape inheriting such objects, so they have to tolerate them in their homes. For instance, S. (a divorced woman in her early forties) kept a stone on a mantelpiece in her house that has been left to her by her mother who had found it on the North Sea coast when visiting her daughter in the UK. S. admitted that, although she did not see aesthetic value in it, she still kept the stone together with several other items inside the display cabinet. For similar reasons, she kept a glass figurine which had been her mother's wedding gift to her. Following Smart (2007), S.'s accounts can be interpreted through the lens of 'sticky' relationships, signifying a sense of connection which cannot be described as simply good or bad but which are 'interwoven and embedded' (Smart 2007: 45) into people's lives in many different ways. According to Smart, 'it is hard to shake free from [such objects] at an emotional level and their existence can continue to influence our practices and not just our thoughts' (2007: 45). S.'s description of the objects that were given to her by her mother indicates this 'stickiness' that reveals both closeness and tension. In the earlier quotation N. also said that she would take the heavy samovar with her because it was given to her by her parents. This also happened in the home of I. and A. (a married couple in their thirties), who had put the Orthodox icons given to them by A.'s mother on the top shelf, where I spotted them almost by chance. A. explained:

2. **A. (married men in his thirties):** It is one of the objects which were given to us 'by force'. There on the top. We had to put them somewhere because we do not have the courage to throw them away.[10]

These descriptions point to the idea that objects, while sustaining connections to people and/or places, may not always reveal straightforward or unproblematic feelings and emotions. As, during my interviews, I followed my participants' lead in showing me their homes, I could not always get to see the objects that evoked such 'sticky' relationships, but they sometimes manifested themselves through abrupt silences, hinted descriptions or closed doors.

To continue with the theme of ambivalence I would like to add a further dimension to the meanings of objects, one that signifies the link that these objects play in both connecting and detaching migrants from their home country and its related culture. I refer to these objects as 'diasporic' to emphasise the existing connections to their origins and the broader cultural references, and at the same time to point to their de-territorialised nature. While objects can refer to and stereotypically represent Russia, not all of them were brought from Russia. Many were acquired while living abroad (for example, bought in the second-hand shops in the UK or elsewhere, or received as gifts) and thus gained their meaning in that context (Pechurina 2020; Savas 2014; Walsh 2006).

To illustrate my point, I will discuss stereotypical Russian souvenirs such as matryoshka dolls, crockery and crafts that I frequently saw on display at my participants' homes and which perhaps usually attract the most attention, at least on an initial visit. As I mentioned before, some of these objects manifested the personal and family connections of my participants. At the same time, participants also admitted that they kept souvenirs because of (sometimes obvious) cultural references. It can be further argued that while, on the one hand, these objects showed a connection with the home country, on the other hand they also underlined the fact that having those objects at all was the result of migration. As N. mentioned in reference to her collection of matryoshka dolls, 'You really do understand the meaning of the objects that are taken for granted in Russia.'[11] I could relate to this experience myself when I bought my first matryoshka doll in a UK charity shop after eleven years of living in the country. While it was a reminder of Russia, it was also a way of acknowledging the time I had been away from it. Thus, souvenirs and

Figure 2.3 My diasporic object: an old matryoshka doll which I bought in a UK charity shop after eleven years of living there.

gifts are diasporic objects in a sense that they are reminders not only of the home country but also of the fact that one is no longer there (Svašek 2012; Vanni 2013). They connect to the experiences of the past while simultaneously they are embedded in the everyday life of the present – the matryoshka doll I bought was one of my British-born daughters' first toys, scattered on the floor or kept in the box and mixed with many other things she played at that time (see also Pechurina 2020).

It should be noted that, while I use matryoshkas and other souvenirs as generalised examples, there can also be other types of diasporic objects such as kitchen or utility items. As migration experiences themselves did not always mean a linear journey from A to B and involved a multiplicity of transnational attachments and relationships, so the meaning of diasporic objects is ambivalent and fluid, continuously balancing between 'here' and 'there', between home and away. L. (a divorced woman in her forties) described a mixture of souvenirs brought from the countries she had lived in and/or visited as well as some items given to her by her friends in the UK in the following way: 'Everything is connected here and represents my key points here. I am not going to leave it.'[12]

LANGUAGE

> 3. **M. (married woman in her forties):** I remember when we had just arrived here and were looking to buy a house, we went to view quite a few and I didn't see a single book in any of the houses we viewed. When we came in to view this house I saw a book about Stalingrad on a coffee table; it surprised me as I hadn't seen any books in any homes here. And here they also had a bookcase, so when we came in here I was surprised to see books. Because I haven't seen books at all in other houses.[13]

> 4. **N. (married woman in her late twenties):** We have fantastic books – you can put them nicely showing their covers – Tolstoy, Dostoevsky, edited volumes, folios, book in red leather with gold lettering and what can they do? What exactly is from England? Will you drag your red telephone box into the house?[14]

Although exploring the role of language was not the main focus of my research, it was inherently present from the start. The interviews were conducted in Russian, and the Russian language was one of the ways of finding and connecting with participants. On several occasions I started conversations with people when I heard them speaking Russian. During my fieldwork I also came across various communities and organisations linked to the Russian language, including student and professional ones. For example, university-based Russian-language student societies offered a useful way into the broader networks of Russian speakers, including students' parents, academics and attendees of the events organised by the societies. Other types of organisation were represented by the various societies and associations that aimed to unite and represent the Russian immigrant community throughout the early 2000s – the Russian language was used by many of them as one of the key defining criteria of the 'Russian diaspora' (for more details, see Byford 2012).

When exploring the attitudes of UK-based Russian-speaking migrants towards the language, Kliuchnikova (2015) shows its significant role in shaping and 'establishing boundaries and senses' (2015: x) within and outside migrant groups and thus impacting on migrants' self-reflection on their own identity as well as on their perceptions of the host society. The quotations by the two women above illustrate these complexities and ambivalences well, and point to how home and sense of home are constructed with objects like books – as something that both indicates belonging to one's community and draws the boundaries between others. These themes were also reflected in the home environments of my participants (where objects, such as Russian-language books, could carry symbolic significance and have representational value).

In the research interviews I had several questions which specifically referred to the Russian language and whether people did anything to keep it, but quite often people mentioned it themselves when they referred to something they missed, such as speaking Russian or when they talked about objects they owned, such as books or music. Books, in particular, were the objects that embodied participants' feelings and attachments towards their roots, culture, heritage, and the experience of living abroad. Books were something that G. brought along on his initial trip to the UK ('to entertain me on the train journey'[15]), the first thing that S. sought out during her first months of immigration ('Of course, I got a library card first thing to get to the Russian-language section'[16]), and that A. gradually accumulated over the years of living in the UK ('... I have five book cabinets. I cannot but read'[17]). To some extent, books represent the types of 'diasporic' objects discussed above as they acquire particular significance after, and because of, the migration experience. For example, L. (a divorced woman in her forties), who defined herself as a 'self-confessed immigrant' and an 'immigrant by calling',[18] said she had brought 'suitcases of books' with her, which helped her stay connected with the Russian language and culture, but not with the country itself, which she had left 'for political reasons'. L. speaks five languages, works as a language teacher, and writes poetry, so language is part of her work, but it is also part of her broader British identity – 'I am British of non-British background, someone who is a little different from other British people', as she put it. For L., migration provided the desired distance from her home country, and she does not aim to cultivate her Russianness in immigration, which she sees as one of the many characteristics of her identity.

In a slightly different way, the interest of T., a university researcher in her thirties, in Russian literature and poetry, which she developed after her immigration to the UK, has led her to rediscover and reflect on her Russianness more than she did before migration. T. started collecting Russian classic literature, which she bought in Russia or on her holidays in the UK and Europe. This hobby invigorated her interest in Russia, which she started visiting specifically to explore and in some way rediscover its culture. The interior of her house reflected this connection, featuring as it did decorative fir cones, pictures of nature and souvenirs, although her books were the most important things for her:

5. **T. (a single woman in her thirties):** I don't think I need objects of one kind or another to feel myself Russian. I do not think that my Russianness can be expressed in any material form. The main thing is the language. The Russian language is what makes me feel myself Russian. If I don't speak or read Russian, I will lose it. So, it's the language. More than anything else. I don't think that we Russians have any particular qualities. What's there? That they are alcoholics or generous people. Maybe, I don't know. I had stereotypes in the past, but they are broken now. Because people aren't pictures. You start to understand what they are like. You understand yourself better and in what way you are different from your neighbour. And in the bigger sense we are not that different. Because all those material expressions do not show the depth. So, I do not suffer without objects. I suffer without language.[19]

This emotional account echoes the notion of home as a process of 'uprooting' and 'regrounding' (Ahmed et al. 2003), in which books – acquired over the years on different journeys – embody the continuous 'search for home' (Boccagni 2017) as well as for one's identity.

Furthermore, Russian books and speaking the language also illuminated T.'s as well as others' ambivalent experiences and the way they viewed their position in the multicultural and multilingual context of the UK (Kluichnikova 2016). This can be seen in the account of K., a university researcher, who had been living with his wife and daughter in the UK for seven years and who described himself as a middle-class intellectual. When introducing his neighbourhood to me, N. (a married man in his thirties) emphasised that he lived in a residential and local (i.e., 'native' British) area, thus implying his level of integration into British life. However, during the interview, his references to British culture were often ambivalent as he talked about his nostalgia for Russia and consequent isolation from both British and Russian circles who did not share his strong feelings. He continued:

> 6. **N. (married man in his thirties):** There is a special group of people who, although they were born in Russia, were not Russians. They set themselves up to go abroad; they learned the language. As they were born in Russia, they speak Russian. They know the language but they could easily do without it. They are a very different type of [Russian] people. I will never be like them. I always need my Russian [language]![20]

N. admitted that he needed regular communication with Russians in the Russian language, as only through using the Russian language could he feel the whole range of emotions regardless of what he does: speaking, reading or watching TV. This example also illustrates the 'sticky' character of this attachment to the native language – something that one is attached to and cannot let go of, even if the connection may not necessarily make one feel better or happier in one's current life.

The relationships to language and the country may not only be expressed through the books that people owned but also through the ones that they did not. G. (a single man in his thirties) prefers not to keep any books as they remind him of *meschanstvo* (philistinism) – which he associates with books arranged by colour in glass cabinets; instead, he prefers to read electronic versions. P. (a recent divorcee in his late forties) told me that he had left four big boxes containing his favourite books in a friend's garage and remembered about them only years later when his friend informed him that the books had rotted due to damp. P. felt sorry about the books, but as soon as he came back to the UK, he forgot about the incident. 'Many of these things I would have liked to have here, but first, I can live without them and, second, I can replace them when I need to.'[21] He remembers his Russianness in the same way as he recalls objects. The following quotation demonstrates both the tension and ambivalence of his experience and the feeling of home.

7. **P. (recent divorcee in his late forties):** The first ten years of my life abroad I didn't miss Russia at all. I don't miss it now either, but I going through a bit of a life crisis now, so I've started [missing it] again. The story is as follows: I don't visit Russia for a year and literally forget about it. But when I arrive in Russia . . . ooh! all the smells, native talk, tastes, views . . . it makes me so excited. How could I live without all these things? And friends, of course. But after ten days or so all the freshness of these emotions withers. I eat *pelmeni* [dumplings], Russian bread and herring. Someone talks rudely to me in a shop, and I drink and eat non-stop. And I want to get out of Russia and go home. I fly, we descend and land in the UK; it's foggy and damp and green all over, and it feels so good.[22]

At the time of the interview P. had only recently moved into a flat and considered it temporary. We sat at a small table in the barely furnished living room. As the interview continued, we listened to some of his Russian music and laughed about at his experience of cooking *morkovcha* – Korean carrots – for his British friends for the first time.

CONCLUSION

This chapter has sought to explore the meanings of objects in the homes of Russian immigrants in the UK. By reflecting on the empirical material and using participants' and my own reflections on the objects, the chapter has aimed to illustrate the ambivalent and complex meanings of the objects that can simultaneously connect people with their home country and culture and emphasise their distance from them. Furthermore, material objects illuminated migrants' relationships and perceptions of the host country and the ongoing challenges and emotional difficulties of their migration journey.

The study is positioned within the broader framework of home and migration (Boccagni 2017; Boccagni and Kusenbach 2020) that considers home as a changing and multidimensional concept. The domestic objects and material cultures of home were used as a way to approach the complexity of home, which is continuously made and remade in the course of migration. While previous studies have shown the capacity of objects to connect with home country and its culture, in this chapter, by offering the concept of 'diasporic' objects, I also aimed to emphasise the significance of objects in the process of creating distance and detachment. The chapter also considered the evocative power of objects in revealing difficult or 'sticky' relationships, such as in the case of S. and N.

Throughout the chapter I have deliberately tried to move away from providing a list, typology or description of possessions found in Russian homes by focusing more on how they can be interpreted in relation to the broader notions of home, feeling of home, identity and belonging. Nevertheless, I have provided a more detailed discussion of the stereotypical 'Russian' objects, such as souvenirs, as these are often the ones that attract attention and are associated with stereotypical notions of Russianness. One of my arguments which was illuminated by the example of souvenirs is that the seemingly visible qualities of some objects do not necessarily imply straightforward meanings attached to them, and even souvenirs can represent deep and complex personal connections, relationships and emotions. Even objects on display could carry the feeling of obligation to keep and show them or refer to personal aspects of biography that are not always joyful. In relation to this, the chapter has shown that home and the possessions found in it are continuous and changing, and that therefore they should be approached in terms of processes and practices rather than as fixed and defined points such as the 'present home' and the 'past home'. Similarly, the feeling of home can change into a 'non-home' and the country left behind can be rediscovered and revisited, and thus continuously reconstructed, as the example of T.'s narrative shows. Objects can play a part in this by providing valuable references to experiences, attachments and feelings about past and present, here and there.

Finally, in this chapter I have brought in reflections on my own objects and about the personal associations evoked by objects I have seen in other people's homes. In so doing, I aimed to emphasise the large role played by objects in reflecting/combining both personal and cultural meanings, as well as their embeddedness in 'the fabric of face-to-face relationships' (Smart 2017: 182). Therefore, researching objects in migrants' homes and revealing something of their stories may bring us closer to the complexities of cultures, biographies, and identities and, thus, to central aspects of ourselves.

NOTES

1 An additional four interviews were conducted in 2012 in London and one in 2018 in Leeds.
2 It is important to note that at the later stage of the project I used the concept of diaspora identity to refer to identity practices of research participants. The concept

was suitable as it enabled highlighting the deterritorialised and ambivalent nature of participants' identities and their relationships with their home country. See also Pechurina 2020.

3   See, e.g., Olesen's (2010) discussion about the connection between 'ethnic objects' and class.

4   Here and in the rest of the endnotes, passages in Russian are the originals of the excerpts from the interviews I quote. 'Он [самовар] ведь в коробке, упакован, я его перла, это же вообще ужас, он еще с подносом, а это ж все. Но это не чугун, но что-то такое. Тульский. Я его когда везла прошлой весной, я думала я с ума сойду.'

5   'Есть такие вещи, к которым пригораешь . . . Пришлось бы мне это самовар тащить.'

6   I have discussed the co-constructed nature of Russianness in the home in Pechurina 2016.

7   Here I mean objects that would be stereotypically recognised as related to 'Russian' culture: Orthodox icons, Khohloma and Gzel pottery, folky souvenirs, traditional wooden decor and handicrafts and 'Soviet' paraphernalia.

8   As my study showed, an Orthodox icon often indicates the connection to home rather than religious affiliation, so in some ways can be compared to other 'souvenirs'. For more on icons, see Pechurina 2011.

9   'рука не поднимается'.

10   'Это такое, что родители насильно дали. Вон на полке. Мама когда-то дала, надо было куда-то деть. А выбросить рука не поднимается.'

11   'Вещи, которые в России воспринимаются как должное, ты именно начинаешь понимать их значение.'

12   'У меня действительно все соединенное. Эти вещи мной подбирались на протяжении лет, и я их не оставлю.'

13   'Я помню, когда мы только приехали и искали дома, и когда мы искали этот дом и ходили по многим домам, я нигде не видела ни одной книги. . . . Когда мы смотрели этот дом, у хозяина на столе лежала книжка про Сталинград, и меня это удивило, потому что я нигде больше не видела книг вообще у людей. И у них здесь раньше стояла полка с книгами, и когда мы пришли этот дом смотреть, я удивилась, что здесь книги. Потому что в других домах я не видела вообще.'

14   'У нас книги тоже замечательные, – поставь корешками их, Толстого или Достоевского, избранные сочинения, фолианты, книги в красной коже с золотыми буквами, что они могут? Что именно английское? Красную телефонную будку в дом приволочете?'

15   'посмеяться в поезде'.

16   'Конечно, первым делом в библиотеку записалась, где русские книги.'

17   'у меня много очень книг. Я не могу не читать.'

18   'убежденный иммигрант', 'иммигрант по призванию'.

19   'Нет. Я не думаю, что мне нужны какие-то вещи, чтобы чувствовать себя русской. Не думаю, что у моей русскости существуют какие-то внешние проявления. Язык, прежде всего. Все равно язык. Язык – это то, что мне помогает чувствовать себя русской, если я не говорю на русском, если я не читаю на русском языке, то у меня он, наверное, пропадет. Все равно, я все-таки считаю – язык. Больше, чем что-либо другое. Я не считаю, что у нас, у русских есть какие-то специфические чувства. Может быть они и есть.

'Стереотипы. Что там? Алкоголик, что они щедрые. Может быть. Не знаю. У меня когда-то были стереотипы, но они все уже давно сломались. Потому что люди не картинки. А ты понимаешь, какие они. Ты начинаешь понимать себя лучше. Ты начинаешь понимать, а чем собственно ты отличаешься от соседа. И получается, что по большому счету мы мало чем отличаемся. И все вот эти внешние признаки, они не касаются глубины. И поэтому я не очень страдаю без вещей. Без языка страдаю.'

20 'Есть особая категория людей, которые родившись в России, уже были не русскими. Они уже настраивались, чтобы жить на Западе, изучали язык. Поскольку они говорили по-русски в своей стране, они знают этот язык – а так, не было бы, не разговаривали. Это другая категория людей, я бы не оказался в такой ситуации. Русский мне нужен!'

21 'Многие из этих предметов я хотел бы иметь здесь, но, во-первых, могу жить без них совсем; во-вторых, могу найти замену им здесь.'

22 'Первые 10 лет, когда я жил за границей, совсем не скучал. И сейчас не скучаю, но сейчас у меня какой-то, наверное, очередной кризис в жизни, и опять начинаю. А картина следующая. Год не бываешь в России, и про нее буквально не помнишь. Приезжаешь в Россию – о! все эти запахи, все эти, конечно, разговор родной на улицах, вкусы, виды. Все это сразу сильно возбуждает. Как здорово, ах, мне не хватает этого, ах, как же я жил без этого, да как же здорово любой человек может зайти за угол и получить вот это. Опять же друзья. Проходит дней 10 или больше, острота этих впечатлений, утрат и прочая немножко ослабевает, поел там пельменей, поел хлеба, селедки. Да. Где-нибудь в магазине нахамили, непрерывные застолья, и, в общем-то, уже хочется убраться восвояси. Летишь на самолете, снижаешься в Англии, туман, сыро, зелено – ах, хорошо.'

REFERENCES

Abbots, E. J. (2016), 'Approaches to food and migration: rootedness, belonging and exchange', in J. Klein and J. Watson (eds), *Handbook of Food and Anthropology*, London: Bloomsbury.

Ahmed, S., C. Castaneda, A.-M. Fortier and M. Sheller (eds) (2003), *Uprootings/Regroundings: Questions of Home and Migration*, Oxford: Berg.

Appadurai, A. (1996), *Modernity at Large: Cultural Dimensions of Globalization*, Minneapolis: University of Minnesota Press.

Blunt, A. (2005), 'Cultural geography: cultural geographies of home', *Progress in Human Geography* 29:4, 505–15.

Boccagni, P. (2017), *Migration and the Search for Home: Mapping Domestic Space in Migrants' Everyday Lives*, New York: Palgrave Macmillan.

Boccagni, P. and M. Kusenbach (2020), 'For a comparative sociology of home: relationships, cultures, structures', *Current Sociology*, 68:5, 595–606.

Burrell, K. (ed.) (2009), *Polish Migration to the UK in the 'New' European Union: After 2004*, Aldershot: Ashgate.

Byford, A. (2009), '"The last Soviet generation" in Britain', in J. Fernandez (ed.), *Diasporas: Critical and Interdisciplinary Perspectives*, Oxford: Inter-Disciplinary Press, pp. 53–63.

Byford, A. (2012), 'The Russian diaspora in international relations: "compatriots" in Britain', *Europe-Asia Studies*, 64:4, 715–35.

Byford, A. (2014), 'Performing "community" Russian speakers in contemporary Britain', in L. Cairns and S. Fouz-Hernández (eds), *Rethinking 'Identities': Cultural Articulations of Alterity and Resistance in the New Millennium*, Bern: Lang, pp. 115–39.

Chapman, G. and B. L. Beagan (2013), 'Food practices and transnational identities', *Food, Culture & Society*, 16:3, 367–86.

Christou, A. and H. Janta (2019), 'The significance of things: objects, emotions and cultural production in migrant women's return visits home', *The Sociological Review*, 67:3, 654–71.

Ehrkamp, P. (2005), 'Placing identities: transnational practices and local attachments of Turkish immigrants in Germany', *Journal of Ethnic and Migration Studies*, 31:2, 345–64.

Finch, J. and J. Mason (2000), *Passing on: Kinship and Inheritance in England*, London: Routledge.

Fog Olwig, K. (1999), 'Travelling makes a home: mobility and identity among West Indians', in T. Chapman and J. Hockey (eds), *Ideal homes? Social Change and Domestic Life*, London: Routledge, pp. 73–83.

Forero, O. and G. Smith (2010), 'The reproduction of "cultural taste" amongst the Ukrainian diaspora in Bradford, England', *The Sociological Review*, 58:2, 78–96.

Frykman, M. P. (2009), 'Material aspects of transnational social fields: an introduction', *Two Homelands*, 29, 105–14.

Giogi, S. and A. Fasulo (2013), 'Transformative homes: squatting and furnishing as sociocultural projects', *Home Cultures*, 10:2, 111–33.

Hall, S. (2000), 'Who needs 'identity'?', in P. Du Gay, J. Evans and P. Redman (eds), *Identity: A Reader*, London: Sage, pp. 15–30.

Hecht, A. (2001), 'Home sweet home: tangible memories of an uprooted childhood', in D. Miller (ed.), *Home Possessions*, Oxford: Berg.

Hondagneu-Sotelo, P. (2017), 'At home in inner-city immigrant community gardens', *Journal of Housing and the Built Environment*, 32: 13–28.

Hoskins, J. (2006), 'Agency, biography and objects', in C. Tilley, W. Keane, S. Küchler, M. Rowlands and P. Spyer (eds), *Handbook of Material Culture*, London: Sage, pp. 74–84.

Kliuchnikova, P. (2015), 'Language attitudes and "folk linguistics" of Russian-speaking migrants in the UK', *Russian Journal of Communication*, 7:2, 179–92.

Kliuchnikova, P. (2016), 'Linguistic biographies and communities of language of Russian speakers in Great Britain', PhD thesis, Durham: University of Durham.

Kopnina, H. (2005), *East to West Migration: Russian Migrants in Western Europe*, Aldershot: Ashgate.

Kopytoff, I. (1986), 'The cultural biography of things: commodification as a process', in A. Appadurai (ed.), *The Social Life of Things: Commodities in Cultural Perspective*, Cambridge: Cambridge University Press, pp. 64–92.

Marcoux, J. S. (2001), 'The refurbishment of memory', in D. Miller (ed.), *Home Possessions: Material Culture behind Closed Doors*, Oxford: Berg, pp. 69–86.

Morgunova, O. and A. Byford (2018), 'Between neo-nationalizing Russia and Brexit Britain: the dilemmas of Russian migrants' political mobilizations', *Revue d'études comparatives est–ouest*, 4: 4, 129–61.

Olesen, B. B. (2010), 'Ethnic objects in domestic interiors: space, atmosphere and the making of home', *Home Cultures*, 7:1, 25–41.

Pechurina, A. (2011), 'Russian dolls, icons, and Pushkin: practicing cultural identity through material possessions in immigration', *Laboratorium*, 3:3, 97–117.

Pechurina, A. (2016), 'Defining the Russian diasporic home and its atmospheres: theoretical challenges and the methodological implications', *Russian Sociological Review*, 15:2, 26–41.

Pechurina, A. (2020), 'Researching identities through material possessions: the case of diasporic objects', *Current Sociology*, 68:5, 669–83.

Rabikowska, M. (2010), 'The ritualisation of food, home and national identity among Polish migrants in London', *Social Identities*, 16:3, 377–98.

Raman, P. (2011), 'Me in place, and the place in me', *Food, Culture & Society*, 14:2, 165–80.

Remennik, L. (2002), 'Transnational community in the making: Russian-Jewish immigrants of 1990s in Israel', *Journal of Ethnic and Migration Studies*, 28:3, 515–30.

Rosales, M. V. (2009), 'Objects, scents and tastes from a distant home: Goan life experiences in Africa', *Two Homelands*, 26, 153–66.

Rosales, M. V. (2010), 'The domestic work of consumption: materiality, migration and home-making', *Etnográfica*, 14:3, 507–25.

Savas, O. (2014), 'Taste diaspora: the aesthetic and material practice of belonging', *Journal of Material Culture*, 19:2, 185–208.

Silva, K. (2009), 'Oh, give me a home: diasporic longings of home and belonging', *Social Identities*, 15:5, 693–706.

Smart, C. (2007), *Personal Life: New Directions in Sociological Thinking*, Cambridge: Polity Press.

Story, J. and I. Walker (2016), 'The impact of diasporas: markers of identity', *Ethnic and Racial Studies*, 39:2, 135–41.

Svašek, M. (2012), *Moving Subjects, Moving Objects: Transnationalism, Cultural Production and Emotions*, New York: Berghahn Books.

Vanni, I. (2013), '*Oggetti spaesati*, unhomely belongings: Objects, migrations, and cultural apocalypses', *Cultural Studies Review*, 19:2, 150–74.

Walsh, K. (2006), 'British expatriate belongings: mobile homes and transnational homing', *Home Cultures*, 3:2, 123–44.

White, A. (2011), *Polish Families and Migration since EU Accession*, Bristol: Policy Press.

Wiles, J. (2008), 'Sense of home in a transnational social space: New Zealanders in London', *Global Networks*, 8:1, 116–37.

Woodward, S. (2015), 'The hidden lives of domestic things: accumulations in cupboards, lofts, and shelves', in E. Casey and Y. Taylor (eds), *Intimacies, Critical Consumption and Diverse Economies*, London: Palgrave Macmillan, pp. 216–31.

CHAPTER 3

'Material Stories' and Cross-referencing: Experiences of Home and Migration among Women from Russia Living in Japan[1]

Ksenia Golovina

As Tonya was showing me around her rented apartment in Tokyo, shared with her husband and two young children, she pointed to a steel stovetop kettle. It was black from long usage.

> 1. Tonya: [I] don't mind that it's so old. I am not throwing this tea kettle away on principle! This is the very first household item I bought when I came to Hokkaido as a student. It was so novel to me that I could use a gas stove! Because, you know, I come from Sakhalin,[2] and Sakhalin is where gas is extracted, but – ta-da! – all the gas just flows away to Moscow and elsewhere, Hokkaido included,[3] while Sakhalinians mostly use electric appliances. In our home, at least, everything was electricity-based. That's why this kettle is so special to me.

In this multi-themed narrative, the kettle emerges as a locus of intersecting experiences and emotions. It serves the purpose – despite having been purchased in Japan – of a physical reminder of Tonya's pre-migratory past. This was a past in which warmth, emanating from hot tea, was facilitated through electricity, despite Sakhalin Island possessing abundant gas reserves (Henderson and Moe 2016). For Tonya, access to this 'native' gas was finally realised once she had crossed the sea to the Japanese archipelago. As her first purchase in Japan, the kettle epitomises the act of Tonya's relocation, embodying her experiences as a cross-border migrant. Here, the 'intrinsic gathering and enduring capacities of materials' (Olsen 2010: 110) come into play. Yet, paradoxically, the kettle also mediates the relationship between past and present, and between two locations – Russia and Japan. The kettle 'pulls in' and throws these temporalities and spaces together through its concreteness as a device that had received the tangible touch of the Sakhalin gas when Tonya first came to Japan. Additionally, despite its worn-out look about which Tonya warned me, the kettle encapsulates the story of upward mobility. For Tonya, this purchase symbolically ensured access to the gas originally meant for capital cities such as Moscow and so-called first-world neighbours such as Japan.

In this chapter I refer to such narratives as 'material stories'. In these stories, a material object emerges as a central actor and a meaning-making component; it attracts and accumulates or distances people's experiences, memories, affects, emotions and aspirations. When analysing such material stories, I focus on the practice that is conceptualised here as 'cross-referencing'. Cross-referencing means that the story-told object is indexed as belonging to multiple experiential dimensions. As this study demonstrates, such a practice often helps migrants from Russia to achieve an unfragmented imaginary of their life, stabilises their being in space and time, and harmonises the relations between the pre-migratory and post-migratory experiences.

I argue that the objects featuring in these material stories appear to collapse, or – as Nancy Munn (1992: 101–2) described it – 'squash' the perceived linearity of time and singularity of space. These objects do not only evoke 'images of home away from home' (Yelenevskaya and Vukov 2017), but also materialise and bring 'home' into one's present moment, even if this might be unwanted; 'home' in this context is both temporal and spatial. One's pre-migratory home is understood as being a range of individually varied experiences, sensations, and perceptions of one's place of birth, origin or upbringing. Although intersected by multiple variables such as regionality, age, status and class, the backgrounds that the interviewed women shared were similar. They were born and brought up in the late Soviet Union, spent their early adulthoods in post-Soviet Russia, and migrated to Japan at the turn of the twenty-first century.

Material practices of Russian-speaking migrants have gained scholarly attention over the past decade (Bernstein 2010; Golovina 2016 and 2019; Pechurina 2015 and 2020; Protasova and Reznik 2020). In many of these studies, the point of departure is objects associated with Russianness, Sovietness and post-Sovietness. The items studied include souvenirs and elements of home decor, seen as contributing to remaking the feeling of home in terms of one's identity as a migrant. Authors have highlighted the complexity of migrant material practices, conceptualised – to cite Anna Pechurina – as 'lived and relational experience that is constantly reconfigured and reinvented within new cultural settings' (2020: 2).

Figure 3.1 Tonya's kettle. Photograph taken by the author.

With the previous research in mind, this study is concerned with the material dimensions of the objects and particularly focuses on the objects' elasticity in terms of spatiotemporality and the meanings that they can enact for migrants who interact with them. It is important to note that none of the three main objects discussed in this chapter, similarly to the 'memory objects' described by Sabine Marschall, had been initially chosen 'for the sake of remembrance' (2019: 264). The objects' mnemonic properties were effectuated through material interaction and storytelling. In the homes that I visited and observed from outside, both the objects directly associated with perceived Russo-Soviet imagery (a building resembling a *khrushchevka* – apartments that were planned and constructed during the era (1953–64) of the Soviet leader Nikita Khrushchev, hence their name) and those outside such imagery (a kettle or a satellite dish) emerged as strongly invested with meanings related to home and migration. The women's material stories brought the objects to the surface, reinforcing the item's position as a focal point of the women's attention. Although formulated and refined by each woman who was affected by the object, the story itself became embedded in the object both discursively and affectively (see also Golovina 2019). Thus, the objects and their accompanying stories served as 'means by which a narrated [. . .] event is given "presence"' (Munn 1992: 113), facilitating the shifting and switching of times.

I find Bjørnar Olsen's concept of 'mixing' times, which is enabled by the objects, to be productive (2010: 108). Many women in this study welcomed such a mixing as it allowed experiential access to the past. For others, however, the reappearance of the pre-migratory past through a certain object was experienced as an invasion of one's status and freedom as a migrant and the object was therefore resisted. Hence, rather than being uncompromisingly welcoming of the physicality of the past home into their 'now', the women sometimes adopted a defensive stance when dealing with the spatiotemporal gateways opened up by these material objects. The women were thus conscious of the often painful ambivalences of the past. These points are illustrated in the current chapter.

PEOPLE FROM RUSSIA WHO LIVE IN JAPAN

In December 2019 there were 9,378 nationals of Russia residing in Japan; this figure was a 20 per cent increase from the number recorded in 2009. Gender-wise, 67 per cent of this population were females (MOJ 2020), and most of these women were in their thirties and forties. It is assumed that many of them have been living in the country for a prolonged period, as illustrated by earlier data. The age of twenty-three years was recorded as the average age for initial female migration to Japan (Golovina 2017).

The population of Russian nationals in Japan is generally characterised by the tendency to settle (Mukhina and Golovina 2017). This point is evident in the prevalence of 'permanent residency' permits these migrants possess. Eligibility details abridged, this permit is generally granted either through marriage to a Japanese national or through a full-time job in the country, spanning several years (Immigration Services Agency of Japan 2020). In terms of location, 32, 10 and 7 per cent of the Russian nationals in Japan live in the metropolis of Tokyo and its neighbouring prefectures, Kanagawa and Chiba, respectively (MOJ 2020).

Currently, most communication between migrants from Russia in Japan takes place in Russian-speaking groups on social networking websites such as Facebook. Facebook hosts several interest groups for Russian speakers, from Russia or other post-Soviet countries, who live in Japan. One of the oldest groups, Iaponomama, originally launched as a forum on an individual website but migrated to Facebook several years later. Here, Russian-speaking women who were married in Japan, mainly (but not exclusively) to Japanese men, converse on topics related to womanhood, wifehood and motherhood (Mukhina 2012: 55, 173). Of interest is Varvara Mukhina's (2012) discussion of the group's name as revealing the women's self-identification and socialisation into Japanese society primarily as mothers of Japanese nationals. I also suggest the presence of a trickster element in this name due to its not so subtle association with a euphemistic swear phrase in Russian. To solicit interviewees for this study, I relied on several such groups, including Iaponomama. The interviews took place in the women's homes and lasted for two to three hours. Written informed consent was obtained from the interviewees. I took photographs and secured permission to use them for research purposes.

A GATEWAY INTO RUSSIA: MAYA'S SATELLITE DISH

I would normally be able to reach an interviewee's home via public transport, but Maya's insistence to meet me by car at the station was most welcome. Otherwise, I might have spent hours waiting for the right bus and then walking to her home in Ibaraki Prefecture. She explained that the location was far away. Although seemingly not too far from Tokyo on a map, the area was on the other side of a river that tended to burst its banks during typhoon season.

As we entered the house, I realised that it was home not only to Maya's family of four but also their numerous pets. These included three rescued starlings, one of which promptly greeted us in Russian. Maya joked that it is hard enough bringing up one's children as Russo-Japanese bilinguals in Japan, yet she had additionally managed to train a wild bird. Our laughter broke the ice and so began the three hours of conversation. Maya had moved to Japan twenty years earlier, having abandoned a career as a paediatrician just as it began.[4] When Maya had already given birth to her children in Japan, she was approached by a Japanese acquaintance who wanted to connect her to a person helping foreign doctors in Japan obtain their medical licence. Maya was warned that the process would require her full devotion (learning Japanese, gathering documents, and cramming for the exam) for several years. She had to turn down the offer, as she lacked a support network; with her husband working a career job, she was expected to care for the children and the household.

Maya shared many material stories with me that day, focusing on her Japanese husband's collection of European porcelain, their children's arts and crafts, and her own childhood teddy bear. The bear had been brought from Russia and carefully hidden away from children and pets.

One story focused on a satellite dish. I was about to leave Maya's place, when we stopped to chat in her garden, and I noticed a large (nearly 2 metres in diameter) satellite dish above the house's entrance. I asked Maya about it, and she replied; the image was directly connected to what she had just been describing during the interview. As Maya talked about it, the satellite dish emerged as enacting properties that served as a gateway to Russia in the semiotic, symbolic and virtual senses.

2. Maya: So, when I first came to Japan and we moved into this suburban house, the Internet wasn't yet as readily available as it is now. I had to use those telephone cards to call Russia, not even Brastel [Japanese telecommunications company], but much more expensive local ones. I think 10 minutes were like 1000 yen. I felt really lonely. And I wasn't working at first [Maya currently works as a cashier at a large retail store – *KG*]. So, my husband immediately purchased this satellite dish which made it possible to watch all sorts of cable channels, including the ones in Russian. You won't see dishes like these anymore anywhere – but it has served me well and removing it is a bit of a hassle, so we are just keeping it.

Indeed, the satellite dish looked unusual; depending on the angle from which one looked at Maya's house, the dish seemed gigantic as it protruded into the gloaming sky. Never have I seen an antenna so big attached to a private house in a town in Japan. As her story illustrated, for Maya, despite the current availability of Internet-based content in Russian and the accessibility of her family and friends in Russia thanks to the Internet telephony, the satellite dish held deep symbolism. It connected her to her hometown through time and space.

The dish was mainly used during Maya's initial years in Japan and was no longer really needed, but it preserved the notion of linear time flowing from the past towards the future; it also preserved the separateness of locations: Russia and Japan. Preservation is enacted in the satellite dish's functioning as a mnemonic device for Maya's past hardships – career abandonment, isolation and separation from loved ones – turning her experience into a material story of a migrant life course. At the same time, since the dish is now mainly a dormant artefact rather than an object-in-use, it collapses the notion of time and space into the present moment. This allows Maya to relive her past in the immediacy of her today-ness. These two functions of the dish – preservation of linear time and separate space on the one hand, and their collapsing, on the other – are explicated in various forms of cross-referencing found in Maya's storytelling. This cross-referencing almost therapeutically invites contemplations of how things once were and how they are now, of what they meant then and what they mean now. Her past is thus constantly revisited and becomes part of her present. Furthermore, the dish – by nature of its physical continuance into the future (as seen in Maya's reluctance to have the dish dismantled) – creates a mark that, similar to how the act of writing is interpreted by Richard Calichman, functions as a 'past inscription' capable of sending itself 'out into the future' (2016: 19).

This inscription creates the possibility to imagine oneself in the future, looking back at the past events in a series of ontological 'will have been' moments (Calichman 2016: 19).

The digitalisation and internetisation of a human experience over twenty years is also explicit in Maya's material story. Although migration made such a transformation feasible, the change was not the result of migration per se but rather occurred in both countries over the course of time. In this regard, the satellite dish, which is oversized for a private household by today's standards, is a powerful metaphor. What once required a device that in its grandeur almost resembled a space station is now accessible via a palm-sized Internet router. Yet, the disproportionately large device had not necessarily meant easy access for Maya to her relatives and friends in Russia, or content in Russian. It is the smaller device that is capable of satisfying these needs, more quickly and cheaply. However, those needs have become more subdued over time, as Maya noted. The size of the dish is thus expressive of Maya's initial emotional state.

While the above interpretation has a somewhat poetic turn, it appears evident that Maya's need to break through the distance brought by migration and the locality of their suburban home, and the resulting isolation, was pronounced when she first came to Japan. Indeed, it required a material object as large as an industrial satellite dish to make the breakthrough possible. Thus, the dish is a memorial to Maya's experiences and emotions, as it tangibly enables the process of multitemporal 'tracing' of events, connections and memory (Calichman 2016: 16).

KHRUSHCHEVKA TURNED *DANCHI*: NATALIA'S NIGHTMARE, OLGA'S NOSTALGIA

Material stories surrounding a type of dwelling in Japan called the *danchi* are of particular interest here (the word is explained in detail below). The interest arises through the shared pattern that can be observed among the interviewees' experiences. Many interviewees in this study associated *danchi* with *khrushchevka*. It is worth mentioning that the word *danchi*, like many other Japanese words describing various aspects of local life, is often used as it is in the Russian-language speech of Russian speakers in Japan. At times, the word appears paired with *khrushchevka* where a person would say: 'We live in *danchi*, you know, *khrushchevka*.'[5]

Some of my interviewees lived in *danchi* or similar apartments in Japan, while others only observed these buildings along Japan's streets – yet cross-referenced them with *khrushchevka* in their material stories.

Some of the women referred to *khrushchevka* when talking about specific features of their apartments in Japan, such as the thin walls, even if the building itself was not particularly reminiscent of the Soviet apartments. Hence, *khrushchevka* emerged as a strong reference point for women from Russia in Japan as they made sense of their living environments. An online survey I conducted in 2016 showed that 11.4 per cent of respondents (n=186, targeting Russian-speaking people from all former Soviet countries) had lived in *khrushchevka* before moving to Japan (Golovina 2016).

In the 1950s the housing question was highly relevant for both the Soviet Union and Japan. One reason was the destruction and displacement caused by World War II; another reason was the poor living conditions of ordinary urbanites in both countries. In the Soviet Union many people lived in communal apartments, barracks and dormitories (Harris 2013 and 2015). In Japan people lived in boarding houses, factory dormitories, barrack huts and one-room wooden apartments (Francks 2009: 80; 154). A separate apartment with one's own kitchen, bathroom and toilet was an aspirational ideal. It was 'the cutting edge of modern life and a harmonious social order' (Harris 2015: 181) – of communist modernisation in the Soviet Union and of westernised modernisation in the case of Japan. The Soviet Union's solution was achieved through the construction of so-called *khrushchevka* in the 1950–60s, initially envisioned as a temporary fix to the housing problem. These were standardised low-cost apartments, each with its own kitchen and a combined bathroom-and-toilet. The entrance to the 5-metre kitchen was from the largest room, which acted as a kind of corridor (Harris 2013: 81–2). People labelled the three-room *khrushchevka* a '6-9-15', where the numbers referred to each of the rooms' square measurements. The respective apartment buildings were three to five storeys high, usually built from precast concrete panels and united into a micro-district with amenities (Harris 2013 and 2015; Jull 2017; Olsen and Vinogradova 2019).

While Japan was tackling the housing question, in the same period several visits were organised to the Soviet Union to observe on-site the implementation of the mass-housing project of the country's communist neighbor (Hara 2012: 44–5; Hobara 2019). The political climate for such visits was favourable: the two countries had signed the Soviet–Japanese Joint Declaration in 1956 (Hara 2012). Following the establishment of the Japan Public Corporation of Housing by Prime Minister Ichiro Hatoyama (Smith 2018: 67; Usui 2016: 114), standardised *danchi*-type apartment buildings were devised in Japan (Neitzel 2016). They were similar to *khrushchevka* in some of their principles and appearance. As time passes, many *danchi* are being bulldozed as they no longer fulfil Japan's revised earthquake safety standards.

The fact that Japan's post-war housing developers took notice of the Soviet mass-housing project, along with other sources, when devising the *danchi* is not widely known. Yet my interviewees did not need to know this: they immediately perceived *danchi* as *khrushchevka* and cross-referenced the two dwellings in their material stories. The extract below is from a narrative by Natalia, a student-turned-professional migrant in Japan. Her first year at the elementary school coincided with the collapse of the Soviet Union, and she came to Japan as a student nearly eighteen years ago:

> 3. **Natalia:** I get a nagging feeling every time I pass this *danchi* complex not far from where we live. Some of the apartments are still in use, but a few buildings are deserted pending restoration. It feels as if I am completely back in Russia, or even more so – in the USSR! I am not a fan of this feeling. It's a bit nightmarish, you know. It feels like I have never migrated, never went through the years of struggle climbing the social ladder, you know, education, marriage and work and all that. [. . .] You should try going through that area today!

The *khrushchevka* might have been ideal for comfortable separate living after the war. By contrast, in modern-day Russia, these decaying buildings have lasted well beyond their envisioned lifetime and are today a reminder of economic hardship, poor living conditions and intergenerational conflicts. In private discourse these apartments are now sometimes referred to as *khrushcheby*. This is a wordplay that incorporates both *khrushchevka* and a Russian word for 'slum'. For many interviewees in this study financial difficulties, poor quality of life, and underemployment were precisely the reasons that they had voiced regarding their migration. The *khrushchevka* buildings may serve as reminders of these pre-migratory conditions.

In Natalia's material story, an encounter with architecture so similar to that of Soviet buildings created a sensation of going backwards in time and space, which emerged as unsettling. As such, it constituted an act of what Olsen and Vinogradova (2019: 13) conceptualised as 'unvoluntary remembering'. For Natalia, the sensation was so powerful that for a moment it eradicated her experience as a migrant – the years of hard work to achieve her current socio-economic status. The Russian philosopher Nikolai Berdyaev (1935: 30–1) stated that one's 'creative act is an active resistance to time', which is also the only way to overcome the melancholy associated with bygone days. In the discussed case, by contrast, the individual's creative struggle to become who she was today was under threat of being erased by the sudden physical reemergence of a time that she had deemed bygone. Unlike the kettle and the satellite dish in the two other cases, for Natalia and several other interviewees, the gateway into another dimension opened by these buildings was dreaded.

In other narratives, *khrushchevka* featured differently. Some of my interviewees, especially those who had migrated through routes other than marriage, had lived in dormitories, shared houses, and one-room wooden apartments when they first arrived in Japan. Many had made the move from the relative comfort of a parental home in Russia. The experience led to the formation of understandings such as the one expressed by Olga, who had moved from the south of Russia to Japan.

> 4. **Olga:** I had this image of Japan as a first-world country, so it was a shock to me to find myself virtually in a barrack, heated by a kerosene stove, and with a prehistoric bathroom! Even the worst *khrushchevka* is well insulated and has running water that heats up fast!

The women in my study often found themselves in wooden apartments shortly after migrating not because of their international migration per se; it had more to do with their entering a certain life stage. They would probably have moved into a dormitory or shared accommodation if they had pursued an independent life in Russia and relocated domestically. Because their move to independence coincided with their migration, relocation to Japan became – in their minds – associated with a lowering of their living conditions. Again, *khrushchevka* emerged as a cross-referencing point around which the material stories were organised. As far from the standard of modern comfortable living as today's *khrushchevka* apartments are, for Olga and others they were still more desirable than barracks in a 'first-world' country such as Japan. People's class, status, age, sex and economic standing naturally come into play here. Having just stepped off a plane, the migrant Olga – like many young single people in Japan – could not afford to live anywhere else than in a poorly insulated apartment.

Additionally, this section shows how material objects such as apartments can flip the conventional discourses related to the dichotomies 'East and West' and 'third world and first world' upside down. One of the core narratives that accompanied the migration of people from Russia following the collapse of the Soviet Union was that domestic housing and products were of poorer quality than those abroad. Thus, the subse-

Figure 3.2 A deserted *danchi* building nearby Natalia's apartment in Tokyo. Photograph taken by the author.

quent encounter with the *khrushchevka*-resembling apartments that can be found not only in Japan but also in Finland (Nikula 1994) and many other industrialised countries,[6] reflective of the urban planning trends of the times, puzzles post-Soviet migrants. Such an encounter evokes the painful question of the difficulty to cross over one's class and status, despite having crossed over the border. On a broader scale, it invites the contemplation of the historical responsibilities surrounding the politics of the Iron Curtain and social traumas associated with it (Ryazanova-Clarke 2014: 10). These evocations and contemplations prompt what Svetlana Boym calls 'an emotional farewell' to the West of 'the unofficial Soviet imagination' (2001: 65). This is the West that never existed in reality, the images of which functioned as a 'countercultural dream' for the Soviets (Boym 2001: 65–6).

CONCLUDING REMARKS

In this chapter material stories surrounding three objects have been discussed. The objects are a kettle, a satellite dish and a *danchi* apartment (associated by many interviewees with the Soviet *khrushchevka*).

Verbalised by the women, these material stories became embedded in the objects and then continued to be expressed non-verbally when the women were in the presence of these objects.

I have shown how, in these stories, the objects have been cross-referenced in regard to the women's pre-migratory and post-migratory experiences. This process unearths a multitude of intersecting meanings. However, the material stories revealed that the women's experience of the objects went beyond the nature of the latter as symbols carrying certain meanings about home and migration. What featured most prominently in the stories was the object's capacity to transform lived time and space. The women's 'varying degrees of attention to time' (Munn 1992: 104) were thus echoed by the objects' intrinsic ability to enact the 'mixing' of times (Olsen 2010: 108). This transformation took various forms. On some occasions, it allowed one to move backwards in time and to immerse oneself in the memories of the past from the safe distance of the present. On other occasions, the objects reminded one of time's progression from past to future, stabilising one's current place in a migrant life course.

Yet, on other occasions, the material items erased perceived linear time by bringing 'then' and 'now' into the present moment simultaneously, enabling a collapse of spatiotemporal conventionality. This capacity of objects to transform – to invite, trace, shift, switch, collapse, squash and mix – time and space was not always celebrated. Sometimes it threatened to destabilise one's current place and made one question the phenomenological realness of years of experience as a resident in Japan.

NOTES

1. This study was supported by the Japan Society for the Promotion of Science Grant-in-Aid 18K12591 (Project Name: Modes of Diversity in Japan: Russian-speaking Migrants and their Material Culture).
2. While this theme did not feature in this particular interview, it is essential to note that, for many Russian migrants from Sakhalin, the experience of Japan started long before their actual migration to that country. This can be attributed to factors such as the presence of consumer goods from Japan and frequent referrals to the topic of Russo-Japanese relations (with the focus on Hokkaido) in the Sakhalin media (Buntilov 2019). With 140 companies throughout Russia's Far East, Japanese businesses are also visible in the region (Petrunina et al. 2018: 534).
3. Gas is reportedly the top imported product in Hokkaido. In 2018 Hokkaido imported from Russia natural gas valued at 22.7 billion JPY. In the same year Sakhalin Oblast exported to Japan natural gas valued at 2.9 billion USD (Hokkaido Sakhalin Jimusho 2019: 17–18). The Sakhalin–Hokkaido Gas Pipeline project, although not yet implemented, has been already discussed for several decades (JPDO 2020). Japan's investment share in the Sakhalin-1 and Sakhalin-2 oil and gas projects is 30 and 22.5 per

cent, respectively (Petrunina et al. 2018: 532). These realities thus provide further food for the public imagination regarding the future of Russo-Japanese relations in the energy sector.

4 While there exists a screening process in Japan that permits a doctor with a foreign diploma to undertake the country's National Medical Practitioners Qualifying Examination (NMPQE), the bar is exceptionally high. The applicants are required to pass the most advanced level of the Japanese Language Proficiency Examination (Level 1) at the beginning of the screening and, if admitted, to take the NMPQE in Japanese.

5 For an account of lexical borrowings and other features of Japan's Russian speakers' language, see Margarita Kazakevich (2013). As for the two other cases presented in this chapter – the tea kettle and the satellite dish – the interviewees used the Russian words *chainik* and *sputnikovaia tarelka*, respectively. The metallic kettle (Figure 3.1) can be called either *yakan* or *ketoru* in Japanese, the second word being borrowed from English. Perhaps due to the identicality of the object across cultures and the importance of the *chainik* ('tea kettle') in Russian culture, the interviewee used the Russian word. This is not necessarily the case for other kitchen-related Japanese objects – especially for a range of multi-shaped and multi-sized utensils and dishware absent in the Russian kitchen. Naturally, the use of Japanese borrowings to describe kitchen utensils and dishware is determined by factors such as whether the migrant has married into a Japanese family, whether they cook often, and whether a somewhat suitable equivalent for a word in question is available in Russian.

6 The case of the American Pruitt–Igoe public housing project in St Louis, Missouri, designed by the American architect of Japanese origin Minoru Yamasaki, provides additional context for this discussion (Bristol 1991).

REFERENCES

Berdyaev, N. (1935), 'Vechnost' i vremia', *Vestnik Russkogo Hristianskogo Dvizheniia*, 3, 27–33.
Bernstein, J. (2010), *Food for Thought: Transnational Contested Identities and Food Practices of Russian-Speaking Jewish Migrants in Israel and Germany*, Frankfurt and New York: Campus Verlag.
Boym, S. (2001), *The Future of Nostalgia*, New York: Basic Books.
Bristol, K. G. (1991), 'The Pruitt–Igoe myth', *Journal of Architectural Education*, 44:3, 163–71.
Buntilov, G. (2019), 'Imagining Japan in Moscow and Sakhalin, and imagining Russia in Tokyo and Hokkaido: contrasting identities and images of other in the centre and periphery', PhD thesis, Hokkaido University.
Calichman, R. F. (2016), *Beyond Nation: Time, Writing, and Community in the Work of Abe Kōbō*, Stanford, CA: Stanford University Press.
Francks, P. (2009), *The Japanese Consumer: An Alternative Economic History of Modern Japan*, Cambridge: Cambridge University Press.
Golovina, K. (2016), 'Nihon ni okeru ijūsha no maihōmu: roshiagoken komyunichi membā no jūtaku erabi to interia wo jirei ni' [Migrants' homes in Japan: practices of finding and organizing dwellings among Russian-speaking community members], *Seikatsugaku ronsō* [Journal of Lifology], 29, 15–29.
Golovina, K. (2017), *Nihon ni kurasu roshiajin josei no bunkajinruigaku: ijū, kokusai kekkon,*

jinseizukuri [Russian Women in Japan: Migration, Marriage, and Life Crafting], Tokyo: Akashi Shoten.

Golovina, K. (2019), 'Skin-to-skin with the house: senses and affect in the relationship of migrant Russian women in Japan with their homes', *Asian Anthropology*, 18:3, 170–85.

Hara, T. (2012), *Danchi no Kūkan Seijigaku* [Spatial Politics of Danchi], Tokyo: NHK Publishing.

Harris, S. E. (2013), *Communism on Tomorrow Street: Mass Housing and Everyday Life after Stalin*, Baltimore and Washington, DC: The Johns Hopkins University Press and Woodrow Wilson Center Press.

Harris, S. E. (2015), 'Soviet mass housing and the communist way of life', in C. Chatterjee, D. L. Ransel, M. Cavender and K. Petrone (eds), *Everyday Life in Russia: Past and Present*, Bloomington and Indianapolis: Indiana University Press, pp. 181–202.

Henderson, J. and A. Moe (2016), 'Gazprom's LNG offensive: a demonstration of monopoly strength or impetus for Russian gas sector reform?,' *Post-Communist Economies*, 28:3, 281–99.

Hobara, M. (2019), 'Iaponskiye jilye massivy: shodstvo mejdu Tokio i Moskvoi', *Opyt antropologii po-russki. Rossiia i russkie v Iaponii*, The University of Tokyo. Course papers' collection, pp. 44–9.

Hokkaido Sakhalin Jimusho (2019), 'Sahalin shū no gaiyō' [Overview of Sakhalin Oblast], at <www.pref.hokkaido.lg.jp/fs/3/0/7/4/5/5/2/_/sakhalin2019.pdf>.

Immigration Services Agency of Japan (2020). 'Eijū kyoka, Nyūkanhō dai 22 jō' [Residence permit, Immigration Law, Article 22], at <www.immi-moj.go.jp/tetuduki/zairyuu/eizyuu.html>.

JPDO (Japan Pipeline Development and Operation Inc.) (2020), 'History of our efforts toward putting the project to commercial use', at <www.jpdo.co.jp/eindex.html>.

Jull, M. (2017), 'The improbable city: adaptations of an arctic metropolis', *Polar Geography*, 40:4, 291–305.

Kazakevich, M. (2013), 'Russkii iazyk v russkoiazychnoi diaspore Iaponii', *Roshiago Kyōiku Kenkyū* [Russian Language Education Research], 4, 75–97.

Marschall, S. (2019), '"Memory objects": material objects and memories of home in the context of intra-African mobility', *Journal of Material Culture*, 24:3, 253–69.

MOJ (Ministry of Justice) (2020), 'Zairyū gaikokujin tōkei' [Japan's Foreign Residents' Statistics], 2006–19, at <www.moj.go.jp/housei/toukei/toukei_ichiran_touroku.html>.

Mukhina, V. (2012), 'Sociology of cross-national marriage: a case of Russian-speaking wives in Japan', PhD thesis, Kumamoto University.

Mukhina, V. and K. Golovina (2017), 'Roshiajin diasupora no genjō: zainichi roshiajin ijūsha no ichizuke ni mukete' [Overview of contemporary Russian diaspora: defining specific features of Russian immigrants in Japan], *Imin Seisaku Kenkyū* [Migration Policy Review], 9, 106–23.

Munn, N. D. (1992), 'The cultural anthropology of time: a critical essay', *Annual Review of Anthropology*, 21, 93–123.

Neitzel, L. (2016), *The Life We Longed For: Danchi Housing and the Middle Class Dream in Postwar Japan*, Portland, OR: Merwin Asia.

Nikula, R. (ed.) (1994), *Heroism and the Everyday: Building Finland in the 1950s*, Helsinki: Museum of Finnish Architecture.

Olsen, B. (2010), *In Defense of Things: Archaeology and the Ontology of Objects*, Lanham, MD: AltaMira Press.

Olsen, B. J. and S. Vinogradova (2019), '(In)significantly Soviet: the heritage of Teriberka', *International Journal of Heritage Studies*, 26:9, 901–18.

Pechurina, A. (2015), *Material Cultures, Migrations, and Identities: What the Eye Cannot See*, Basingstoke and New York: Palgrave Macmillan.

Pechurina, A. (2020), 'Researching identities through material possessions: the case of diasporic objects', *Current Sociology*, 68:5, 669–83.

Petrunina, Z. V., D. V. Kiba, and G. A. Shusharina (2018), 'The Far-East vector for Russian–Japanese investment cooperation', *European Research Studies Journal*, 21:1, 529–41.

Protasova, E. Y. and K. L. Reznik (2020), 'Functions of the migrant home: Russian-speakers in Finland', *Historical Courier*, 4:12, 204–16.

Ryazanova-Clarke, L. (2014), 'Introduction: the Russian language, challenged by globalisation', in L. Ryazanova-Clarke (ed.), *The Russian Language Outside the Nation*, Edinburgh: Edinburgh University Press, pp. 1–32.

Smith, D. M. (2018), *Mass Media, Consumerism and National Identity in Postwar Japan*, London: Bloomsbury Academic.

Usui, K. (2016), *Marketing and Consumption in Modern Japan*, London and New York: Routledge.

Yelenevskaya, M. and N. Vukov (2017), 'Images of home away from home' (Migration and Mobility Working Group), panel held at the 13th Congress of International Society for Ethnology and Folklore (SIEF) in Göttingen, Germany, on 29 March 2017.

CHAPTER 4

The Role of Material Objects in the Home Interiors of Russian Speakers in Finland

Ekaterina Protassova and Kirill Reznik

THE RUSSIAN-SPEAKING HOME AND MIGRATION

Habitation is the intersection of spatial and material, storage of memory, continuation of personal space, realisation of oneself in culture, relation of private and public, epoch and individuality, financial possibilities and aesthetic principles. Recently, linguists and anthropologists have become more and more engaged in understanding the importance of the house in the construction of discourse. Folklore tradition assumes strict continuity in the maintenance of the house, passed down from generation to generation and associated with the mythological reading of small and large spaces (Adon'eva 2011). As a stronghold of the family, as protection and as place of self-reflection, the home becomes an anthropological centre for the formation and maintenance of identity (Dushakova 2005). The idea of the house as a starting point of existence, continuity, and spiritual and physical strength grows in the language consciousness through a variety of associations and phraseological units (Fedorova 2016). Each nation has its own persistent stereotypes about the significance of the house, its parts and its furnishings (Filippova and Archakova 2013). Despite many real losses, people constantly re-examine and reimagine things that they have ceased to own (Gramatchikova 2018).

In Soviet times, the boundaries between the external and internal world of housing became blurred, traditional values were destroyed, symbols of housebuilding changed, and a new housing culture was formed, which, in turn, broke down during the transition from a disciplinary society to a society of achievements, where less attention was paid to the home and more to work (Kim Joon Seok 2018). In the aftermath of the Soviet Union, different generations formed diverse cultures of living, from refurbished old apartments in city centres to cheap dwellings in the suburbs, from giant mansions in the countryside to small family dachas or village *izbas* (log houses) inherited from grandparents. Different waves of Russian speakers have moved abroad with their own ideals of a proper or decent lifestyle. In general, in the philosophy of culture of the twentieth century, the idea of home appears as a place of peace and tranquillity, protection and reliability; however, in parallel, thoughts about permanent or temporary homelessness or about the entire universe as a home are actively discussed (Rymarovich 2013).

In traditional Russian culture, as in many others, the space of the house symbolically reflected the structure of the world; the home was a living being and the embodiment of the universe (Baiburin 1983; Boal 2000). Traces of this metaphorical relation to the immediate and remote environment are still visible. Whether homes are typically rented or purchased varies from culture to culture; it may be rich or poor, empty or full, large or small. Windows – the 'eyes' of the house – can be uncovered during the day and curtained at night. The threshold and the entrance to the house in general still have a special significance (e.g., a Russian never shakes hands on the threshold). Few people are able to show true independence in the decoration of their houses; most adhere to traditions and group conventions (e.g., the front gardens of neighbours living on the same street or the apartments of people of the same social class may be similar). Makhlina (2009) considers housing as the main site of everyday life. Houses contain items that are partly shared property and seem to belong to everyone, partly jealously guarded and kept inaccessible to others.

The home seems to grow up from the ground, and when migrants use expressions such as 'without roots', 'our roots are here', 'uprooted', 'rootless', 'to take root' or 'tumbleweed', they often refer to the image of a person as a plant or the house as having an underground, deep part. The house in a broad sense always belongs to a family endowed with history and traditions. Gapova (2004) believes that the idea of the national home and food are inextricably linked, while food is the main metaphor of native culture. Books and films belong to the same circle of national identity, and for some this includes going to church, celebrating New Year, International Women's Day and other holidays. From the point of view of the researcher, such signs of entering the community are imaginary and help people to position themselves through a certain self-determination. In diaspora, however, a new collective identity emerges, and 'we' does not only mean the community of the pre-immigration life but also those who are around now.

An emigrant can give up his or her former home, discard everything, and strive to create a new home (Mostikov 2015). The pressing need to organise their living space was also experienced by the first Russian emigrants, for example in France (Rudkovskaya 2019). The special attitude of post-Soviet migrants to home has been studied in the United Kingdom (Pechurina 2011; 2016), Amsterdam and London (Kopnina 2016), Germany (Ivanova-Buchatskaya 2010), Israel (Fialkova and Yelenevskaya 2007), Italy (Odynets 2018; Talalay 2012), Japan (Golovina 2017 and 2019), the United States (Gapova 2004) and Finland (Gurova 2013; Protassova 2004; Protassova and Reznik 2020). Dushakova (2019) has shown the objects that are important to Romanian Old Believers when they returned to Russia and left it again in the twentieth century: documents, means of transportation, daily tools, photographs and letters. 'Home' is also a shelter for children or elderly people (Semenova, 2012; Volpjansky 2002). In migrant fiction, the word is associated with a special sense of homelessness, which some seek and from which some flee, and which evolves throughout life outside the homeland (Koznova 2019; Mineeva 2013; Tsepennikova 2014). Historical traditions and modern features of the Russian home, whether in the metropolis or abroad, may appear peculiar to non-Russians (Gunn 2019; TDR).

For centuries, immigrants from the east came to do business or settle in Finland. In the eighteenth century, under the rule of Catherine II, Russian merchants, clergy, missionaries and military men started settling in Finland, which became part of the Russian Empire. Migration from Russia to Finland continued in the nineteenth century, including peasants who were resettled and bureaucrats representing imperial offices. The Russian military stationed in Finland when it was an autonomous duchy of the Russian Empire contributed to an increasing number of Russian-speaking migrants. These 'Old Russians' (Baschmakoff and Leinonen 2001; Protassova 2004; Schenschin 2008) kept memories of Russianness in their homes and transmitted them to their children.

Figure 4.1 Icons and old books in the homes of the 'Old Russians' in Finland.

The image of Russians in Finland is ambivalent. On the one hand, they come from the neighbouring country that has waged several wars against Finland and Sweden; on the other hand, the common border has enabled the rapid transit of goods and tourists, thus contributing to the economic growth of Finland (Varjonen et al. 2017; Viimaranta et al. 2017, 2018 and 2019). So, while this factor may not soften hearts, it makes laypeople understand that economic ties connecting the two countries are essential for their prosperity. According to statistics, in Russia, Finland is highly rated as a place of study and recreation (Honkanen et al. 2016; Laine 2017). It may seem to a visitor that Russian is spoken everywhere, but this is primarily because there are many tourists here (fewer during the pandemic, naturally). Learning Russian is included in the mandatory training programme for hotel business employees. In major tourist destinations Russian is one of the most frequently used languages on signs, in advertisements and on social media advertising sites. The composition and content of such sites shows that they have two addressee groups, aimed at both foreign and local Russian speakers.

The words for 'integration' and related processes in Finnish are *kotoutuminen*, *kotiutuminen*, *kotouttaminen*, all of which derive from the word *koti* (*koto* in poetry), meaning 'home', contrasting with *talo*, 'house' (Moilanen 2004). Russian-speaking immigrants integrate into the Finnish labour market and society, yet they do not really feel Finnish; neither are their salaries among the highest paid to immigrants (Päivinen 2017). Russian speakers in Finland usually perceive their group status to be fairly high, but this does not necessarily contribute to their full integration into the host society (Renvik et al. 2018). When dealing with everyday issues, they rely primarily on their family and official organisations; entering the host society requires immersion in new relationships, which is not always easy, as it requires language proficiency and adjustment to different communication patterns and cultural habits (Heino and Veistilä 2015). Biographical narratives reflect ideas about having two homes, living on the border, finding one's own place in the new life and in the new country, and creating a third mixed space saturated with nostalgia (Yarovaya and Yarovoy 2019). Russian grandmothers shuttling between Finland and Russia contribute to these mixed feelings (Tiyainen-Qatar 2016).

In this chapter, we consider the attitude of Russian-speaking immigrants in Finland to space and the things that fill it. To do this, we analyse virtual discussions that took place on forums of Russian-speaking people in Finland as well as face-to-face group discussions, individual interviews, and essays and self-reports written by participants in the project. In total, more than a hundred people took part in this study. The

Figure 4.2 Balalaika, realistic paintings and photographs in the homes of the 'Old Russians'.

majority of the participants were women, aged between eighteen and seventy. Most took part in the project anonymously, but some wanted their names to be published. The majority were from the capital region, but other places in Finland were presented as well. Our goal was to understand how Russian-speaking immigrants in Finland determine what their home is (regardless of the type of house), what role it plays in their lives, and how they position themselves through it. We wanted to know what they consider important to preserve from their past life and what has changed in their perception of home during their lifetime. We explored what types of hybrid culture are manifested in the organisation of space (including iconic objects and interiors). In the process of self-description, the participants relied on family legends and inherited artefacts, rather than on national traditions and symbols.

OBJECTS, INTERIORS AND MEMORIES

While thinking about the place where they live, the participants analysed what had changed when they moved to Finland, whether they wanted their home to be and look Russian or Finnish. They reflected on their choice of things they wanted to bring with them. There were dilemmas of where to place these objects in their new homes and what to do with them when they were no longer needed. Above all, should one maintain traditions just because they existed in their family? It turned out that some participants even brought along their favourite antique furniture,

Figure 4.3 Gzhel and Khokhloma ware, dictionaries and books, portraits of Sergei Yesenin and Alexander Pushkin. Photographs by the owners of the objects.

causing something of a headache on the border, and they had to restore the objects which were in poor condition. Several participants mentioned that they had brought folding tables (*stoly-knizhki*), which are very useful for receiving guests and which are not available in Finland.

Other participants emphasised that the bright Finnish homes meet their needs: 'We did not change the style of our furniture and *sisustus* [Fin. 'interior']; we had about the same in Moscow. We had a different style. Moscow is a dark city; we had light walls, light furniture, and here, it is about the same. We brought our collection of symbolic items and paintings.' A grandmother's plate could not be left behind 'because something from our previous life had to remain'. Russianness generally meant having famous metal trays from Zhostovo, delftware from Gzhel, samovars, Pavlovsky shawls, wall units (popular in the 1960s) and crystal chandeliers. In folklore studies, such items are commonly referred to as 'ethnic objects'. Some immigrants put them up as decoration; for others these are functional objects. Children play with matryoshka (nesting) dolls, learning to disassemble and assemble them, wooden Khokhloma boxes are convenient for storing salt and sugar, and spoons for stirring soup when it is being made. All these everyday things are often hidden from sight, instead of being put on display, as one might think (Figure 4.3).

1. **Aleksei:** These are the things I remember as long as I remember myself. My parents, I recall, had a nightstand, on the nightstand was some kind of a napkin, it was 1957, right? And there was a

radio on it, and Dad was listening to the football. Siniavsky's [a famous football commentator] voice is one of my earliest childhood memories.

The radio was brought to Finland. When going away, many immigrants pack their wedding and anniversary gifts if they have nobody to leave them to. No matter what their cost, 'there are things that cannot be thrown away, because they are the very symbol of the family'. People tell stories associated with getting things in the Soviet past when there were shortages of everything. Acquired with great difficulty, they are difficult to get rid of even when they are no longer used (Rezanova 2011). Thus, the older generations do not want the younger ones to forget about the pains and exploits of those who managed to 'catch' these goods. In 'Soviet-speak' this meant queuing for hours on end, or, worse still, pre-registering for the purchase. Then the customer would have to leave a postcard with his or her address which would be sent by the shop when the ordered item arrived. Sometimes customers made a list of those in the queue for goods but would have to come in person several times a day for roll calls. When, finally, the desired items were available, people would carry their trophies home, sometimes from a remote district of the city. Some objects lose their material value and are stored as markers of their owners' life events. In the USSR, things were often bought, not because they were needed, but because they were in short supply and there might be no other opportunity to get them later. Sometimes people would buy 'deficit' goods for family and friends. Accumulation of possessions seemed

Figure 4.4 Souvenirs from Russia and bookshelves. Photographs by the owners of the objects.

like a lifetime achievement. Many scarce items had not been unpacked, and a multitude of identical items remained stored in the factory packaging with a warranty card. These were also brought to Finland.

The uniformity of Soviet mass-produced consumer goods caused people to have identical household objects. During the 1970s–80s books were on the top of the 'treasure list' and not easy to purchase. 'If the library in the house where you come to visit is 90 per cent similar to yours, you will make friends with this person,' commented the participants in our study with irony. According to the narratives, when planning to emigrate today, people donate books to prisons, bring them to waste collection points, or simply stack them in the inner courtyard of their apartment block. Reading migrates from paper to electronic formats; old books are often of poor quality and low artistic value. Nevertheless, poetry and dictionaries stay in the household and are apparently considered to have eternal value. Tools are also considered to be very important. Two men who do not know each other confessed that they took their drills with them whenever they moved from place to place throughout their lives, claiming that 'they don't produce such things anymore'. Note that drills, hammers, screwdrivers and similar tools are considered to be essential components of the male material world while sewing kits are their female counterparts. This gendered division of tools is a reflection of persisting traditional gender roles in the Russian household.

Migration is an opportunity to start a new life, but there is no need to throw old things out, whatever they are, said the older participants. At first, parents share furniture, tableware and linens with their children who become independent and do not have enough money; later, children who are less connected with Russia return them to their parents and buy new things that speak more to their hearts. Parents are surprised by the taste of their children: how can they replace high-quality, 'good' things with the flashy, poorly manufactured items that you can find in every Finnish home? Where is their individuality? Paradoxically, parents seem to be unaware of the monotonous sameness of the Soviet consumer goods while labelling Finnish things as boring and devoid of individuality. At the same time, parents appreciate that their children are more interested in what is happening in Finland than in Russia, that they know the local customs and language well, and are involved in their work life. One participant said, 'We do not live in a country; we live on the Internet that has no borders.' Today, when a grandmother asks her grandchild, 'Why are you putting a new T-shirt on? The old one is still in good shape,' the youngster does not understand what she means, because things have a different value for the young generation: they can just purchase a new one any time.

2. Irina: Indeed, we have a rather sad life, because when we lived in the Soviet Union, we only bought what we could get, [but] when we came here, we had so little money that we only bought the cheapest of what we could afford, and now there are so many unnecessary things with histories that, if we wanted to replace something and buy what we want and what we like, there is simply nowhere to put old stuff. And we can't throw things away, because we're not brought up that way. Nobody will ever know what our taste is like.

Those who are more adapted to the modern culture of recycling do not agree that there is nowhere to put things: you can, after all, give them to acquaintances or to charities in your country of birth or offer them to other immigrants.

When people migrate, inevitably things go missing: someone forgets what is in which box and throws valuables into the trash; another stores some objects in a neighbour's pantry from where they get sent to a landfill; someone else sends items by post, but they never arrive. First, these persons are upset, and later they accept the loss: 'We will leave this world, and we will not be able to take it all with us'; 'We must also think about children, so that they do not have to sort out these things after our death'; 'Understanding comes with age.' Some believe that the house should have a soul, a heart, and that things can create an appropriate atmosphere; others argue that only people make a house a home.

Participants shared their observations that Russians love reproductions of Russian Realist art (Ivan Aivazovsky, Ilya Repin, Ivan Shishkin), portraits of classic Russian authors, especially Alexander Pushkin and Sergei Yesenin, which are decorated with embroidered cloths as people used to do with icons. Some purchased paintings depicting Russian land- and cityscapes (Figure 4.3). Orthodox Christians value baptismal crosses and have a lot of icons. Some have family jewellery, but usually explain that it is not the price that makes its value but the stories behind these pieces. One participant said, 'We believe in education, social justice, and beauty instead of icons and pictures.' The Old Russian love of icons and paintings was visible in their homes, and pre-Revolution books are often preserved in home libraries passed from generation to generation (Figures 4.1 and 4.2). Icons are found in the homes of both Lutheran and Orthodox participants. Several respondents noted that Finns who worked in the USSR have real Russian houses, with all the 'mandatory' visual attributes, and had put together collections of Russian art.

Wall clocks and Leningrad or Chinese fine porcelain tea sets were exported from the participants' country of birth. A dispute broke out among the participants about *meshchanstvo* (philistinism): is it right to always label something thus just because it pleases the eye? Some lack of taste concerning decorative Russianness was condemned: 'I would not hang up such a thing even if I were threatened with execution.' Deliberating on the objects in their house, people say how many years they have lived in Finland, whether they plan to leave, how their attitude to Finland has changed, how they found or did not find their place in the new country. One participant stated:

3. Elena: Russian interior design hasn't reared its head in my house for a long time, but the interior itself was and remains stylistically atypical, so a visitor is almost always surprised: a lot of colour, a pronounced 'density' of furniture, and yes, of course, the books in Russian are not going anywhere. Lately, however, I have noticed a certain tendency towards ethno-cultural 'markers' added to the interior: a couple of Khokhloma bowls, tins for spices with views of Tallinn (flea market provenance), and I have one important artefact, exposing my Soviet roots, and, apparently, a certain kind of mentality: it is a spinning crystal combination plate with five sections and a round centre. Of course, it is not immediately visible – the tableware is placed only on a very festive table. But it has its own history: once it belonged to my mother's stepmother, a great lover of and expert at organising festivities. I visited her from my early childhood, and the plate began to symbolise fun, the easy life, holidays, abundance, overall the Soviet *savoir vivre*. Now, of course, filling the five crystal sections does not require any connections or corruption, and I take it out once a year at Christmas, but still, the memory is very specific. And the object is recognisable. Russianness is not striking in the interior, rather there is something pan-European: coloured plaster, brightly striped curtains, dark wood, a Chinese cabinet bar, open shelves in the kitchen and tile mosaic . . . The Khokhloma bowls simply fitted in because of the colour.

Visitors from Russia keep bringing crystal vases as gifts, 'which we do not even look at – however, it seems a pity to get rid of them'. Crystal chandeliers are usually liked by people from the East, but also in old Finnish houses, in the areas of Katajanokka, Eira, 'there are a lot of crystal chandeliers, but they do not look "Soviet" (in the sense of the period, not the country of origin)'. Huge crystal salad bowls are put on the table at celebrations or to create a festive mood. Participants compare themselves with other local and foreign groups of people. Russian speakers hang carpets on the walls and put them on the floor, while Finns hang *ryijy* (handwoven tapestries) on the wall and put *matot* (handmade rag rugs) on the floor. In a Russian house, there is often a piano. The television set is in a prominent place; in living rooms the television is the centre of life, a true 'member of the family'. While children are small, it remains a means of transmitting the Russian language. Adults watch it less often, but for the elderly, even for the Old Russians (those speakers of Russian whose families had lived in Finland already before 1917 when Finland became independent of the Russian Empire after the Revolution), it is an important way to feed their souls with events and experiences. Curtains brought from Russia, multi-layered, multi-tiered, made of tulle and guipure, and edged with lace, are also liked by Arabic and Roma speakers and are cheap to buy on the market, but expensive when sewn to order. These curtains require appropriate furniture, which is difficult to find in Finland. 'We don't like minimalism and pure forms. Where in the Finnish house will you see such an outrage?' 'I remember how I met a Ukrainian neighbour. She said that she had recognised our windows by the net curtains. And now, we don't have any. Only books and music,' says one interviewee, while another one jokes: 'You mimicked [the locals].' Curtains in Finnish homes usually cover only the lower part of the window or hang down only at the sides, while Russians always draw the curtains when they come home.

Igor told us what he had brought with him:

4. **Igor**: Paintings, books, records, equipment. I arrived light, and then, like an ant, dragged and dropped whatever I could fetch from Ukraine. Clothes, though not much is left from that time, a couple of scarves. All my life is with me – a children's photograph album; my father was a good photographer, and he and my mother added to the album from my birth on. A Vietnamese vase, although I got it from my relatives. Glued, black, they were sold in the Soviet Union. A pre-Revolution gold watch – I don't wear it – and a pre-Revolution rusty corkscrew.

The historical items in this participant's collection include an invitation to meet the Finnish president Urho Kekkonen (served 1956–82), for whom his grandmother interpreted when he visited Kiev. This person preserves valuable items like postcards, war letters from his grandfather, and his father's camera. He gave away the rest or sold what would sell to earn some money. He kept only one miniature car from his collection: 'You can't bring everything, and there is nowhere to put it; the apartment is small.' His house does not look typically Russian. A lot of his decorations come from flea markets. His furniture is from IKEA, except for an English equipment stand shaped like a pagoda. On the walls, he has hung photographs by a famous Kiev photographer of the 1970s and 1980s and paintings by Ukrainian primitivists. 'We live with a Kiev spirit. We have more pictures than we had before.' The house appears clean and tidy to visitors. Finnishness is salient in the two ornamental Arabia plates illustrating scenes from the national epic, the *Kalevala*. In Soviet times, both were gifts from the Finnish part of the family, and they returned to their country of production, along with a traditional Finnish coffee machine, household items, Fiskars knives, and Hackmann forks and spoons – all of those renowned Finnish brands. The walls are painted white in the Finnish style.

Another participant reports how the stereotype of Russianness offends Russian speakers and makes them negotiate their image with those who come with ready-made opinions and prejudices:

5. **Konstantin:** About ten to twelve years ago, a film crew of a large Finnish TV channel came to my home in Helsinki. They were shooting a TV series, and they had to show the interior of a typical Russian home in Finland (as I understood, all natives of the former Soviet Union were and are still perceived as Russian, except, perhaps, people from Lithuania, Latvia and Estonia). I tried to dissuade them. I had nothing especially Russian at all, but they invaded us and took pictures of the piano and bookshelves (at that time, I had about 1,500 books, well, most of them in Russian) . . . Their very first question was 'Where are the icon corner and balalaika?' . . . the samovar, the matryoshka dolls, the gold of the lady of the house, her miniskirts, her 14-cm stiletto heels and knee-high boots? (They couldn't believe [we didn't have them] and asked to have a look at what was in our wardrobes!)

Similarly, other respondents said that they felt they were expected to show signs of Russianness, but do not need to do so. Along with purely Russian products, they display Dutch statuettes, Finnish Iittala glassware, and souvenirs from all over the world. One special place for memorabilia in the apartment is a refrigerator with magnets. Some participants mention that, during their adolescence, boys sometimes become interested in military caps, uniforms and other paraphernalia. Teens also like T-shirts with currently fashionable slogans. Those who served in the army keep their army jackets and so on. For fun or in earnest, some keep Russian flags and portraits of the leaders. One participant believed that, as a Russian citizen, she should have a Russian flag, bast (traditional bark) shoes, and a map of Russia at home (Figure 4.4). Others disagreed, saying that displaying the state symbols of a neighbouring country was inappropriate; however, maps are popular with Russian speakers when children are small. As with the language ideology, the map somehow defines the worldview and the language use (Wright 2014).

Apparently, people who moved to Finland at an advanced age (including many Ingrian repatriates and ethnic Finns), reproduced Russian-style home interiors more often than their young compatriots, while making adjustments for the typical layout of Finnish apartments. The majority of young and middle-aged people, however, do not differ much from their local peers in terms of their interior decoration. Children born in Finland perceive this differently and cherish special things inherited from the family, since this confirms that they have roots somewhere else. Russians often put plants on shelves and windowsills, while Finns are more likely to hang them in the windows. Someone hypothesised that the style of the home decoration (the prevalence of items from the country of departure) may correlate with the children's Russian-only circles and friendships with other Russian speakers.

In many New Year posts on Facebook, immigrants shared photographs of their decorated *elka* (Christmas tree) and mentioned that they had brought Christmas tree decorations used in their families when they were still little children. Some of these decorations are truly antique pieces dating from before 1917; some others are from the 1930s and later periods. These decorations were carefully packed in old shoeboxes, isolated from one another by layers of cotton wool. This is how they were kept throughout the year in old suitcases and trunks, and this is how they travelled to Finland. According to the participants, these bright and silvery glass baubles, stars and animal figurines, were dear to their heart; they were like sweet symbols of hopes and dreams, of treasures and riches of the poor (Figure 4.5). Surprisingly, it is common practice among migrants to drag these tokens of joyful times along with them across borders (Barsukov 2021). Valentina sent us a photograph of her Christmas tree and wrote:

> 6. **Valentina:** These [Christmas] decorations are from my childhood, somewhere in the early 1960s, not earlier). We brought them from Karelia; some of them, unfortunately, have not been preserved. We cannot put up all the decorations at once; the older ones are hanging on the upper part of the tree, the newer ones are at the bottom. We should probably make an inven-

Figure 4.5 A decorated Christmas tree, Old New Year tree decorations and an old suitcase.

tory of the old decorations and photograph them while they are still intact. They are the things that remind me of my parents, my brother and my childhood. In our family, the tradition was to install and decorate a living tree [not artificial], even before my mother's birthday, just before Christmas, although we celebrated only the New Year. The Christmas tree stood in the house for a long time, until the Old New Year [according to Julian Calendar, 14 January], and sometimes until Epiphany, on 19 January, and now [we remove it] much earlier. Revisiting this sparkling past is stirring up pleasant memories, and I am happy to share them.

All respondents in different groups agreed that the only thing that unites everyone is the presence of a large number of books: 'Again, everything was reduced to Russian literature as a national idea.' However, Finns have large home libraries as well, and in both countries one can find houses with no books at all. One person was of the opinion that, in some Russian houses, Finns could make a study of minimalism and asceticism. Some time ago, participants had a lot of DVDs and CDs which replaced collections of video and audio cassettes. The topic of food that emerged in many conversations completed the image of home: nobody objected to traditional delicacies like buckwheat blinis, *pelmeni* (dumplings) and *riazhenka* (fermented baked milk). For Russian speakers, a table full of food crowns the house, which becomes a real home when there are guests in it. Someone added that the contents of the refrigerator say more about the people who live in the house than what they watch on TV.

CONCLUSION

In the process of discussing their representation and ideas of home, the Russian-speaking immigrants to Finland confessed that their primary reference point is the way of life of significant others – parents, friends, neighbours and even favourite film stars. Shadows of the Soviet/Russian past that are visible in the homes we visited give an insight into the sentimental remnants of the inhabitants' past life and its hierarchy of values: first books, then icons, paintings and so on. Cherished mementos continue their life in Finnish interiors where pure form reigns. The meanings of the objects change, their preservation or loss in the process of migration are remembered for a long time, and immigrants care about what other people think about their dwellings. The research shows that documents and photographs are the most valued things, as well as icons and crosses for those who are Orthodox. The 'Old Russians' kept memories of Russianness in their homes and transmitted them to their children. Not many people have objects that have accompanied them from birth onwards, but they keep belongings connected to the memory of their relatives and friends. Some people tend to keep the way of life they had before emigration; others want to have a very modern European home. Some try to materialise their former dreams; others try to find out who they are.

Participants demonstrated all versions of typical migrant relations to home: nostalgia, a break with the past, lives between two homes, hybrid housing, attempts to recreate one's former lifestyle in a new place or to make dreams come true, and adaptation to the dominant culture. We heard reflections on themselves as agents but also as victims, desires to go with the flow or to change everything. The proper space created in the new environment turns out not to be the same as before because the conditions are inevitably different. Before leaving their homeland, Russian speakers in Finland lived like everyone else, mostly having very modest means. In their new homes, they have a lot of objects, in fact so many that they have to get rid of some. No one we met possessed any really expensive items. Any clothes brought to Finland have long since worn out, but some children's things have been kept, such as homemade carnival costumes, ethnic craft objects, photographs, letters, postcards and notes. Immigrants often buy second-hand items, not only for economic but also for ecological reasons: a chance to give things a second life. Many

Russian-speaking immigrants think that their tastes coincide with those of their Finnish neighbours, and therefore it is impossible to distinguish what is Finnish from what is not.

When space acquires particular meanings, it turns into a place with its own identity, and most aspects of human identity have place-related implications (Dixon and Durrheim 2000). Some Russian-speaking immigrants to Finland may become – or want to become – more local than the locals themselves, and others want to redefine themselves. 'Someone at first throws out the matryoshka dolls, and then hurries to buy them again!', claimed one participant. There are also differences in what exactly is depicted in the photographs, how things appear in the house, for what purpose, and what associations with these objects are stored in owners' memories. A wish to become a member of the local society, to preserve one's own identity, the fear of being 'misplaced' or despised, and the joy of realising a previously inaccessible dream intertwine. Periods of passion for a specific design replace periods of indifference to it. Self-identification of a migrant is a long process, and everyone goes through a variety of stages.

Moving to another country is an experience of reformulation. A new language and surrounding values have a huge impact on the evaluation of one's own goals and habits. Migrants need the ability to admit losses and reconcile with them by emphasising the inner core of their being. Everyone is aware of material comforts, but not everyone delights in them. According to our participants, a 'typical' Russian house is a hospitable place where guests come, eat together, talk about 'Russian' topics, and sing Russian songs. This actually means that any home could be transformed into such a place, because 'Russianness' lies mostly not in material things (although food plays an enormous role in it), but in a long history of human gatherings. Do immigrants need to adapt in such manner? In fact, unconsciously, immigrants discover new semantics and semiotics of everyday life and learn about their selves anew. Psychologically, immigrants accept their evolving identity. They find that their new homes reflect their inner and outer transformations and are formed by the experiences and preferences of the people inhabiting them.

REFERENCES

Adon'eva, S. B. (2011), *Simvolicheskii poriadok*, Saint Petersburg: Amfora.
Al-Ali, N. and K. Koser (eds) (2002), *New Approaches to Migration? Transnational Communities and the Transformation of Home*, London: Routledge.

Baiburin, A. K. (1983), *Zhilishche v obriadakh i predstavleniiakh vostochnykh slavian*, Leningrad: Nauka.

Barsukov, A. (2021), 'Gosudarstvennaia ideologiia – v ukrasheniiakh dlia elki. V Novosibirske otkrylas' unikal'naia vystavka', *Radio Svoboda*, 6:1, available at: <sibreal.org/a/31032962.html> (last accessed 14 November 2022).

Baschmakoff, N. and M. Leinonen (2001), *Russian Life in Finland, 1917–1939: A Local and Oral History*, Helsinki: Institute of Russia and Eastern Europe.

Boal, F. (ed.) (2000), *Ethnicity and Housing: Accommodating Differences*, Aldershot: Ashgate.

Dixon, J. and K. Durrheim (2000), 'Displacing place-identity: a discursive approach to locating self and other', *British Journal of Social Psychology*, 39, 27–44.

Dushakova, N. S. (2019), 'Materiality of mobility: objects in migration memories of Old Believers', *Culture of Slavs and Culture of Jews: Dialogue, Similarities, Differences*, 21, 232–45.

Fedorova, L. L. (2016), 'Svet v okoshke: dom kak istochnik metafor i frazeologicheskikh obrazov', in D. Sukhovei (ed.), *Podrobnosti slovesnosti*, Saint Petersburg: Svoe izdatel'stvo, pp. 367–78.

Fialkova, L. and M. Yelenevskaya (2007), *Ex-Soviets in Israel: From Personal Narratives to a Collective Portrait*, Detroit: Wayne State University Press.

Filippova, S. and N. Archakova (2013), 'The "house/home" and "homeland" associative fields in the Yakut and Russian linguistic consciousness', *Karadeniz*, 5:19, 469–76.

Gapova, E. (2004), 'Zheny "russkikh" programmistov ili zhenshchiny, kotorye edut vsled za muzhchinami', in S. Ushakin (ed.), *Semeinye uzy: modeli dlia sborki*, Moscow: NLO, pp. 409–31.

Golovina, K. (2017), 'Material culture and bricolage: Russian-speaking migrants in Japan who make and procure objects', *Anthropological Forum*, 34, 178–211.

Golovina, K. (2019), 'Skin-to-skin with the house: senses and affect in the relationship of migrant Russian women in Japan with their homes', *Asian Anthropology*, 18:3, 170–85.

Gramatchikova, N. B. (2018), 'Lost and invented: places and things of/in the family history', *Labirint*, 1, 17–30.

Gunn, D. (2019), 'Russian properties: a history of Russian housing', *Expatica*, 30.01, available at: <expatica.com/ru/housing/housing-basics/russian-properties-a-history-of-russian-housing-105578> (last accessed 14 November 2022).

Gurova, O. Y. (2013), '"To look Russian": Russian migrants in Finland: social characteristics and consumption of clothing', *Economic Sociology*, 14:2, 17–41.

Heino, E. M. and M. H. Veistilä (2015), 'Integration, recognition and security: discourses on social support by families of Russian background living in Finland', *Nordic Journal of Migration Research*, 5:2, 91–8.

Honkanen, A., K. Pitkänen and M. C. Hall (2016), 'A local perspective on cross-border tourism: Russian second home ownership in Eastern Finland', *International Journal of Tourism Research*, 18:2, 149–58.

Ivanova-Buchatskaya, Y. V. (2010), 'Rossiiskie nemtsy v Germanii: znakovye ob'ekty povsednevnoi zhizni i identichnosti', *Diaspory*, 2, 137–66.

Kim, J. S. (2018), '"Home-life" in Soviet society: social psychology in the works by Mikhail Bulgakov', *Siberian Philological Forum*, 4, 37–49.

Kopnina, H. (2016), *East to West Migration: Russian Migrants in Western Europe*, London: Routledge.

Koznova, N. N. (2019), 'The transformation of the image of the house in the diaries of Irina Knorring', *RUDN Journal of Studies in Literature and Journalism*, 24:2, 196–203.

Laine, J. (2017), 'Finnish–Russian border mobility and tourism: localism overruled by geopolitics', in D. Hall (ed.), *Tourism and Geopolitics: Issues and Concepts from Central and Eastern Europe*, Wallingford: Cabi, pp. 178–90.

Makhlina, S. (2009), *Semiotika kul'tury povsednevnosti*, Saint Petersburg: Aleteia.

Mineeva, I. N. (2013), 'Materials to the dictionary of plots, images, motives "culture of Russian expatriate community of the XX–XXI centuries": the concept of emigration', *Universum*, 2:2, 1–12, available at: <7universum.com/ru/philology/archive/item/396> (last accessed 14 November 2022).

Moilanen, R. (2004), 'Miten uudissanat kotoutua ja kotouttaa ovat kotiutuneet kieleemme?' [How have the new words *kotoutua* and *kotoutia* become at home in our language?], *Kielikello*, 4, available at: <at kielikello.fi/-/miten-uudissanat-kotoutua-ja-kotouttaa-ovat-kotiutuneet-kieleemme> (last accessed 14 November 2022).

Mostikov, S. V. (2015), 'Correlation of migration processes and the social concept of "home"', *Journal of Siberian Social University. Humanities and Social Sciences*, 8:9, 1990–7.

Odynets, S. (2018), 'Home without walls, walls without home: constructing physical and symbolic transnational locations in Ukrainian women's migration to Italy', *Laboratorium*, 2, 34–51.

Pechurina, A. (2011), 'Russian dolls, icons, and Pushkin: practicing cultural identity through material possessions in immigration', *Laboratorium*, 3, 97–117.

Pechurina, A. (2016), 'Defining the Russian diasporic home and its atmospheres: theoretical challenges and the methodological implications', *Sociological Review*, 15:2, 26–41.

Protassova, E. (2004), *Fennorossy: zhizn' i upotreblenie iazyka*, Saint Petersburg: Zlatoust.

Protassova, E. and K. Reznik (2020), 'Funktsii migrantskogo doma: russkoiazychnye v Finliandii', *Istoricheskii kur'er*, 4, 204–16.

Päivinen, J. (2017), *Mitä tiedämme maahanmuuton taloudellisista vaikutuksista? Selvitys maahanmuuton taloudellisten vaikutusten kokonaisuudesta* [What do we know about the economic effects of immigration? A report on the overall economic effects of immigration], Helsinki: Sosiaali- ja terveysministeriö.

Renvik, T. A., A. Brylka, H. Konttinen, R. Vetik and I. Jasinskaja-Lahti (2018), 'Perceived status and national belonging: the case of Russian speakers in Finland and Estonia', *International Review of Social Psychology*, 31:1, 1–10.

Rezanova, Z. I. (ed.) (2011), *Nostalgiia po sovetskomu*, Tomsk: Tomsk State University.

Rudkovskaya, M. M. (2019), 'Urban everyday life of the Russian military emigrants in Toulon in the 1920s–1930s: housing and living conditions', *Izvestiia Smolenskogo gosudarstvennogo universiteta*, 4:48, 374–86.

Rymarovich, S. N. (2013), 'Idea of home in the philosophy of 20th century culture: the main approaches', *Uchenye zapiski. E-Journal of the Kursk State University*, 2:26, 144–53.

Schenschin, V. (2008), *Venäläiset ja venäläinen kulttuuri Suomessa*, Helsinki: Aleksanteri-instituutti.

Semenova, S. U. (2012), 'Russian house in the environs of Paris', *Russian History*, 3, 83–4.

TDR, 'Top 10 facts about the Russian House', available at: <todiscoverrussia.com/top-10-facts-about-the-russian-house> (last accessed 14 November 2022).

Tiaynen-Qadir, T. (2016), 'Transnational grandmothers making their multi-sited homes between Finland and Russia', in K. Walsh and L. Näre (eds), *Transnational Migration and Home in Older Age*, London: Routledge, pp. 25–37.

Tsepennikova, A. N. (2014), 'Transgression of the "home"-concept in Russian émigré literature of fourth wave', *Ural Philological Bulletin, Series: Russian Literature of the 20th and 21st centuries*, 4, 39–48.

Varjonen, S., A. Zamiatin and M. Rinas (2017), *Russian-speaking Population in Finland Here and Now: Statistics, Surveys, Organisation Field*, Helsinki: Cultura Foundation.

Viimaranta, H., E. Protassova and A. Mustajoki (2017), 'Aspects of commodification of Russian in Finland', *Russian Journal of Linguistics*, 21:3, 620–34.

Viimaranta, H., E. Protassova and A. Mustajoki (2018), 'Russian-speakers in Finland: the ambiguities of a growing minority', *RECEO*, 49:4, 8–40.

Viimaranta, H., E. Protassova and A. Bursa (2019), 'Family language policy and Russian–Finnish bilingualism: preliminary data and directions for further research', in S. Haque and F. Le Lièvre (eds), *Politique linguistique familiale. Enjeux dynamiques de la transmission linguistique dans un contexte migratoire*, Munich: Lincom, pp. 87–100.

Volpjansky, P. (2002), 'Belaia Gvardiia v strane Suomi', *Trud*, 1 July, available at: <www.trud.ru/article/29-06-2002/42627_belaja_gvardija_v_strane_suomi.html> (last accessed 14 November 2022).

Wright, S. (2014), 'The map, the group and language ideology', *Journal of World Languages*, 2, 81–98.

Yarovaya, A. and G. Yarovoy (2019), 'How immigrants from Karelia live in Finland', *The Barents Observer*, 5 June 2019, available at: <https://thebarentsobserver.com/en/node/5475> (last accessed 14 November 2022).

CHAPTER 5

The Role of Possessions in Adaptation to a New Life[*]

Marika Kalyuga

INTRODUCTION

The possessions people are attached to help us to identify who they are. In migration, when people uproot their lives and adapt to another country, material objects from the place of their origin are likely to be especially meaningful and play an important role in the understanding of immigrant identity. This chapter examines the effect of a new culture on the life of immigrants by comparing possessions that people bring with them to Australia with possessions remaining in their households years later. Altogether, there have been several major waves of immigration from Russia and the Soviet Union to Australia: (1) from the late nineteenth century to World War I (pre-revolutionary labour and political immigration); (2) from the early 1920s to World War II (post-revolutionary immigration); (3) from the late 1940s to the early 1950s (post-war immigration); (4) from the mid-1950s to the second half of the 1980s (immigration from China and Europe) and (5) from the late 1980s to the present day (*perestroika* and post-*perestroika* immigration) (Gentshke et al. 2014; Kanevskaya 2008; Ryan 2005; Usuyama 2015). Some researchers, however, prefer different divisions of these flows. Thus, Ryazantsev (2013) singles out six immigration waves, whereas Ters (2015) claims there have been eight, and both of them give a finer division relying on differences between contingencies and motives. I focus on immigrants who moved to Australia from Russia and Ukraine or from the corresponding republics of the Soviet Union at the end of the 1980s and after the collapse of the Soviet Union in the early 1990s, as well as in the 2000s.

---

[*] I would like to thank my responders, who made this study possible, for their time and willingness to share their stories.

Possessions are viewed as providing valuable insights into how people present themselves and identify their membership in society. Various prior studies have examined possessions of immigrants and their role in securing identity, including the identity of Russian immigrants. For example, Pechurina (2011) focuses on the possessions of Russian immigrants in the UK that serve as a 'symbolic representation' of Russia and 'Russianness'. Protassova and Reznik (2019) examine why Russian immigrants to Finland value some objects as special possessions and get rid of others. Some studies focus on the classification of migrants' possessions. Suleimanova (2015), for example, distinguishes three main types: (1) one's own everyday household items (e.g. furniture, electrical appliances, dishes); (2) 'symbolic items' that satisfy spiritual needs (family photographs and other memorabilia) and (3) everyday household items provided by landlords (e.g. furniture and appliances). Her classification is based on two very different criteria, namely: whether possessions are owned or borrowed and whether they have any symbolic representation or not. Another classification is presented by Belk who divides possessions into categories according to the meanings they acquire for migrants. Analysing personal documents from the 1847–69 Mormon migration, Belk (1992: 339) differentiates between the following five major categories of possession symbolism: (1) sacred; (2) material; (3) personal; (4) familial and (5) communal meanings. According to this classification, possessions that have personal meanings are those that help to create or re-establish feelings of competence and domesticity, such as tools, musical instruments, furniture or china. Possessions having familial meaning include heirlooms and ritual artefacts (they are unique and family-related), while community meanings are those shared by a community (such as religious attributes or objects of stereotypical handicrafts, symbolising the ethnic belonging of their owners).

The present chapter adopts Belk's (1992: 339) classification and focuses on such categories of possession symbolism as: (1) material meanings; (2) sentimental or personal meanings and (3) ethnic meanings. The differentiation between these types is rather conditional since the same item may have material, sentimental and ethnic meanings. Moreover, the meaning of a possession can change. Such changes are especially common during periods of unsettled lives, migration being a case in point (Swidler 1986).

Attachment and migration, fixation and loss, as well as transnational mobility and diasporic belonging, can all be associated with home and possessions. New kinds of uprootedness and boundary transgression may have intertwined meanings including mobility and location technology in a globalising world (Ahmed et al. 2003). The presence of cultural artefacts in diaspora fosters a sense of belonging to a common homeland, even if it is only virtual (cf. Abu-Ghazaleh 2011). The clear goals for acquiring material property may change over time.

DATA COLLECTION AND METHODOLOGY

The material for this study was drawn from in-depth semi-structured interviews and relied on content analysis and the photographic method. Both approaches play a crucial role in social semiotics and linguistic ethnography. Content analysis accepts in-depth interpretations of the oral and written narratives and adds to triangulation of the results obtained (see, e.g., Krippendorff 2010). The photographic method does not only allow for a better documentation of the setting of the fieldwork but also permits a rethinking of the anthropological significance of things in the space of a person's existence, where culture and the surrounding world continually interact (e.g., De Leon and Cohen 2005; Schultz 2005). The data collection and investigation procedures involved continuous comparative analysis of possessions that people bring with them to Australia with possessions remaining in their households years later. Circulating a questionnaire was the primary means of collecting data. It contained questions about: (1) demographic data; (2) the types of possessions brought from the homeland to Australia, and (3) the items that were useful and the items participants regretted bringing. The questionnaires were sent by email. They were presented both in Russian and in English, and the responders could answer either in English or in Russian. Yet everyone chose Russian. No names of participants are mentioned in this chapter to ensure anonymity. The excerpts from the Russian-language interviews were translated by the author. The criterion for selecting participants was the length of their residence in Australia. The dates of arrival ranged between 1987 and 2019. There were sixteen participants, and these include men (3) and women (13) born and raised in the Soviet Union, as well as in post-Soviet Russia and Ukraine. All migrated to Australia as adults. Participants were recruited through snowball sampling.

The interviews were not the only method of data collection. To support the findings from the interviews, the data collection process also included the examination of blogs and forums in which experienced Russian-speaking Australians recommend those who are planning to immigrate what to bring to Australia and discuss such important issues as building a new home away from the homeland, domesticity in the new surroundings and attitudes to a new culture. These blogs and forums were monitored for four years. Discussion threads with suggestions were translated into English.

Table 5.1 Demographic information on participants.

Age at arrival in Australia	20–35
Country of birth	Soviet Union (5 participants), Russia (6 participants), Ukraine (5 participants)
Years in Australia	0–5 (4 participants), 6–10 (6 participants), 11–33 (6 participants)

Photographs of household items used in this chapter were provided by members of the Russian and Ukrainian community in Australia, who were asked to send photographs of the items that they had brought from the country of origin and still held in their possession. Table 5.1 summarises the demographic information on the participants.

Many factors influence the choice of what people take with them to a new country and what they still keep in the house years later. These factors include country of origin, age, gender, occupation and personal taste, as well as the influence of family members. For example, Csikszentmihalyi and Rochberg-Halton (1981) observed that men and adolescents, unlike women and the elderly, tend to indicate objects that symbolise their personalities as their favourite possessions. Men are also more likely than women to mention expensive electronic goods as their favourites (Mehta and Belk 1991: 405), while older people 'tend to be strongly attached to contemplative possessions that help them survey their past' (Mehta and Belk 1991: 399–400). The main focus of this chapter is on the possessions of those Russophone Australians who migrated with families, rather than alone, and, therefore, whose households contain items chosen by or belonging to different family members. Thus, this chapter will trace the general tendencies of what people bring with them to Australia and keep in their household for years.

MATERIAL MEANINGS OF POSSESSIONS

Due to the large distance between Russia and Australia, the number of individual possessions brought is limited by the cost of moving them. Immigrants have to decide on which items are important enough to justify the cost and effort of transporting them. As stated in one of the online articles in my sample:

1. **Mila:** I thought that the more expensive the 'contenders' for being moved [to Australia – *M.K.*], the better.

Recent immigrants often comment on bringing expensive small electronic goods, such as mobile phones, iPads and computers. They discuss the question of compatibility of devices, their price and quality. They talk about prestige items and about what new immigrants can afford to buy in the first stages of their life in the new country and what they cannot, and therefore should try to bring with them from their homeland.

Some immigrants, when moving to a new place of residence abroad, try to take as much as possible:

> 2. **Vera:** It seemed foolish to us to give away our property acquired by hard work to a stranger. We found boxes at a nearby store and skilfully wrapped our small appliances and tableware in clothes, blankets and linens . . . There was a question about the compatibility of household appliances with Australian appliances, and we found out that the voltage in the network is the same. When we delivered our goods, all appliances could be turned on. All equipment worked, and the TV 'spoke' without problems.

However, others advise to buy electronic appliances locally, in Australia:

> 3. **Monia:** Buy a device with a warranty and a connector adapted to the local power grid.

Some possessions that once were considered status objects may no longer play this role in the new country. For example, rugs, crystal vases or Madonna china sets, which were viewed as having high material value in the 1980s and at the beginning of 1990s and were proudly displayed in the houses of immigrants (Figure 5.1), are not that popular anymore. Crystal vases and carpets/rugs were fashionable in the Soviet Union in the 1970s–80s and in short supply, which increased their value. Madonna porcelain was imported from Eastern Germany.

Among the possessions that lost high material meanings are expensive clothes. For example, people report regretting bringing an evening dress trimmed with Italian lace, made by a professional dressmaker, expensive high-heeled shoes, or fur jackets. Many have noted that Australians prefer to wear plain, comfortable clothes. On the forums, the answers to such questions as 'Is the Russian/Ukrainian "I wear all my best clothes at once" style different from the Australian style?' are:

> 4. **Nelly:** No, there is no cult of clothing per se; no one bothers.

Figure 5.1 Madonna china sets.

5. **Valia:** In everyday life, Australians wear comfortable clothes – shorts, T-shirts, jeans – something that does not hinder movement, and it is not a pity if they become crumpled when one sits on a lawn participating in a picnic. Of course, when it comes to visiting a decent restaurant or a business meeting, then Australians observe the rules of etiquette and put on business suits.

6. **Joe:** The casual style is mostly jeans or shorts and a T-shirt, usually not ironed (so as not to waste time). In such clothes it is convenient and comfortable in the hot Australian climate; you can sit on the grass or just on the footpath in them . . .

7. **Bella:** The standard look of an Australian on a day-off in the morning or afternoon is yoga pants, bright sneakers and a sweater or sports T-shirt on top.

Some even wrote:

8. **Joe:** When I first came to Australia, I was surprised at how plainly Australians dressed. I brought my best outfits, and when I was going to meet my friends who have been living here for a long time, I put on the most beautiful dress. When I saw that they came in ripped jeans and wrinkled T-shirts, I felt offended. And the first question they asked me was: 'Why are you dressed up like that?' It took me two years to understand, appreciate and accept the Australian clothing style.

There are also suggestions:

9. **Sue:** Chances are good that most of your old wardrobe will not suit your new life. Leave warm scarves and mittens at home!

10. **Joe:** After living in Australia, the Russian way of dressing seems strange to me. Everything is so pretentious, in the Russian–Turkish style, with some kind of sequins, trimmings, stitching and made of synthetic fibres . . . People are dressed in the morning as if for an evening reception, made up, perfumed, and even when it is very hot, they still wear nylon . . .

11. **Bella:** Gradually, I got into the local fashion, put my heels and dresses away in the wardrobe, and began to buy T-shirts, sports tops, leggings with animal prints, jeans with holes everywhere, dresses with all sorts of stripes and cuts, and, of course, sneakers . . . By the way, in Russia I often dressed classically, and I had only one pair of sneakers, but hundreds of dresses, each of which was vital to me and each of which was carefully transported to Australia . . .

Many also note changes in immigrants' wardrobe, caused not by the influence of how the majority dress, but by the conditions of life, for example the absence of central heating in Australia. Buying stylish and even decent-looking clothes was one of the challenges of Soviet times. Immigrants, who moved to Australia from Russia and Ukraine or from the corresponding republics of the Soviet Union at the end of the 1980s and after the collapse of the Soviet Union, may have a very diverse cultural background. As a result, their material culture, including clothing, as well as decorative items, may reflect a mix of different influences. Having found themselves in the West, Soviet immigrants were often amazed at the informal style of clothes worn in the host countries and mocked it in their narratives (see, e.g., Fialkova and Yelenevskaya 2007: 104–5). Such a mundane thing as clothes can be an indicator of the lifestyle and societal values. It is also a question of etiquette: for example, ex-Soviets may consider it impolite to wear worn-out jeans and T-shirts to an evening event. Americans think it is impolite to use perfumes which can be unpleasant for someone. It is also a question of age: a lot of young Russians in big industrial cities wear the same style of clothes as their peers in the West. At the same time, some girls wear shoes with 10–12-centimetre heels in the daytime.

12. **Jenny:** If it was plus-12 degrees outside, then it was about the same in our studio flat! First of all, we went to buy a fan heater, warm clothes and UGG fur boots. By the way, I finally understood the true purpose of these Australian analogue of Russian felt boots. Australians wear UGGs at home during the Australian winter!

13. **Zhenia:** Here, there's such a paradox: despite the fact that the winters here are not severe, the lack of central heating and 'cardboard walls' make me feel colder than in Russia. Therefore, sheepskin slippers were my first purchase. Usually in winter it is even warmer outside than at home: once in my friend's apartment the thermometer rose to a maximum of plus-9, while the temperature outside was about 13 . . . Australians make themselves warm as best as they can: they use heaters and simply dress more warmly. UGG fur boots worn outside in the whole world are worn at home here.

14. **Sasha:** At home I wear UGG fur boots. I put them on today for the first time in the season, and it immediately warmed my heart. Amazingly comfortable footwear.

Although the majority of migrants say that their style of dress has become more casual and regret bringing to Australia clothes or shoes that are too expensive or warm, there is also another trend. Several respondents said that they had bought a sheepskin coat or a fur hat during a trip abroad only because, many years ago, in an era of scarcity in the Soviet Union, it was a cherished dream to have such a thing (see Figure 5.2):

15. **Tatiana:** I saw a sheepskin coat in Turkey and could not resist. I knew that it would only collect dust in my wardrobe in Sydney, and I would rarely wear it during my trips abroad, but I really wanted to buy it . . .

16. **Anna:** I felt that I absolutely had to buy that mink earflap hat even though it was too warm for the Australian winter. It was the fulfilment of a youthful dream.

In such cases, the purchased items had a sentimental rather than material value. Some emigrants living abroad borrow warm clothes from friends when visiting northern parts of Russia, especially in winter. Maybe the realisation of youthful dreams ticks a box on a wish list con-

Figure 5.2 A fur coat (*shuba*).

nected to migration and therefore contributes to the general satisfaction with the decisions made once in the past.

SENTIMENTAL AND PERSONAL MEANINGS OF POSSESSIONS

Immigrants' homes contain a variety of items that have special personal importance and remind their owners of life in the country of origin: photographs, personally crafted objects or items that were crafted by loved ones (father, mother or grandparents), as well as everyday household items brought from the homeland. In the immigrants' houses I visited I was shown traditional Ukrainian shirts embroidered by the owner's great-grandmother, a vase that was presented to my interviewee in her childhood and which is now carefully stored. Her family members are not even allowed to use it for flowers. In another house I was shown an old self-made book with poems that the participant's father wrote to her mother. Responders from Russia and Ukraine said that they had also brought with them linen bedding, duvets and down pillows because they were used to them. Natal'ia B. noted that she had brought a little *kazanok* – an iron pot traditionally used for cooking food – and was very happy that she had, because in Australia she could not find pots of that size and type.

Having familiar possessions from home may help people to gain a sense of security in the new environment and facilitate adjustment to a new country (Halpern 1968; Kahne 1967; Nemy 1986). Mehta and Belk (1991: 400) argue that 'this seems likely to be especially true for objects that are linked to continued behavioral rituals', for example eating, sleeping and grooming. No wonder that immigrants from Russia and Ukraine living in Australia advise newcomers on forums:

17. Olia: Take all the usual kitchen accessories, which you cannot buy here. [smiley face] An aluminium spoon with holes or a favourite mug. [smiley face] For example, take gauze for cottage cheese, because it is difficult to find big pieces of gauze. Pharmacies sell only small shreds of gauze ... Take everything that is 'non-disposable', which you are used to, that can sweeten your life.

Despite the availability of all sorts of white cheeses in English-speaking countries, as well as in Germany, France and so on, the Russian soul cannot imagine happy life without the Russian one called *tvorog*. So, some immigrants make it themselves. Milk is first left to ferment, and then the pot with it in is put inside another, bigger pot on a low heat. The resulting semi-liquid substance is put into gauze and hung to drain. When it stops dripping whey, the desired consistency of the cheese is achieved and the *tvorog* is ready. The process is time-consuming, and the quantity yielded meagre, yet the resulting product is praised for its excellent taste and health-giving qualities. Some women use the whey as a treatment for their skin and hair. People may use gauze for other purposes, and small swatches available in the pharmacies are not satisfactory.

Some responders claiming origin in the former Soviet Union trust the 'Russian' medications they were used to in their pre-immigration life, attributing to them an almost folkloric power. These can be prescription drugs or over-the-counter items available in pharmacies, believed to be potent remedies, such as drinking soda, iodine, brilliant green (*zelionka*), potassium permanganate (*margantsovka*), mustard plaster (*gorchichnik*), and lime or rosebay willowherb infusions (*lipovyi tsvet / ivan-chai*). Moreover, Russian drugs are not only more familiar than Western medications but also substantially cheaper.

18. Sveta: Australian healthcare is of the highest standard, with pharmacies operating everywhere. However, the prices of many medications we are used to, such as absorbents, are far from cheap. Therefore, to save money, take a minimum set of medications and other self-care stuff with you.

19. Vera: We should take more medicine with us. Since all the medications here are unfamiliar, and most are only by prescription; in order to buy, for example, ear drops, you must first go to see your doctor. He will write a prescription and then you can buy the medication. A visit to the doctor will cost 30–50 local dollars until a Medicare card is received. Prices for medications are also rather high, so it is better to take them with you. And, in general, in the first days, there is so much to do and such a huge amount of information to digest that going to the doctor would be a completely unnecessary extra effort.

Many everyday items from the country of origin are stored and used in immigrants' homes for many years after migration: a dish for jellied meat (Figure 5.3), a garlic press (Figure 5.4) or favourite tea towels (Figure 5.5). Even outdated electrical devices, for example a travel iron (Figure 5.6), can be kept in the house as metonymic associations with a home back in Russia or Ukraine.

Moreover, bringing dishware, travel irons and the like was typical of immigrants who lived in the days of consumer goods shortages and, therefore, found it difficult to part with such 'hard-won' items. At present, these items have mostly lost their material value but have retained sentimental meanings. Such items which remain in the homes of immigrants are usually small in size and still have a presentable appearance. Thus, for example, one responder said that she kept her old small travel iron but had thrown away a bulky meat grinder that had once belonged to her grandmother, despite all the effort of bringing it to Australia.

As noted by many scholars, when people leave favourite possessions behind, they may experience feelings of sadness and nostalgia (Belk 1991; Boschetti 1986; Grinberg and Grinberg 1984; Howell 1983; Pastalan 1983; Pollock 1989; Rivlin 1982; Sherman and Newman 1977).

Figure 5.3 A dish for jellied meat.

Figure 5.4 A garlic press.

20. Nelly: Of the little things that used to be my favourites and dear to my heart, I took only a little teddy bear. I regret this a little, and I miss my favourite porcelain cup and a small statuette in the shape of an angel.

21. Vera: Ah, my pots and pans! I still regret not taking them with me. We used to have the right approach – multiply the weight of the item by the cost of transportation and, if the amount is less than the amount of the purchase of a new item, then take

THE ROLE OF POSSESSIONS 109

Figure 5.5 Linen tea towels.

Figure 5.6 A travel iron.

it with you. This absolutely correct and rational approach was almost forgotten when we were packing. There is not a single thing that we brought here about which I would say that we wasted money on transportation. But I still regret many things I left behind.

Hage (1997: 108) argues that it is usually 'positively experienced nostalgia' that 'does not necessarily involve a desire to "go back"; more often than not . . . it is a desire of being there here.'

However, the immigration process is not only a spatially and culturally transitional stage, but it is also often linked to changes in education, career and marital status. It introduces an opportunity to build a new identity. Many immigrants also mention that their taste and, therefore, personal possessions have changed since their arrival in Australia.

22. Mila: The point is that in Australia your lifestyle and your taste will change a lot. With the change of a country, you will live in a new climate, will have a new job and a new house [in Australia – *M.K.*]. I bought things that I would not have even looked at in Ukraine.

ETHNOCULTURAL MEANINGS OF POSSESSIONS

Among the treasured items in immigrants' homes there are also those that represent their ethnic identities. Such artefacts are often not from their Russian or Ukrainian homes but were purchased later – during trips back to their home countries. Therefore, they may have been brought not because they remind immigrants of their pre-emigration homes but rather of their homeland in general. In Ukrainian houses one can see, for example, pillows and scarfs embroidered with traditional ornaments, painted Easter eggs (*pysanka*) from Kosmach (a village located in the Ivano-Frankivsk region of Ukraine) and *motanka* dolls (traditional knotted dolls which are among the most ancient family protective charms). Various scholars note that Russian immigrants tend to decorate their homes with traditional Russian artefacts and souvenirs, such as '*matryoshka* dolls, painted wooden spoons, and Khokhloma bowls' (bowls made of natural wood and hand-painted in the Khokhloma style, known for its red-and-gold flower patterns over a black background) or symbols of Orthodoxy (Boym 2002; Pechurina 2011). Participants value such possessions as a 'symbolic representation' of their country of birth. As Pechurina (2011: 98) notes, these items 'index "Russia" and "Russian" at the same time as they mediate complex feelings and engagements with notions of "Russianness" and "home" for migrants'. It is difficult to find a household of Russian immigrants that does not contain any of the popular Russian souvenirs: matryoshka dolls, Pavlovo Posad shawls, Khokhloma lacquer boxes, Gzhel ware (a Russian-style blue-and-white pottery which bears the name of a village south of Moscow where this craft originated), samovars, birch-bark crafts and so on. People who visit the homes of immigrants note that their homes have 'clear signs of Russianness':

23. **Musia:** One can find Russian books, albums with coloured photographs of Russian cities and museums, tablecloths, Khokhloma and icons.

After living in Australia for several years, many immigrants on trips to their homeland begin to bring back souvenirs:

24. **Seva:** And from Russia I brought back ... a samovar! I also brought crystal glasses, vodka, wooden Khokhloma dishes, books, and something made of malachite. I bought as much chocolate as allowed: Australian chocolate is made with additives and, to my taste, not as good as Russian chocolate! My children were delighted with the samovar and the chocolate.

Scholars also mention books and DVDs in the Russian language as common immigrants' possessions. Some immigrants collect them purely out of personal interest. However, for others, Russian books and DVDs are also 'an important part of reaffirming Russian identity' since these books and films 'represent Russian language and Russian culture in material form' (Pechurina 2011: 109; 110). Since new technologies have spread, DVDs, like video cassettes before them, are becoming objects of the past. So, like members of host societies, immigrants face the dilemma: to keep them or get rid of them? For immigrants it may be a harder decision because their sentimental value is high.

The presence of books in the mother tongue is typical of houses of Russian and Ukrainian immigrants in Australia. However, the attitude to books often depends on the time of migration and the number of years spent in Australia. Factors that should be taken into consideration include historical contexts and technological progress. For recent immigrants, books are something that is easy to obtain. Some even argue that books, as heavy objects, should not be carried to a new country. On forums you can find sarcastic remarks following other participants' advice to take Russian or Ukrainian books to Australia:

25. **Sue:** Yeah, and also take your favourite dumbbells and weights [smiley face] ... What to take with you to Australia? Books? Paper? All of these can be bought in Australia.

26. **Robby:** Books can be downloaded from the Internet or, if you really want, you can buy them online.

However, for immigrants of the 1980s and the beginning of the 1990s books had not only ethnic and personal but also material (and status) meanings. Some immigrants of that period even mentioned that books were the main items brought to Australia:

27. **Nadezhda:** We carried suitcases with books and nothing else.

There have been cases of immigrants leaving for Australia donating their unique book collections to museums. For example, the Odesa historian Miron Fisher, when immigrating to Australia, donated his lifetime collection of rare editions of works by Pushkin, Gogol, Chekhov, Bunin and Kuprin, including a rare copy of the 1824 edition of Pushkin's *Polar Star*, as well as many other books to the Odesa Pushkin Museum (Perstniova 1997). At the end of the 1990s Miron Fisher organized a club for book lovers in Sydney for Russian-speaking immigrants.

However, not only rare or unique books were considered as highly valuable possessions. During Soviet times even ordinary books were prized since it was difficult to buy them: 'books were bragged about, they were put on display next to crystal glasses and the Madonna china sets' (Dontsova 2007). This ironic statement by a popular author of pulp literature is true about many a Soviet household. Today the situation has changed. For example, some immigrants of the 1980s and the 1990s complain that books are poorly preserved in the humid climate and so some of them have had to be thrown away. An important role is also played by the language shift. It starts with dictionaries, textbooks and children's books, but gradually immigrants add to their book collections professional textbooks, books related to their hobbies and even fiction in the majority language. When books have only ethnic and no personal or material meanings, their number in immigrants' homes tends to dwindle.

Other possessions that have ethnic meanings are images of snowy winter scenes or birch trees. What is typical of these people, who have changed their environment and, now far from the familiar European landscapes, have immersed themselves in Australian ones, is that they miss snow and familiar trees. For example, on the Internet, among posts written by immigrants from Russia, one can often see nostalgia for familiar nature:

28. **Sergei:** I was going from Brisbane to Sydney along the New England Highway. About 600 kilometres before Sydney, I stopped to refuel in the town of Glen Innes. There was a school next to the petrol station, and in the courtyard in front of the school there were birch trees! For the first time in seven years, I saw birch trees in Australia . . . I stroked their rough trunks, touched their small smooth leaves and felt a lump roll

up to my throat. Well, what was so special about these white trunks that I'd seen thousands of times before but which had never before really drawn my attention? And here you go! A sentimental old man! And the rest of the way to Sydney I was in a good mood.

29. **Nata:** These towns [Wentworth Falls, Bilpin and Berrima – *M.K.*] are united by the European spirit: many of them have trees that are familiar to us – birch trees, maples and oaks. Coming here in the autumn is a joy to my eyes, yearning for the homeland.

In many homes of immigrants from Russia and Ukraine you can find paintings of winter landscapes. These can be pictures of fields covered with snow, a winter forest, or winter city streets with the gilded domes of churches in the distance. My mother, who was an artist, used to paint her landscapes somewhere near a creek in Sydney and then transform them into images of the Russian winter by adding white colour for snow (Figure 5.7) or by turning eucalyptus into birch trees (Figure 5.8).

Figure 5.7 A landscape.

Figure 5.8 A landscape.

White birch trees are a recognised symbol of Russia, so images of these trees in the houses of immigrants have not only personal but also ethnic meanings. 'People's spirit and mentality are expressed in the landscape because they always have sufficiently rich symbolic "equipment", in other words, social consciousness binds its own national (or ethnic, or religious) self-identity with certain symbols, such as birch trees, vast expanses, crosses and churches in Russia' (Diomin and Konovalova 2013: 146).

CONCLUSION

This study focused on the meanings and functions of the possessions of immigrants who moved to Australia from Russia and Ukraine and from the corresponding republics of the Soviet Union from 1987 to 2019. The following categories of possession symbolism were examined: possessions that have (1) material, (2) personal and sentimental, and (3) ethnic meanings. Migration is linked to cultural, economic and personal changes and therefore in many cases involves the revaluation of possessions and their functions. The responses of my informants reveal that possessions often change their meanings: they can lose their material or personal significance and change their meanings from material to sentimental or ethnic. During periods of adaptation to a new life familiar items become very significant. They help migrants maintain their identity and provide comfort in unfamiliar surroundings.

People everywhere cherish memories of their youth. Different artefacts that stir memories of events and people of the past may acquire special value for migrants. In a society where consumer goods were difficult to obtain, a piece of clothing, a pair of shoes, a gadget or an electric appliance could become an object of a dream. Some people buy these things years later when they no longer need them, just because they can afford them and obtain them without any obstacles.

The wish to combine old dreams and new opportunities may result in an excessive accumulation of things that still have a symbolic significance for some time. Changing storage conditions, such as the dimensions of a house, alters people's perceptions of property. Age-related attitudes towards maintaining continuity or starting from scratch have an impact on 'warehousing'.

In the initial stages of post-migration life newcomers may be critical of the layout and interior decoration of the houses in their new homeland. They are either viewed as too ascetic or too posh. Moreover, newcomers often fail to take into account that different climates impose different standards on making dwellings sustainable and economical. Yet, with time they get used to the local styles and gradually introduce their own elements into their houses. With some of the artefacts still preserved in their homes to bring comfort and foster memories, Russian immigrants' homes in the diaspora can often look rather eclectic.

BLOGS AND FORUMS (ONLINE SOURCES)

1. Chto ne nado vezti v Avstraliiu, at <www.ua-au.net/что-не-надо-везти-в-австралию>
2. Pereezd iz Pitera v Brisben, at https://mystoryaustralia.com/2011/06/12/moving-from-petersburg-to-brisbane/.
3. Chto pochiom, at <https://eduau.com.au/australia/going-on-a-journey/>
4. Chto vezti s soboi v Avstraliiu, at <www.ua-au.net/что-везти-с-собой-в-австралию>
5. Avstraliia, at <https://turpogoda.ru/about.php?country=avstraliya>
6. Chetyre goda v Sidnee, at <www.strana-naoborot.com/1au/4years/Sydney.htm>
7. Avstraliiskie magaziny odezhdy, at https://katrin-from-aus.livejournal.com/4407.html?ysclid=ld7zfanfeq29452177.
8. Chto vziat' s soboj v Avstraliiu, at <www.hotcourses.ru/study-in-australia/essentials/packing?

9. Avstraliiskaia zima. Mify i real'nost', at <https://myaustralia365.com/2015/07/16 австралийская-зима-мифы-и-реальность>
10. Ia zhivu v Avstralii 5 let i khochu rasskazat' o liubopytnykh veshchakh, s kotorymi stalkivaius' zdes' kazhdyi den', at <www.adme.ru/svoboda-puteshestviya/ya-zhivu-v-avstralii-5-let-i-hochu-rasskazat-vsyu-pravdu-ob-etoj-udivitelnoj-strane-1892215/>
11. Avstraliia: +20°C v iiune, liudi nadevaiut shuby i mekhovye, at <https://blogs.elenasmodels.com/australia-temperature-june/>
12. Chto veziom s soboi v Avstraliiu iz Rossii?, at <www.gday.ru/forum/>
13. Chto s soboi vziat' v Avstraliiu?, at <www.turizm.ru/australia/articles/chto_s_so boj_vzyat_v_avstraliyu/>
14. Dmukhovskii, M. (2013), Gde nashe ne propadalo. Kak zhivut russkie v Avstralii?, at <https://sobesednik.ru/obshchestvo/20130209-gde-nashe-ne-propadalo-kak-zhivut-russkie-v-avstralii>
15. Immigrantskie istorii: Ekaterinburg – Kanberra, at https://www.canberranovosti.com/2016/12/22/22573.
16. Kakie veshchi i lekarstva vziat' s soboi v Avstraliiu, at <www.votpusk.ru/story/article.asp?ID=9144?>
17. Miroshnik, D. (2001), 'Avstraliia. Shtrikhi k portretu', at http://lib.ru/EMIGRATION/australia2.txt.
18. Sochinenie na temu 'Kak ia provela vykhodnye', at https://www.instagram.com/p/Bj92fXagxZ2.

REFERENCES

Abu-Ghazaleh, F. (2011), *Ethnic Identity of Palestinian Immigrants in the United States: The Role of Material Cultural Artifacts*, El Paso: LFB Scholarly Publishing LLC.

Ahmed, S., C. Castada, A.-M. Fortier and M. Sheller (eds) (2003), *Uprootings/Regroundings: Questions of Home and Migration*, London: Routledge.

Belk, R. (1991), 'Possessions and the sense of past', in R. Belk (ed.), *Highways and Buyways: Naturalistic Research from the Consumer Behavior Odyssey*, Provo, UT: Association for Consumer Research, pp. 114–30.

Belk, R. (1992), 'Moving possessions: an analysis based on personal documents from the 1847–1869 mormon migration', *Journal of Consumer Research*, 19:3, 339–61.

Boschetti, M. (1986), 'Emotional attachment to homes past and present,' in D. G. Saile (ed.), *Architecture in Cultural Change: Essays in Built Form and Culture Research*, Lawrence, KS: School of Architecture and Urban Design, pp. 31–44.

Boym, S. (2002), *The Future of Nostalgia*, New York: Basic Books.

Csikszentmihalyi, M. and E. Rochberg-Halton (1981), *The Meaning of Things: Domestic Symbols and the Self*, London: Cambridge University Press.

De Leon, J. P. and J. H. Cohen (2005), 'Object and walking probes in ethnographic interviewing', *Field Methods*, 17:2, 200–4.

Diomin, G. and Iu. Konovalova (2013), 'Individual and social expression in painting', *Tyumen State University Herald*, 10, 145–50.

Dontsova, D. (2007), 'Prividenie v krossovkakh', available at: <www.youbooks.com/book/D-Donczova/Privedenie-V-Krossovkah> (last accessed 14 November 2022).

Fialkova, L. and M. Yelenevskaya (2007), *Ex-Soviets in Israel: From Personal Narratives to a Collective Portrait*, Detroit: Wayne State University Press.

Gentshke, V., I. Sabennikova and A. Lovtsov (2014), 'The archival Rossica in Australia', *Herald of an Archivist*, 1, available at <www.vestarchive.ru/2013-1/2591-arhivnaia-rossika-v-avstralii.pdf> (last accessed 14 November 2022).

Grinberg, L. and R. Grinberg (1984), 'A psychoanalytic study of migration: its normal and pathological aspects', *Journal of the American Psychoanalytic Association*, 32:1, 13–39.

Hage, G. (1997), 'At home in the entrails of the west: multiculturalism, ethnic food and migrant home-buildingm', in H. Grace, G. Hage, L. Johnson, J. Langsworth and M. Symonds (eds), *Home/World: Space Community and Marginality in Sydney's West*, Pluto Press: Annandale, pp. 99–153.

Halpern, H. (1968), 'Transition phenomena: constructive or pathological?', *Voices*, 4, 44–60.

Howell, S. (1983), 'The meaning of place in old age', in G. D. Rowles and R. J. Ohta (eds), *Aging and Milieu: Environmental Perspectives on Growing Old*, New York: Academic Press, pp. 97–107.

Kahne, M. (1967), 'On the persistence of transitional phenomena into adult life', *International Journal of Psychoanalysis*, 48, 247–58.

Kanevskaya, G. (2008), *History of Russian Immigration in Australia (the End of the 19th Century – the Second Half of the 80s of the 20th Century)*, St Petersburg: SPbGU.

Kemppainen, L., T. Kemppainen, N. Skogberg, H. Kuusio and P. Koponen (2018), 'Immigrants' use of health care in their country of origin: the role of social integration, discrimination and the parallel use of health care systems', *Scandinavian Journal of Caring Sciences*, 32:2, 698–706.

Krippendorff, K. (2010), 'Content analysis', in N. J. Salkind (ed.), *Encyclopedia of Research Design*, Thousand Oaks, CA: Sage, pp. 234–8.

Mehta, R. and R. Belk (1991), 'Artifacts, identity, and transition: favorite possessions of Indians and Indian immigrants to the United States', *Journal of Consumer Research*, 17, 398–411.

Nemy, E. (1986), 'Security blankets never really vanish', *New York Times Magazine* (16 February), 73.

Pastalan, L. (1983), 'Environmental displacement: a literature reflecting old-person-environment transactions', in G. D. Rowles and R. J. Ohta (eds), *Aging and Milieu: Environmental Perspectives on Growing Old*, New York: Academic Press, pp. 189–203.

Pechurina, A. (2011), 'Russian dolls, icons, and Pushkin: practicing cultural identity through material possessions in immigration', *Laboratorium*, 3:3, 97–117.

Perstniova, N. (1997), 'Vsemu svoio vremia, i vremia vsiakoi veshchi pod nebom', *Zerkalo nedeli*, 33, available at https://zn.ua/ART/vsemu_svoe_vremya,_i_vremya_vsyakoy_veschi_pod_nebom.html> (last accessed 14 November 2022).

Pollock, G. H. and M. D. Madison (1989), *The Mourning-Liberation Process*, 1, Madison, WI: International Universities Press.

Rivlin, L. (1982), 'Group membership and place meanings in an urban neighborhood', *Journal of Social Issues*, 38:3, 75–93.

Protasova, E. and K. Reznik (2019), 'Russkie doma v Finliandii: predmety i diskursy', *Ural'skii filologicheskii vestnik, Iazyk. Sistema. Lichnost': Lingvistika kreativa*. 2:28, 122–33.

Ryan, N. (2005), *Rossija – Kharbin – Avstraliia: sokhranenie i utrata iazyka na primere russkoi diaspory, prozhivshei XX vek vne Rossii*, Moscow: Russkii put'.

Ryazantsev, S. V. (2013), 'Migration from Russia to Australia and formation of a Russian community', *ANU Centre for European Studies Briefing Paper Series*, 4:5.

Schultz, W. T. (ed.) (2005), *Handbook of Psychobiography*, Oxford: Oxford University Press.

Sherman, E. and E. Newman (1977), 'The meaning of cherished personal possessions for the elderly', *International Journal of Aging and Human Development*, 8:2, 181–92.

Suleimanova, O. (2015), 'Veshch' kak sredstvo adaptatsii na novom meste zhitel'stva (na primere pereselentsev Kol'skogo Severa poslednei treti XX – nachala XXI vv.) *Perspektivy nauki*, 6, 43–7.

Swidler, A. (1986), 'Culture in action: symbols and strategies', *American Sociological Review*, 51:2, 273–86.

Ters, K. (2015), 'Many routes of those who made a home Down Under', *Russia Beyond*, 17 March, available at www.rbth.com/arts/2015/03/17/many_routes_of_those_who_made_a_home_down_under_44537.html (last accessed 14 November 2022).

Usuyama, T. (2015), 'The assimilation process of Russian immigrants and preservation of the Russian language and culture in Australia', *Russian Journal of Communication*, 7:2, 229–35.

CHAPTER 6

The Hollywood *Kazwup*: Historic Russian Restaurants in Los Angeles, 1918–1989

Sasha Razor

The Romanoffs (2018), a recent online television series, was met harshly by critics, with the self-declared Duchess Marie of Russia calling it 'fatally indulgent' (Marshall 2018), not unlike the tsars themselves. Yet, the series has brought the continuity of Hollywood's fascination with Russian royalty to the fore. The origins of this discourse go back to the symbiotic relationship between Hollywood and its colony of White émigrés, which, in the 1930s, counted about 1,500 members (Day 1934: 1). Its economic commodification can be best illustrated by a 1932 exhibition of Russian decorative art objects belonging to the Romanovs, chosen from the collection of Dr Armand Hammer at Bullocks, a luxury department store on Wilshire Boulevard. Russian actor Ivan Lebedeff and American pianist and actress Norma Boleslavsky (Drury) posed for the *Los Angeles Times* holding an empty royal champagne bucket, a testimony to the refugees' social drama, albeit with a price tag attached.

In his review of the exhibition, Arthur Millier expressed his disapproval of the tsarist regime while simultaneously examining the meaning of this spectacle within the context of multicultural Los Angeles: 'So don't be astonished if, in the near future, when you dine in Hollywood, some blond lady of the screen says casually: "Oh, yes – these belonged to my great aunt, the late Czarina. The double eagle was our family crest, doncherknow"' (Millier B13).

Back in 1932, Millier's class-conscious example was certainly plausible because Los Angeles restaurant goers had long been familiar with those double-headed avians, among other heraldic paraphernalia, of Hollywood's Russian colony. While many cities across the world, including Berlin, Paris, Shanghai and New York, also hosted large populations of Russian émigrés with their own restaurants, it was the proximity of the

Figure 6.1 Ivan Lebedeff and Norma Boleslavsky with an artefact from the collection of Dr Armand Hammer, on exhibition at Bullocks Wilshire, Los Angeles, 1932.

Hollywood film industry that contributed to the uniqueness of the local Los Angeles nightlife. The exilic identity struggles that these restaurants endured mimicked the way in which Russia itself was captured on screen, described by Olga Matich as a 'slippery relation between invented and authentic Russianness, between simulacra and their originals' (Matich 2005: 209).

This chapter is dedicated to the history of Los Angeles's restaurants of the first wave of Russian immigrants, also known as the White emigration, and the complexities of its identity as gleaned from these establishments' interior decorations, menus and biographies of their owners. Building a home away from home – both metaphorically and metonymically – is also a way to create a space where an immigrant can socialise with his or her compatriots, exchange information and satisfy their cultural needs. Restaurants fulfil this socio-communicative function. They are at once culture hubs open to the public as well as private businesses, where the owner's personality, their taste and preferences impact how the place represents the entire community and shape the visitors' perception of an ethnic enclave in question. The span of this study begins in the 1920s and continues until the 1980s, when the few remaining eateries owned by the first-wave migrants and their children went out of business. Its primary sources include archival photographs, newspaper articles and commercial advertisements. These semi-public and semi-private spaces became contact zones between the host community and exiles of various creeds, from former White Army officers to Jews who had fled the pogroms. Informed by nostalgia for a country that no longer existed, this unfolding émigré identity was performed cabaret-style on stage, building communities of spectators, while the dream factory next door toiled at manufacturing Russian reveries on screen.

A historic reconstruction of this kind is difficult because many of the restaurants in question went out of business too quickly to be documented. For example, little is known about De Blumenthal-Russian Tea House, which opened in Pasadena, other than that it was part of the Slavic Handicraft Center (35 North Euclid Avenue) that is first mentioned in 1918 in *Thurston's Pasadena City Directory* (including Altadena and Lamanda Park). Unlike the flamboyant Russian tearoom interiors of the period, described in Jan Whitaker's history of tearooms in the United States (Whiteker 2002: 153), the decor of this tearoom was rather simple and featured modest wicker furniture, folksy clay jugs above the window, a samovar and paintings of Orthodox religious scenes.

Figure 6.2 De Bluhmental-Russian Tea House. Slavic Handicraft Center, 135 North Euclid Avenue, Pasadena, 1920.

The restaurants that opened in the following years enjoyed multiple connections to Hollywood's industries, be it by virtue of location and clientele (the Double-Headed Eagle, Romanoff's and Bublichki), the personality of the owners who worked in cinema themselves (Michael Vavich, Theodore Lodijensky, Alexander Drankoff and Michael Romanoff), the restaurant's names referencing specific productions (Katinka and the Volga Boat Cafe), or the inspired decor of Mischa's and Violet's.

In the late 1920s the lifespan of Los Angeles's ethnic restaurants was so short that, in a parody of the restaurant business, *Los Angeles Times* journalist Weare Holbrook describes the opening of a Russian restaurant in a following way:

> Then the restaurant underwent another transformation and came out Russian. 'Kazwup,' it was called – 'Kazwup' meaning 'the little-white-birch-tree-beside-the-rabid-whirlpool-knocktwice-and-ask-for-Sweeny' – and it was enlivened by a balalaika orchestra and entertainers in Russian blouses. Some of the entertainers sang 'The Volga Boat Song', and 'Roaminoff in the Gloaminoff', while others just spun around on their heels and shouted 'Hi!'. The Russian regime ended a week later when wreckers began to demolish the building. (Holbrook 1929)

The aesthetics of emotional excess is inscribed in the made-up name, Kazwup, which combines phonetic allusions to *kazak* (the Russian word for Cossack) and *katsap* (a Ukrainian derogatory term for a Russian person) with the 'up' morpheme, which denotes a vertical, ascending movement (as in 'Bottoms up!'), produces a simulacrum born at the intersection of nostalgia, exemplified by 'The Song of the Volga Boatmen', and a parodic title of a popular entertainment song.[1]

But what exactly is this *Kazwup* spirit if not a figment of the journalistic imagination, and how did it come about? The very first Russian restaurants to appear in Hollywood functioned as community clubs. The Russian-American Art Club (5525 Harold Way) is mentioned in city directories from 1929 to 1934. Its president, Michael Vavich, was a well-known Russian singer, impresario, Hollywood actor and active member of the Orthodox Church community. In his dissertation titled *The Russian Colony in Hollywood: A Study of Culture Conflict* (1930), American sociologist George Martin Day describes this club as a two-storey culture centre, with a restaurant and stage on the first floor and a lounge and art room on the second:

> To add to the artistic delight of the club, the walls have been exquisitely decorated with mural paintings representing legendary

things familiar to and beloved by every native Russian, and this work was marvelously executed by artists of rare talent. The guest steppes off Western Avenue and finds himself in the twinkling of an eye in the heart of old Russia [. . .] The upstairs room of the club is well fitted out with a lounge and with an art room where the paintings of a celebrated Russian painter who recently died are on exhibit. (Day 1934: 107)

The stage was rather spacious and designed to accommodate twenty-five to thirty performers at a time. Their repertoires consisted of folk songs as well as military, dramatic and operatic numbers. Day describes the audience as one-third Russian, one-third American and one-third Jewish. The programme created a special atmosphere that matched the interior to amplify a feeling of Old Russia:

[The] Balalaika Quarter were entertaining the diners with music until nine o'clock, when the regular program was scheduled to begin. These players dressed in their bright colored Russian shirts (rubashkas) and the doorman attired in Cossack uniform, together with the candle lighting and the rich mural decoration, gave a very picturesque atmosphere to this strictly Russian restaurant-club. (Day 1934: 108)

The Hollywood Russian Club/Russian Artcrafters Club (5311 Hollywood Boulevard) was closer to the idea of an art centre. Located in a deserted building, which was believed to be haunted, it housed a Russian and English library and a reading room. It opened its doors only twice a week, on Thursday and Saturday nights, for performances and some refreshments following (Day 1934: 122). The club was active for one year and was registered in the 1930 *Los Angeles City Directory*. Today, Silom Thai supermarket occupies the club's former address, located in Thailand Plaza and the heart of Los Angeles's Thai community. The Russian-American Art Club and the Hollywood Russian Club both functioned as organising centres for the community in an effort to embody a spirit of Russianness their members sought in exile. By the 1930s, after a decade of major Hollywood productions about Russia,[2] outsiders began to perceive these authentic community spaces through the prism of cinema.

If there were a precise scale to measure the amount of *razvesistaia kliukva*, a parody of foreign misconceptions of Russia,[3] that Los Angeles Russian eateries served, the next three restaurants – the Russian Eagle Cafe, the Volga Boat Cafe and Katinka – would raise the imaginary *Kazwupness* index – the main reason being that they worked to attract a wider audience, including key Hollywood players, acting as the cultural envoys of a country which no longer existed, except for when it came alive on screen. The most prominent restaurant was the Russian Eagle Café or Double-Headed Eagle, described by Day as 'more refined and elegant' than the Russian-American Art Club.

> Acquaintance with the personnel of the club management and of the performing artists makes clear how prominent is the motion picture industry in the life of the club. Practically every Russian affiliated with it depends upon the movies for a living, and the club in return depends largely upon the patronage of the motion picture people. Hence the movies people are bound to influence to a large degree the type of performance presented on the club stage. Quite naturally attitudes and values centering about the motion pictures have become dominant once at the club.[4]

Theodore Lodijensky[5] (1896–1947) (Theodore Lodi) was a Russian general[6] who came to Los Angeles from New York in the mid-1920s where he had operated the millinery store and original Russian Eagle Cafe, which has been celebrated by Russian refugees. When film director Dmitry Buchowetzki, who stopped by the café, recognised the proprietor as his former commanding officer, Lodijensky found himself moving to Hollywood shortly after to aid Buchowetzki in making *The Midnight Sun* (1926), a spectacular romance set in Tsarist Russia.

In Hollywood, Lodijensky opened another Russian Eagle restaurant at 1631 North Vine Street that was frequented by key figures from the movie industry. The restaurant burned down in 1928 as a result of an explosion caused by an arson attempt (Branch 1925). Lodijensky nearly died from his wounds, but he made a full recovery and would go on to receive charity money to reopen another restaurant. *Novoie russkoie slovo* wrote about this venture:

> Lodijensky opened his second restaurant with 'donation' money. Charlie Chaplin cut him a check for a thousand dollars, and Marion Davis followed with $6500. He has spent it all, the restaurant is now closed, and Lodijensky left Hollywood for New York.[7]

Prior to his move back to New York, Lodijensky reopened Golden Eagle in 1931, this time in the Hollywood Plaza Hotel (1633–1637 North Vine Street), which hosted a garden grill section called the Russian Eagle Garden Cafe. In 1935 Lodijensky unveiled another restaurant, this time the Russian Eagle Dinner Club, at 8428 Sunset Boulevard.[8] This loca-

Figure 6.3 Poster for *The Midnight Sun* (1926).

tion remained open through the late 1930s, although newspaper obituaries state that Lodijensky returned to New York in 1935.⁹ In 1937 Russian Eagle Garden Cafe at the Hollywood Plaza Hotel changed ownership and became the 'It Cafe' owned by Clara Bow, the original 'It' girl.

The Volga Boat Cafe, geographically removed from the Hollywood's Russian colony, was designed to attract an even wider, touristic audience. Opened on Christmas 1929, it exemplifies yet another facet of the connection between the movie and restaurant business. The restaurant's owner, Alexander Drankov (1886–1949), made a name for himself as a pioneer of the Russian motion-picture industry. His film studio, Drankoff and Co., produced both documentary chronicles and feature films, including, among others, the very first Russian feature film, *Stenka Razin, Life of Brigands from the Lower Reaches* (1908), *The Three Hundred Years of the Romanoffs Tsardom* (1913) and the six episodes of *Sonia Golden Hand* (1914–16).

After his immigration to Hollywood and a failed attempt to produce a feature about the love affair between the late Tsar Nicholas II and Mathilde Kschessinska, Drankov bought the Ship Cafe, a boat permanently docked by Abbot Kinney Pier in Venice Beach.

This boat, already famous for being a site of Hollywood parties, reopened as a Russian restaurant, commemorating the wild revels of Stenka Razin on the Volga River of Drankov's pre-revolutionary past, and capitalising on the success of Cecil B. DeMille's 1926 blockbuster, *Volga*

Figure 6.4 Poster for *Stenka Razin, Life of Brigands from the Lower Reaches* (1908).

Figure 6.5 Postcard image of the Ship Cafe, Venice, California (c. 1920s).

Boatman, written by Konrad Bercovici. The *Los Angeles Times* article 'News of the Cafes' provides a detailed account of the opening:

> A capacity crowd attended the grand opening last Saturday evening of the Volga Boat, formerly the famous Ship Cafe, Venice Pier, remodeled and redecorated in typical Russian style. Dancing to Boris Kamarenko's Russian Balalaika Orchestra was enjoyed by the guests until the break of dawn. A diversified program of entertainment, which consisted mainly of Russian, Egyptian, and Hawaiian dance novelties and song numbers by well-known entertainers, was thoroughly enjoyed by everyone. George Lloyd acted as master of ceremonies and Rue Shepard as hostess. A noted chef prepared an excellent dinner of Russian and French cuisine and, according to management, he has been permanently retained to supervise the culinary department.[10]

The café existed for only one year; in August 1930, the US Attorney General recommended padlocking its doors for its frequent violations of the National Prohibition Act. Afterwards, the Volga Boat Cafe became the Ship Cafe once again until its final closure, along with the pier, in 1946.[11] Perhaps the closest place of comparison, in its commemoration of Russian imaginary geography, was the Garden of Allah Hotel on 8152 Sunset Boulevard, which operated from 1927 to 1959 and belonged to Alla Nazimova, a Russian-Jewish-American actress of the silent cinema who had built for herself the largest private swimming pool in town in the shape of the Black Sea.[12]

Another curious example of *Kazwup* is Katinka, a restaurant named after the popular 1915 Russian-themed operetta written by the Czech composer Rudolf Friml and the American librettist Otto Harbach. A photograph taken by the Walt Disney Studio photographer Herman J. Schultheis on 7351 Beverly Boulevard conveys the restaurant's traditional Russian exterior decor: a balalaika and a mural depicting dancers. The restaurant was mentioned by the *Los Angeles Times* in 1939, although little is known about its proprietors. Katinka is an example of how cultural appropriation (an American production about Russia) materialised in the form of a restaurant serving a mixed Russian and American menu.

Are there any limits to the development of *Kazwup*, or can it continually keep evolving? While there are no straightforward answers to this question, the examples that follow offer two distinct trajectories of its evolution. A new vestige in the Russian restaurant business belongs to the owner of the famous Romanoff restaurants in Beverly Hills. American fascination with the Russian aristocracy created fertile ground

Figure 6.6 Katinka Russian Restaurant on Beverly Boulevard (c. 1939).

for one con man of sorts: the famous, internationally known impostor Michael Romanoff (1890–1971; also known as Harry F. Gerguson and as Hershl Geguzin). Geguzin was born into a Lithuanian Jewish family and immigrated to New York at the age of ten. He began his career by passing himself as Prince Michael Aleksandrovich Dmitri Obolenski Romanoff, behaving as 'a latter-day Robin Hood, extracting cash from the wealthy and joyfully sharing the benefits occurring therefrom with his friends' (Niven 1975: 156). Depending on the gullibility of his audience, he 'operated the sliding scale of claims of kinship to the murdered tsar' by employing other suitable names and titles like the tsar's nephew, the tsar's half-brother, the son of Prince Yusupov, and, occasionally, Prince Yusupov himself (Niven 1975: 157). From 1927 to 1931 he engaged in a number of activities in Hollywood including occasional work as a technical advisor for the film studios. Thus began a life of 'a continuous swirl of cocktail parties, movie premiers, and overnight stays in local jails' (Kistler 1971, A1). The fun lasted until he was exposed in 1931 by Theodore Lodijensky, whom some also suspected of embellishing his biography and exaggerating his closeness to the tsar (Matich 2002: 409).

Lodijensky's exposure of Michael Romanoff was likely guided by a desire to snuff out competition in the world of Hollywood technical advisors as well as to avoid being exposed himself. Curiously, Romanoff's subsequent career as a restaurateur closely resembled the trajectory of

Figure 6.7 Prince Michael Romanoff, popular Hollywood pretender to Russian royal blood, Los Angeles, 1934.

Lodijensky himself, thereby morphing him from con man to capitalist. In his account of Romanoff's opening, David Niven states:

> In 1937 Mike struck gold. He obtained an option on the lease of a defunct restaurant on Sunset Strip. His friends became stockholders in the shoestring enterprise, and the place reopened in the blaze of black ties, mink, well-known faces, and publicity. (Niven 1975: 162)

The enterprise was so successful that, from its humble beginnings without an operational kitchen, Romanoff managed to create one of Hollywood's most popular restaurants (ibid.). In 1941 the restaurant moved from Sunset Strip to 326 North Rodeo Drive, and later, in 1951, to 240 South Rodeo Drive in Beverly Hills with a sister location, Romanoff's on the Rocks, in Palm Springs. Both locations finally shut their doors in 1961 on New Year's Eve.

Unlike the Moscow Inn Restaurant (8353 Sunset Boulevard), which existed for one year, from 1929 to 1930, under the ownership of Prince Yuri Dolgoruky, and featured a 'Russian atmosphere', 'folk dances' and a 'native orchestra',[13] Romanoff's left a deep mark on Los Angeles's nightlife scene. Parallel to the personality of its owner, Romanoff's ambience was far removed from any attempt to create either an 'authentic' feel or its simulacra. All of the Romanoff locations featured a monogrammed *R* on the restaurant's exterior, upscale interior fixtures, and an array of French items on the menu with several namesake signature dishes ('Noodles Romanoff', 'Romanoff Style Chocolate Soufflé' and 'Strawberries Romanoff'). The interiors paid homage to modern Californian design, with only a royal monogram to denote the Russia connection. Yet, the story of a Jewish boy from Lithuania who was to become the toast of Hollywood and its celebrated con man encapsulates the spirit of the time. *Hellzapopping* (1941), the Universal Pictures adaptation of the eponymous Broadway musical, provides an inversion of the Romanoff's restaurant story. Russian-born American actor Mischa Auer plays a Russian prince who passes himself off as a fake Russian prince, explaining to his fellow expats: 'Better that everyone should think I am a fake Russian prince. If they knew I was a real Russian prince, the novelty would wear off, and nobody would want me!' Michael Romanoff, on the other hand, 'pretended to be a great comic pretending to be Prince Michael Romanoff of Russia' (Weiss 2001: 32), and it is the Hollywood magic of his persona, not the missing *Kazwup*, that explain his popularity.

Bublichki Russian Cafe, which operated at 8846 Sunset Boulevard from the late 1930s to the early 1950s, is a perfect antipode to Romanoff's. Its last owner, Alexander Danaroff, was born in Kharkiv (now Ukraine), where he graduated from the local university with a law degree, becoming an actor shortly after. Fighting in World War I, Danaroff travelled to Romania, Poland and Germany, where he organised his own theatre company, The Firebird. In September 1923 the company went on tour to South America (Argentine and Brazil) and came to New York afterwards, where the troupe was disbanded. Danaroff's family, wife Maria Vladimirovna (Moussia) and daughter Irene, joined him in New York. In 1928–9 Alexander Danaroff ran the Russian-American Concert Bureau. In 1930–31 he was the organiser of the circle of Russian artists in Los Angeles. After moving to Florida sometime in the 1930s, Danaroff managed the La Fayette Hotel in Miami Beach and opened his own restaurant, the Russian Bear. Danaroff purchased Bublichki Russian Cafe in 1943 from Russian émigré Konstantin Sankarzhevsky.[14] Staying in Hollywood for the last decade of his life, the former was a regular participant in Russian charity concerts and artistic gatherings, where he performed by reading poems by famous Russian poets. Danaroff also acted in two films: *Black Magic* (1949), in the role of Dr Duval, Baron von Minden, and *Everything Can Happen* (1951). He died in 1952 at the age of sixty-four from heart disease, survived by his wife and daughter. Danaroff's grandson Alex Bruce lives in Florida. Irene Rabinowitsh-Abosh, the daughter of accordion player Jack Rabinowitsh, who would also perform at the restaurant, recounts that it was owned by Moussia and Alexander Danaroff, and that their daughter, Irene, used to work there as a hostess.[15] Hollywood actors and celebrities, including Guy Madison, Gail Russell, Marion Davies and Leonid Kinskey, frequented the restaurant.[16]

A postcard print of the restaurant's interior and menu denote a different, hybrid take on Russian identity. A contemporary typescript and logo are combined with ornate murals coloured with the palette and floral motifs reminiscent of Ivan Bibibin's illustrations of Russian fairy tales. The postcard also features two Cossacks guarding the door; these figures, typical of the 1920s émigré cabarets, look anachronistic for the 1940s and clash with the German-style timber frame of the building. A welcome sign in Russian – *Dobro pozhalovat* (Welcome) – provided the sole linguistic marker. The menu featured a wide selection of vodkas and a variety of Russian items, such as *pelmeni* (Russian dumplings), *borshch* (beetroot soup), *bliny* (crêpes) with black and red caviar, and even Caucasian *shashlik* (the Russian word for kebabs). Their signature dish was Cutlet à la Bublichki, featuring Bublichki special black caviar, turkey, chopped eggs and onions. Despite the popular location, the *Los Angeles Times* mentions Bublichki only briefly in connection to the city's social events; there were no detailed reviews or interior descriptions, although

Figure 6.8 Postcard of Bublichki Russian Cafe (c. 1940s).

there is one newspaper that alludes to 'Balalaika orchestras and flaming dagger dances' (Weiss 2001: 31). If the Cold War had any bearing on the restaurant business, it seemed to bypass both Romanoff's, a product of Hollywood's obsession with foreign royalty, and the native Russian ethos of Bublichki, which also drew in the filmmaking crowd.

From the 1960s onwards the Hollywood *Kazwup* elements were adulterated by several competing trends: the political and cultural liberalisation, the widening gap between the exilic community and the metropole, and immigration from the Soviet Union.[17] The diversification of American cuisine beginning in the 1960s, along with the growing Armenian population of Los Angeles, made it possible for the Markarian family to successfully open and operate three Russian–Armenian restaurants from the 1960s to the 1980s: Kavkaz, Mischa's and Violet's. The proprietors of Kavkaz, Yerevand and Mariam Markarian, had fled from China where, in the 1940s, their families had owned restaurants in Harbin and Shanghai. Yerevand Markarian was born in 1920 in China in a family of refugees who fled the Armenian genocide and grew up in the French concessions of Tientsin (Tianjin) and Shanghai, attending Jesuit school and later serving in the French Foreign Legion. After marring Mariam (née Kardashiantz), he became the manager of Kavkaz restaurant in Shanghai owned by his father-in-law, while opening his own restaurant, Renaissance, right across the street (Markarian: 103). Later, all restaurants owned by Yerevand Markarian were named Kavkaz (Markarian: 190–1). When the communists took over Shanghai in 1949, the Markarians were forced to close their businesses down. They managed to immigrate to Brazil where Mariam 'developed into the first-class cook' (Markarian: 160), first cooking outdoors in their first lodging on the outskirts of São Paulo, and later opening a boarding house of her own. The Markarians arrived in Los Angeles in the early 1960s via San Francisco. They opened a new Kavkaz on 1235 North Vine Street, which served 'standard Russian and Armenian fare', including shish-kebab (or *shashlik*), beef Stroganoff, chicken Kiev, stuffed cabbage, *lahmajoun*, Armenian flatbread, and 'the best rack of lamb in the city called sedlo or shepherd's delight', among other dishes (Andrews 1976). Among the well-known people who enjoyed their food were Charles Aznavour, Roman Polanski, Dan Duryea, Simone Signoret, Peter Ustinov and Armand Hammer (Markarian: 218). Not only did Hollywood filmmakers frequented Kavkaz, but Yerevand Markarian himself acted in a film titled *Beau Geste* (1966), in which he had an episodic role as a French legionnaire.

In 1969 the Markarians relocated to Sunset Strip (8795 Sunset Boulevard), which provided an attractive view of the city (Andrews 1976).

Figure 6.9 Commercial advertisements for Kavkaz and Mischa's restaurants in Los Angeles Russian press, from the mid-1960s to the mid-1980s.

While the original Kavkaz restaurant in Shanghai boasted performances by Alexander Vertinsky, Kavkaz on Sunset Strip also featured weekend entertainment, ranging from occasional singing and dancing to violin and piano performances by composer and virtuoso accordionist Nick Ariondo, singer Viquen, violinist Hrach Yacoubian, Roma violinist Rima Rudina, exotic dancer Tamara, as well as a husband-and-wife Roma duo they brought from Brazil (Markarian: 242–4). The absence of any descriptions of its decor suggests that Kavkaz did not feature any ethnic markers that would attract food critics. The Sunset location was sold in 1981 to Los Angeles chef Wolfgang Puck and became home to the first Spago restaurant, now a chain of flagship restaurants serving upscale Californian cuisine.

Unlike Kavkaz, Mischa's Restaurant and Cabaret was remembered for its flamboyant decor, another iteration of *Kazwup* by the second generation of restaurateurs. Owned by Mischa Markarian, the son of Yerevand and Miriam Markarian, it operated on 7561 Sunset Boulevard from 1977 to 1989. It would be the last of Los Angeles's restaurants to be owned by someone from the second wave of immigration from Russia and a meeting place for the immigrants of the third wave. Known for his alternating roles as a chef in the kitchen and a dancer of *gopak* at the cabaret, Mischa served Russian and Armenian dishes, filled glasses with Californian wine, and offered elaborate cultural entertainment. The establishment's supportive staff included his wife, Irina, and his parents (after they sold Kavkaz in 1981). Extensive restaurant reviews from the *Los Angeles Times* archive provide a glimpse into the evolution of the restaurant and how it reflected the identity of its owner.

In 1977 Mischa's opened while still half-finished. It was separated into two parts: the dining room, which aimed to be 'quiet and fairly formal', and the cabaret. 'The Cabaret half of the restaurant is not finished either, but it is workable, with booths and tables, entertainment – both casual and permanent – in progress. I rather like the feeling of no limits – a brick wall disappearing into an invisible ceiling, a mysterious blackness beyond the upright piano.'[18] In the following years, *Los Angeles Times* food critic Lois Dwan returned to Mischa's on several occasions and meticulously described its interior details. After a remodel in 1982, Dwan's review emphasised the excessiveness of the decor:

> Mischa's cabaret (7561 Sunset Blvd., 874-3467) signs outside and murals inside since I was there. Too many signs, and possibly too many murals, but murals are more difficult. The restaurant is meant to represent a solid chunk of old Russia in all its onion-domed grandeur. If it must be exaggerated, if the colors must shout out to convince, so be it. After all it is only paint trying to recreate the heroic legends of Cossacks and fair maidens. The murals are stage settings, giant, stylized Christmas cards set to create a mood. They are extravagant, incomplete, refreshing in contrast to decorator perfection. It is clearly Mischa's restaurant – and we do not need all those glittery signs in front to tell us so. (Dwan 1982)

By 1983 the restaurant had come together and 'achieved a congruity it did not have in its formative years. By lowering the ceiling with draped canopies, the huge Cossack murals take on a proper proportion and their bright colors become quite compatible with the more sober Byzantine room, now become part of the whole. The bar is merry, adding to the party feeling' (Dwan 1983). In 1985 it unveiled a new 'Romanoff room' and commissioned 'Follies à la Russe' – a 'miniature Muscovite musical' directed and costumed by Jean Blanchette, which consisted of a combination of peasant folk appeal and Soviet shticks (Ellis 1985). The 1988 article announced that the owner of Mischa's had made plans to sell the place (Andrews 1988); the sale went through a year later.

Mischa's Restaurant and Cabaret became the subject of literature, film and memoirs. It is also well documented in restaurant videos featuring performances by Alyosha Dimitrievich and Natalia Medvedeva. A short story titled 'Uncle Izya's Anniversary' ['Iubilei diadi Izi'] by Eduard Limonov and *Hotel California* (1992), a novel by Natalia Medvedeva, also mention it. Anatoly Fradis, the actor, director, producer and entrepreneur, published a memoir about the restaurant, and his description reflects the socio-cultural status that Mischa's had garnered among the immigrants of the third wave:

> Mischa's – Russian restaurant on Sunset Blvd. – was our club and a cozy corner of Russia in the middle of Los Angeles. Natasha [Medvedeva] was singing 'The Golden-Domed Moscow', and we were singing along with her: 'Candy and bagels, sleighs graceful as swans. / "Oh, you disobedient horses!" cries the coachman from his seat.' . . . It had an atmosphere of a wild Russian party from the thickest of which one could hear the rumbles of exquisite Russian obscenities. (Fradis 2019)

In 1982 Violet's restaurant (1712 Colorado Boulevard, Eagle Rock) joined the list of ventures of the Markarian family. It belonged to Violet (Manoushak), Mischa's younger sister, who had married Andy (Hambarstum) Pashinian, also a Shanghai-born Russian-Armenian from a restaurant family. The restaurant advertisements ran in the émigré press, particularly in the 1986 issue of *Soglasie*. The *Los Angeles Times* reviewed Violet's only once. The reviewer, Max Jacobson, emphasised Violet's multicultural menu, which reflected the trajectory of her family's history (her speciality dishes were rack of lamb and chicken Kiev, but the menu also included oriental-style beef as a nod to the family's years of exile in China) (Jacobson 1987). On the one hand, Jacobson differentiates the restaurant's atmosphere from the stereotype formed by Russian literary culture:

> I have this romantic vision of Russian Restaurants taken from old movies like 'Doctor Zhivago' and older novels by Dostoevsky. I picture a roadside tavern surrounded by coaches, and inside, noblemen and Gypsy musicians singing, drinking and eating caviar until dawn. Violet is hardly like that . . .

On the other hand, Jacobson uses another marker for describing the interior of Violet's. *Anastasia*, a historical drama produced in 1956, already looked anachronistic in the 1980s:

> Violet is not what you'd call splashy. The restaurant, which attracts an older crowd, is distinctly lacking in chic. The dining room with its dark shadowy ambiance looks like it was borrowed from the set of 'Anastasia'; it is filled with dimmed chandeliers, czarist art, royally crested wallpaper, and reddish-purple tablecloths. There is an illusion of dining by the candlelight that borders on the mystical.

In Violet Pashtinian, we see an example of a heritage restaurateur so far removed from the native tradition that she included Chinese items on the menu, refused to serve vodka, and made her restaurant look like a movie set. It is not known how long the restaurant stayed in business, or even if it did well. Jacobson's description denotes a tension between the representational clichés of Hollywood blockbusters and a second-generation immigrant restaurateur's attempt at fusion, which encapsulates the very spirit of Californian gastronomic culture.

This chapter examined how refugees from the Russian Empire recreated their home away from home by looking at ethnic Russian restaurants in the Greater Los Angeles area. For Russian-American restaurateurs, recreating their lives in exile also went hand in hand with the manufac-

Figure 6.10 Scene from *Anastasia* (1956), directed by Anatole Litvak. Commercial advertisement for Violet's restaurant in *Soglasie* magazine, 1986.

turing of Russia's image on screen. Beginning as community cultural clubs in the 1920s, these restaurants expanded to include the American audience, especially the city's filmmakers who brainstormed their new Russian-themed production while enjoying authentic Russian dishes and tunes from faraway lands.

Gradually, from the late 1930s and into the 1940s, the simulacra of Russian identity competed with the original, and the social popularity of Michael Romanoff and his restaurants inaugurates this shift. While the original prince restaurateur, Yuri Dolgoruky of Moscow Inn, went out of business, this impostor thrived and expanded his affluence on screen for a time. Cinematic blockbusters produced at the height of the Cold War – *Anastasia* in 1956 and *Doctor Zhivago* in 1965 – furnished versatile, rhetorical tropes for restaurant criticism to come. These films were released all over the world, but the identities they cultivated struck a chord in Hollywood where many of the restaurants' clients and reviewers were familiar with these productions first-hand. Simultaneously, the gap between the exilic community and the metropole intensified: the Russian cuisine that they served continued to evolve in exile.

In the years marking the centennial of the Russian Revolution, the forgotten restaurant names of the first wave resurrected in Los Angeles in the shape of their uncanny, morpheme-shifting doubles: Romanov Restaurant and Lounge on 12229 Ventura Boulevard and Kavkaz on 5341 Santa Monica Boulevard. The name of Grigori Rasputin, whose daughter, Maria Rasputina, lived in Los Angeles in the 1960s and 1970s, seems to have a special significance for the city. The old Rasputin Restaurant on Ventura Boulevard has gone out of business, but a brand-new incarnation called Raspoutine Nightclub has opened on Melrose Avenue (long live Rasputin!). While the club's name sports French vowels suggestive of European sophistication, its advertisement relies on the hackneyed cinematic tropes from 1960s Hollywood: 'Raspoutine's formula is straight out of a scene from *Doctor Zhivago*, complete with dark red wallpaper, leather booths, and lots of vodka' (Holmes 2018). The last remnant of Los Angeles's Russian imperial craze is the double-headed eagle adorning Petit Ermitage Hotel on 8822 Cynthia Street; and who knows, it may only take another season of *The Romanoffs* to conjure an actual *Kazwup* restaurant inspired by the history of Hollywood's famous princes and impostors, generals working as extras and extras playing generals on screen. After all, this double-headed relationship between the original and the simulacrum is what informs homemaking in exile for Hollywood's Russians, doncherknow?

NOTES

1. 'Roamin' in the Gloamin" was a popular song written in 1911 by Sir Harry Lauder (1870–1950), an internationally known Scottish singer and comedian.
2. For more information, see Robinson 2007.
3. *Kliukva*, literally a 'cranberry', is a derogatory term for an artistic portrayal – of any kind – that betrays ignorance of the original. 'The expression has been dated by scholars to a play parodying foreign misconceptions of Russia staged in 1910', (Evans-Romain 2007: 301–2).
4. Day 1934: 111–12. The author goes on to make an apologetic disclaimer about Russian Eagle still keeping the community and identity values at its core (ibid.), but these claims are difficult to verify.
5. Although in her article titled 'The White emigration goes Hollywood', Olga Matich spells this name as Lodyzhensky in accordance with the accepted contemporary transliteration norms, the original spelling (Lodijensky or Lodijenski) is preferable for conducting archival research in the United States.
6. Both Matich (2005: 196) and Iangirov (2007: 189) cast their doubt on the general title of Lodijensky.
7. 'Novoie Russkoie slovo', 26 May 1930. Cited by Rashit Iangirov in 'Govoriashchiaia fil'ma ubila aktiora-inostrantsa', in Seans No. 37–8 'Istochniki nevozmozhnogo', available at <http://seance.ru/n/37-38/flashback-depress/yangirov/> (last accessed 14 November 2022).
8. 'Halloween at the Cafés', *Los Angeles Times*, 31 October 1935.
9. Obituary 3, *Los Angeles Times*, 7 March 1947.
10. 'Volga Boat News of the Cafés', *Los Angeles Times*, 25 December 1929.
11. 'Move Started to Lock Cafés,' *Los Angeles Times*, 24 August 1930.
12. Alla Nazimova (née Marem-Ides Leventon) had immigrated to Los Angeles before the Russian Revolution; her hotel, therefore, cannot be included in its own right in the corpus of White immigration restaurants.
13. 'News of the Cafés', *Los Angeles Times*, 5 June 1929.
14. *Novoe russkoe slovo*, 13 May 1943: 3/6.
15. According to Irene Rabinowitsh-Abosh (2020), her father Jack Rabinowicz played piano and accordion at Bublichki along with Sasha Lukas and his ensemble: Sigmund Shutz, accordion player Bill Keller and Jack Rabinowicz. Their repertoire consisted of the romantic songs of the 1920s, 30s and 40s, both Russian and American, which they played on demand. The name of the restaurant itself alludes to a popular Odesa song written in 1926 by Yakov Yadov. Performed by Leonid Utesov, the song entered the popular circulation and became a staple at the émigré cabarets. It was also performed in Yiddish by the popular American klezmer and jazz performers The Barry Sisters.
16. Martin Turnbull, 'Bublichki Russian Café at 8846 Sunset Boulevard', *Martin Turnbull* (blog), 20 December 2013, available at <https://martinturnbull.com/2013/12/20/bublichki-russian-cafe-at-8846-sunset-boulevard/> (last accessed 14 November 2022).
17. The new wave of the immigration, also known as the third wave, started in 1971 and lasted until the collapse of the Soviet Union in 1991.
18. 'Cabaret in Progress', *Los Angeles Times*, 9 October 1977.

REFERENCES

Andrews, C. (1976), 'Dining out on Mother's Day: the busiest Sunday of the year', *Los Angeles Times*, 5 May.
Andrews, C. (1988), 'A tumble for tumbleweed', *Los Angeles Times*, 13 November.
Branch, B. (1925), 'Life of Russian officer weird', *Los Angeles Times*, 2 August.
Day, G. M. (1934), *The Russians in Hollywood: A Study in Culture Conflict*, Los Angeles: University of Southern California Press.
Dwan, L. (1982), 'Revisiting the scene of the find', *Los Angeles Times*, 28 March.
Dwan, L. (1983), 'Restaurants: if music be the love of food . . . In Old New York New York', *Los Angeles Times*, 3 March.
Ellis, K. (1985), 'Stage beat: Muscovite musical opens new room', *Los Angeles Times*, 11 January.
Evans-Romain, K. (2007), 'Kliukva', in Smorodinskaya, T., H. Goscilo and K. Evans-Romain (eds), *Encyclopedia of Contemporary Russian Culture*, London: Routledge, 301–2.
Eyman, S. (1993), *Ernst Lubitsch: Laughter in Paradise*, New York: Simon & Schuster.
Fradis, A. (2019), 'Kak Andron Konchalovskii pokorial Gollivud', Facebook, 14 January, available at: <www.facebook.com/anatoly.fradis/posts/10215149834271731> (last accessed 14 November 2022).
Holbrook, W. (1929), 'Where do we eat?', *Los Angeles Times Sunday Magazine*, 19 May.
Holmes, M. (2018), 'Celeb-friendly Euro club Raspoutine takes over in West Hollywood', *Eater Los Angeles*, 27 July, available at <https://la.eater.com/2018/7/27/17618736/celebrity-club-raspoutine-west-hollywood-villa-lounge> (last accessed 14 November 2022).
Iangirov, R. M. (2007), *'Raby Nemogo': ocherki istoricheskogo byta russkikh kinematografistov za rubezhom, 1920-1930-e gody*, Moscow: Russkoe zarubezh'e.
Jacobson, M. (1987), 'Violet's – Russian cuisine without the vodka', *Los Angeles Times*, 28 August, available at <http://articles.latimes.com/1987-08-28/entertainment/ca-2926_1_russian> (last accessed 14 November 2022).
Kistler, R. (1971), 'Mike Romanoff, restaurateur and self-styled prince, dies', *Los Angeles Times*, 2 September.
Markarian, Y., *Kavkaz. A Biography of Yerevand Markarian*, [Publisher unknown], [year unknown].
Marshall, A. (2018), 'A Romanoff is not too happy with *The Romanoffs*', *The New York Times*, 19 October.
Matich, O. (2002), 'Russkie v Gollivude/Gollivud o Rossii', *Novoe literaturnoe obozrenie*, 54, 403–48.
Matich, O. (2005), 'The White emigration goes Hollywood', *The Russian Review*, 64:2, 187–210.
Niven, D. (1975), *Bring on the Empty Horses*, London: Hamilton.
Rabinowitsh-Abosh, I. (2020), Phone interview with author, 24 July.
Robinson, H. (2007), *Russians in Hollywood, Hollywood's Russians: Biography of an Image*, Boston, MA: Northeastern University Press.
Weiss, M. (2001), *Star Grazing in Hollywood: Reminiscence of a Beverly Hills Restaurateur (Recollections and Recipes)*, San Jose: Writers Club Press.
Whitaker, J. (2002), *Tea at the Blue Lantern Inn: A Social History of the Tea Room Craze in America*, New York: St. Martin's Press.

CHAPTER 7

Language as a Home Tradition: Linguistic Practices of the Russian Community in San Javier, Uruguay*

Gleb Pilipenko

INTRODUCTION

When we talk about Russian immigrants in Uruguay, the city of San Javier, which was founded as a Russian colony in 1913, is the first thing mentioned. Immigrants from the southern provinces of the Russian Empire, followers of the religious movement New Israel, created under the leadership of Vasily Lubkov, settled there. After unsuccessful attempts to establish colonies in Russia, a decision was made to migrate to Uruguay, where between 1,500 and 2,000 migrants arrived in 1913–14 (Antonova 2010: 136; Petrov 2019a: 378).

At the beginning of the twenty-first century, about half of the population of San Javier were descendants of Russian settlers (Petrov 2010: 76). The language situation in the Rio Negro department is unique because another group of Russians live in the vicinity of San Javier; these are the Old Believers who moved there in the mid-1950s from neighbouring Brazil. Russian communities in Uruguay, in addition to San Javier, can be also found in Young, Fray Bentos, Salta, Paysandú, Salto and Montevideo. The latter communities emerged as a result of both a secondary migration from San Javier and a primary migration of Eastern Slavs (Russians, Belarusians and Ukrainians).

Recently, many scholars have published research on the language and culture of the Old Believers of Uruguay and neighbouring countries, specifically their identity and isolation; this has contributed to the preservation of their traditions (see Boiko de Semka 2009; Rovnova 2010, 2011,

---

* The field research carried out in Uruguay in 2018 was supported by the Russian Science Foundation grant No.16-18-02080 (Russian Language as the Basis for Preserving the Identity of the Old Believers of Central and South-Eastern Europe).

2014a and 2014b). However, there are no studies on the language of the descendants of Russian immigrants in San Javier. An exception here are papers about the religious movement New Israel as well as the history of San Javier itself (Dubovik 2009; Martínez 2013; Moseikina 2003; Petrov 2010, 2019a and 2019b; Putiatova 2008; Roslik 2009). Studies of the San Javier Russian community present only fragmentary information about the language competences of the descendants of Russian immigrants. There is evidence that Russian is not spoken by the majority of the first immigrants' descendants, and their language loss is associated with the lack of Russian language teaching at school (Roslik 2009: 66). The speakers' language competences are characterised as 'rudimentary' (Petrov 2010: 66), as only a few are able to speak Russian (ibid.: 77); most of them are over sixty (ibid.: 78). In the scholarly literature we can also find information about the dynamics of language competences. Russian was still actively used in San Javier forty years after migration (Putiatova 2008: 271), but thirty years later there was already a noticeable language shift. The first generation spoke fluent Russian, the second generation spoke a little Russian, and the third (young people) spoke only Spanish (ibid.: 273).

FIELD STUDIES IN URUGUAY: GOALS, MATERIAL AND METHOD

The 2015 and 2018 field research projects that I carried out in Montevideo, San Javier and Guichón were aimed at analysing the language and culture of the Russian community in Uruguay (Pilipenko 2018a). Semi-structured interviews were used, and the topics that were discussed focused on agriculture, traditional culture, migration stories, language biographies, and stories about school, as well as interethnic and intercultural relations. The interviews were conducted in Russian, but, where necessary, if my interviewees did not speak any Russian, in Spanish. Thirty residents of San Javier were interviewed, and the speech corpus collected totalled forty-five hours.

The main work was conducted in San Javier, which is the centre of the Russian community. It is a small town with 1,600 inhabitants (Petrov 2010: 76). San Javier's architecture is no different from that of other Uruguayan cities, the city being made up of houses typical of the area. Similarly, San Javier residents are not distinguished by their clothing, nor by special religious prohibitions, since religion no longer plays a significant role. The residents of San Javier work in agriculture growing wheat, sunflowers and soy; they also breed livestock and are engaged

Figure 7.1 Fields of sunflowers in the vicinity of San Javier.

in dairy farming. Nowadays, Russian is being gradually replaced by Spanish as children do not speak Russian anymore. This is encouraging researchers to record and describe the type of language that still exists in Uruguay. This language is very interesting because it is not influenced by the norms of the Russian literary language. Most interviewees cannot read or write in Russian, with the exception of those who studied in the USSR, or those who are engaged in cultural activities of the New Israel community. Most of them are elderly people. A significant number of the first settlers were peasants, and many were illiterate, so they transmitted the Russian language to their children orally.

A special feature of San Javier is the cultivation of sunflowers, the seeds of which were introduced by the Russians. Sunflower oil was a local product, and fields of sunflowers can still be seen in the vicinity of the city today (see Figure 7.1). Uruguayans also adopted the Russian immigrants' habit of nibbling sunflower seeds, which is an integral characteristic of local residents and often surprises tourists and visitors from Montevideo. Russian names of recipes and dishes are still preserved in everyday family life, even where the Russian language has already been forgotten (e.g., квас / kvas – a fermented honey-based alcoholic beverage – and вареники / vareniki – boiled dumplings with sweet or savoury filling). On the other hand, the Russians adopted the Uruguayans' custom of drinking mate which they dubbed *зеленуха* / *zelenukha* (from *зеленый* / *zelenyy*, 'green'). Thus, a house has always been a place where fragments of the Russian language, traditions and culture have been preserved by immigrants and their descendants.

This chapter discusses the language situation in San Javier and is based on interviews from the perspective of language use and Russian–Spanish bilingualism. Other sources are also included, both those obtained by the author during the field research and those already published in other scholarly works. It is necessary to analyse language use in the home domain and in the public sphere and explore the dynamics of this process; that is, to study how language use has evolved, and how the Russian community's attitude towards the language situation has been shaped. I will examine the elicited narratives not only qualitatively but also structurally (see the discussion on verb adaptations in the section 'Russian *sanjavierino*'). The peculiarities of integrating Spanish words into Russian will also be explored.

THE LINGUISTIC LANDSCAPE

The linguistic landscape of San Javier demonstrates how widely the Russian language is represented in the public sphere. When studying the linguistic landscape, scholars refer to the inscriptions in public spaces as the primary source of information about the language situation in a particular territory (Sikimić and Nomaći 2016: 8). San Javier is known in Uruguay as a tourist destination. Its 'Russian heritage' along with its natural features (its location on the banks of the Uruguay River) is the main attraction for visitors. In San Javier and the surrounding area, the visual presence of the Russian language is quite rare and, where it does appear, is often in the Latin script. These are unofficial inscriptions and advertising signs, for example the names of small hotels and private business enterprises: Валерка Дом / Valerka Dom ('House of Valery / Valerka'); La Matryoshka ('Matryoshka doll'). A well-known Uruguayan transportation company Sabelín is named after Vladimir Zabelin,[1] a native of San Javier (Roslik 2009: 60). Russian-language items are found in the names of cultural and social institutions, for example the Pobieda ('Victory')[2] cinema (see Figure 7.2.) and Hogar de ancianos Valodia[3] ('Valodia nursing home'), a nursing home named in honour of Dr Vladimir Roslik.[4] Note that both 'Valerka' and 'Volodia' are hypochoristic forms and would hardly be used as names of public institutions in the metropolis. The football club, the city children's park Parque infantil Vladimir Roslik, and the association Fundación Dr Vladimir

Figure 7.2 The Pobieda ('Victory') cinema in San Javier.

Roslik[5] also bear the doctor's name. The San Javier Cultural Centre is named after the Russian writer Maxim Gorky.[6] Many of these names and places are more stereotypical, being a more recent representation of Russia, rather than preserved original names and items from the area of migration.

The building of the religious association stands out in the urban landscape. It carries a bilingual sign: Sabraña[7] Culto. Новый Израиль ('New Israel'). A bust of Vasily Lubkov is located next to this building, and the inscription is entirely in Spanish: *Basilio Lubkov / Jefe spiritual de la congregación religiosa / Novay Izrail / Intendente de Río Negro Dr. Omar Lafluf Hebeich / 31 de mayo de 2014* ('Vasily Lubkov, the spiritual leader of the New Israel religious group, Head of the Rio Negro Department, Dr Omar Laflouf Hebeich, 31 May 2014'). The transformation of the name of the religious association is noteworthy; an attempt has been made to transliterate the Russian name New Israel (in the adjective *Novay*, the Cyrillic letter ы corresponds to the Latin letter *a*).[8] On other inscriptions that mention New Israel, we find a translation in Spanish: *Nuevo Israel*.

At the entrance to the city from Colonia Ofir, a banner with greetings in four languages is installed: Russian (in Cyrillic), English, German and Portuguese (see Figure 7.3). The main inscription is in Spanish: *Bienvenidos a San Javier. Welcome! Willkommen! Bem vindo!* The main street of the city is named after the founder of the New Israel movement: Basilio Lubkov. Russian anthroponyms are also found in the names of other streets: Demetrio Gurin, Demetrio Golovchenko.

Figure 7.3 A banner in four languages at the entrance to San Javier.

The museum in San Javier has a bilingual inscription: *Музей белый дом Museo casa blanca 2008* ('Museum White House 2008'). On the Square of the Founders there is a monument to the first settlers, a sculptural composition: father, mother and child. Next to central stone, there is another memorial stone, erected in honour of the thirtieth anniversary of the founding of the colony; it also bears a bilingual inscription: *1913–21 JULIO – 1943 / '30' / ANIVERSARIO FUNDACION / COLONIA RUSA EN URUGUAY / ЮБИЛЕЙ 30ти ЛЕТИЯ / ОСНОВАНИЯ РУССКОЙ / КОЛОНИИ В УРУГВАЕ / Fdor: B.S. LUBKOV* ('The 30th anniversary of the founding of the Russian colony in Uruguay. Founder V. S. Lubkov'). The inscription *San Javier / colonia rusa* ('San Javier / Russian colony') confirms the Russian origin of this settlement and its founders, and can be found on many signs. Another visual symbol of the presence of Russians in San Javier, not so much linguistic but cultural, are six matryoshka dolls in the city centre.

On the basis of the analysed data, I can conclude that Russian is not actively used in the urban linguistic landscape; some Russian inscriptions mainly perform a symbolic function, often for commercial purposes (anthroponyms in hotel names, shops, some formulaic expressions, etc.). Cyrillic inscriptions are very rare, often with a confusion of letters. Russian words in Latin show a variety of phonetic features; two strategies are noticeable here – the transfer of the phonetic form of the Russian word (for example, Valodia, the reflection of the unstressed [o] as [a]), or its spelling in other words, for example Pobieda, when the unstressed [o] is rendered as 'o'. The instability of spelling is often observed in diasporic communities, even where Russian is more widely used.

The inscriptions given in this chapter are only a small part of the linguistic landscape of San Javier, where the Spanish language is absolutely predominant (both on official signs and in private inscriptions, including advertisements). The small number of Russian-language inscriptions and their symbolic rather than utilitarian nature indicate that the Russian language plays a rather insignificant role in the lives of migrants' descendants. Nevertheless, the visual presence of all these items allows us to speak about the ethnic identity of San Javier, which makes it noticeably different from the neighbouring settlements in Uruguay.

THE RUSSIAN LANGUAGE AS A HOME LANGUAGE

The language shift is almost complete in Russian immigrant descendants' families living in San Javier, as Russian is now used only to a very limited extent. Even in families where both spouses are of Russian origin, Spanish is used. The ethnolinguistic vitality of the Russian language is maintained not in San Javier, but beyond its borders on the *chacras* (farms). During the field research, an interview was recorded with two brothers (born in 1939 and 1942) who live on a *chacra* in Colonia Ofir, a few kilometres from San Javier. The brothers were born in a Russian-speaking family, so they learned Spanish when they went to school. They still use Russian in conversations between themselves, although with frequent Spanish insertions. Their Russian – more precisely, the dialect of the Russian language brought in by their parents from Russia[9] – is the language they use at home, but this rarely happens today. Here is an extract from an interview in which the interlocutors talk about their language competence in Russian:[10]

1. **Dem'ian (male, 78 years old):** Када мы то родились ... отец и мама наўчили нас по-русски ... а спрашвали, када мы начали ходить у школу испанскую, как мы буэм разаварывать: 'А они там буйуть у школу буйуть ходить, они там научутся, а русский язык они не буйуть вучить!' Нас уверёд отец научил по-русским. (When we were born ... our father and mother taught us Russian ... and people asked them, when we started at the Spanish school, how will they communicate? They said they would go to school and they would learn Spanish, but they would not learn Russian. Our father taught us Russian first.)

Almost all my interlocutors noted that the language they used at home with their families was Russian. On entering the elementary school, they knew no Spanish. This was all the more important if relatives settled nearby, since neighbours used to communicate in Russian. This is how **Kaleriia** from San Javier describes her language biography:

> 2. **Kaleriia (female, 85 years old):** Када в школу пошла, так пошла в школу, ничего не знала, и прошла. Я маленькяя с мамкой разуваривала по-русски, с братьями тоже.
>
> (When I went to school, I didn't know anything, but I passed. When I was a little girl I spoke to my mother in Russian, with my brothers too.)

The interviewees often admitted that they associated Russian with their grandparents, who took care of them as children, as their parents, having to work hard, did not spend much time at home. The primary language socialisation was in Russian, and the secondary socialisation was in Spanish. Veniamin comments on the use of languages in his childhood in the following way:

> 3. **Veniamin (male, 55 years old:** *No, pero* эта школа испанская *o sea*, я учился говорить по-русски из моёю бабушка, потому что я из дедом и з баба ничего не мох уоворить по-испански!
>
> **Interviewer:** Они не понимали по-испански?
>
> **Veniamin:** Чуть-чуть, а знали *sí*, бабка, она ничего не знала *practicamente* по-испански, деда, а, уоворил, а я научился примерно по-русскы, а потом, када пошёл сколу здесь [научился по-испански].
>
> (**Veniamin:** The school was Spanish. I learned to speak Russian with my grandmother because I could not speak Spanish with my grandfather and grandmother!
>
> **Interviewer:** They did not understand Spanish?
>
> **Veniamin:** A little bit, grandmother, she didn't know any Spanish. Grandfather spoke and I learned Russian, and then when I went to school here, I learned Spanish.)

Another type of a language biography can be found in Sevast'ian's narrative. He also comes from Colonia Ofir. According to him, when he was a child, communication with relatives in the family was only possible in Russian. However, the children acquired Spanish before starting school, because hired help worked on the farm, and they practised speaking to them in Spanish.

> 4. **Sevast'ian (male, 92 years old):** У моего отца было́ у молотьбу ў его-о, пятнадцать рабочих, и ўсе были́ здешние; все ɣуляли со́ мной. И нам не запрещали, шоб мы учились [по-испански] . . . я с бабушкой по-русски ɣоворил, а с рабочими, со всемы по-испански . . . бабушка *no*, мало [говорила по-испански], понимала *pero* мало!
>
> (During threshing, my father had fifteen workers, and all were local; they played with me. And we were not forbidden to learn Spanish . . . I spoke to my grandmother in Russian, and I spoke to the workers, to everyone in Spanish . . . My grandmother did not speak much Spanish, she understood, but not much!)

On the basis of this information, we can conclude that large families were common, and many households were intergenerational, at least in the initial stages after immigration, and this helped maintain the Russian language. In the same extract, there is another important topic, that of the first settlers' competence in Spanish. What was the level of the Spanish language proficiency among the first migrants? Did they learn the language orally or through special education? Unfortunately, it is impossible to answer these questions today. Since the first settlers are no longer alive, we can only draw conclusions through indirect data. Sevast'ian (4) says that his grandmother did not speak Spanish, and the same is found in excerpts from Veniamin's narrative (3) (cf. Martínez 2013: 36). Communication with older relatives could only be in Russian. In the following interview excerpt, Domna describes the language competence of her parents:

> 5. **Domna (female, 92 years old):** Попалси между сорок, по-сорочьи крякай! Мама прыўыкла, по-русськы моɣла, по-испански моɣла разɣаварывать и понимать. Мноɣо понимаў, ну отец никоɣда.
>
> (If you are among the magpies, quack like a magpie! My mother was used to it, she could speak Russian, she could speak Spanish and understand it, she understood a lot, but my father never learned it.)

Domna's mother learned a second language and could use it, while her father did not actively master it. However, this does not mean that the first settlers did not have any contact with the new language. In Mikhail

Futin's diary, we find information which shows that even in the early period, Spanish loanwords penetrated written speech, for example *aduana* ('customs') and *lancha* ('boat') (Dubovik 2009: 52). In addition, Spanish words are found in the correspondence of the 1920s inhabitants of San Javier with their compatriots in the USSR (Petrov 2019b: 137).

LANGUAGES AT SCHOOL

In the interviewees' narratives, the language used at home is different from the language used at school. Most children became familiar with Spanish for the first time when they started school, and this often led to communication difficulties (cf. Pilipenko 2017: 157–68). The first school in San Javier opened in 1914, with more than 150 students who did not speak Spanish, and a teacher who did not understand Russian (Roslik 2009: 57). The schoolchildren's lack of competence in Spanish and the teachers' lack of competence in Russian caused many problems.[9]

Domna tells a story giving an example of specific lexical problems. The story is about a lesson in a Spanish school, where most of the children were from Russian families, and the teachers, Spanish-speaking, were of Uruguayan origin. This extract can also be viewed as a detailed metalinguistic narrative explaining the linguistic competences of Russian children in the 1930s. It is also a metalinguistic anecdote recalled by Domna and transmitted in her family from generation to generation.

> 6. **Domna (female, 92 years old):** Я пошла з моим племянником [в школу], и мы ж босаи, больше ходили чем. И купили тухли такие. И душили, и болели ноуы, потому что прывышные босыи ходить. И он начáл плакать, а я: '*Mateo*! Матьвей! Молчы!' А он плачеть, а учительша уўидала, прышла: '*¿Qué pasa, qué pasa?*' '*¡Ah, señorita, mi apreta la tujla!*' [смех]. '*¿Qué pasa Mateo? ¡Vení, Futina, Futina!*' Футины уже знали хорошо по-испански: 'Ну что?' 'Туфэль душить!' И сказала: '*¡Ah!*' Она ўзяла, учительша, скинула: 'Ны плачь Матео, *¡no llores*! Када будешь выходить, наденес.'
>
> (I went with my nephew to school; we mostly went barefoot. We bought a pair of shoes, but the shoes were too tight and hurt him. We were used to walking barefoot. and he started crying. I said to him, 'Mateo, Matvey, be silent!' And he cries, and the teacher saw him and came up to us. 'What is going on?' 'The shoes [*tujla*] are too tight for me.' [laughter] 'What

is going on, Mateo? Come, Futina!' Futina's family already knew Spanish well. 'What is it?, 'The shoes are tight!' And she said, 'Ah!' She removed his shoes and said, 'Don't cry Mateo, don't cry!' When you leave the classroom, you will put your shoes on!'

The situation the interviewee recalls is from her nephew's childhood, more than eighty years ago. The nephew knew little Spanish. The teacher did not speak Russian, and so, one of the schoolchildren, whose family was fluent in Spanish, had to act as an interpreter. The difficulty was caused by the lexeme *тухля*, a dialect form of the Russian noun *туфля* [shoe] (SRNG 2012: 301). In the Spanish utterance, this word is adopted to the morphology of this language – it is provided with a definite feminine article *la*. This is what causes the comic effect (Domna's laughter after the quoted statement in Spanish), and the story is perceived as a linguistic anecdote of the time.

This excerpt (6) exemplifies differences in the functioning of the languages in the home and outside the family circle. Dual names are often used in diasporas, including the Slavic ones in South America (see Pilipenko 2018b). Domna calls her nephew first by his Spanish name (Mateo), followed immediately by its Russian counterpart (Matvey). The Spanish name is also used by the teacher since she speaks only Spanish to the children. Russian names thus belong to the home communication within the family and the Russian community.

Reconstructing the episode of her childhood, the narrator resorts to code switching[12] to 'perform' the exchange and to reveal how language contacts affect the speech of the people in her environment. All three participants in the conversation speak both Russian and Spanish, the teacher speaks only Spanish. Using the reiteration strategy for transparency of meaning, the narrator alternates Russian and Spanish and is visibly amused by the mix. The recording shows how the narrator ameliorates her performance by 'changing voices', imitating the intonation of the interlocutors, the tearful voice of the suffering nephew and the compassionate tone of the teacher.

The story is told in order to show the absurdity and comicality of using Russian words in a Spanish context, when they are incomprehensible to the addressees. However, we can also draw other conclusions. Thus, the dominant language for most children at that time was Russian while Spanish was mastered only at school, and there were communication difficulties at the initial stages.

THE RUSSIAN LANGUAGE AMONG URUGUAYANS

According to my interlocutors, even local Uruguayans could speak Russian, because they learned it from their neighbours. We also find evidence that the children of Uruguayans, the neighbours of the immigrants, knew Russian in the 1950s (Putiatova 2008: 271). An extract from an interview recorded from a Spanish-speaking resident of San Javier, who does not belong to the Russian community by origin, is interesting from this point of view. Nicolás speaks about his childhood memories, about life on the farm (the interview took place on his farm outside the city), and communication with neighbours. At the beginning of our conversation Nicolás shows me where the Russians lived and lists the names of their farms.

> 7. Nicolás (male, 70 years old): Then there was a Russian living down there, then there were others across the street, no relatives were left. We were friends, neighbours here; sometimes we got together. My father spoke Russian better than it is spoken by a Russian person. He was a child when the Russians came, started working with them, and learned the language. He spoke Russian, so, when Russians came, they wondered how come he spoke the language. It was easy for him to speak. It was amazing! But he understood Russian ... If a Russian came here to his house, he spoke Russian all the time!

Russian was an active language of Nicolás's father, which he learned by communicating with his Russians neighbours. However, Nicolás does not speak Russian. Many farms have changed owners, and if there are still Russians, many do not speak the language anymore.

REASONS FOR LANGUAGE LOSS

At the beginning of their life in Uruguay, members of the community considered interethnic marriage inappropriate and banned it. Now they blame deviation from this principle for the language loss among the young.

> 8. Emel'ian (male, 75 years old): Не дюже нравылось нашим тут что, диўвкы́ женились испанцамы. Это нехорошо, но тада попереме́шались. Наша колония русская, как приехали, толькы русскый, и слова по-испански-то не

говориль. Ну тада началы́ мешаться, мешаться, и уже русский и не найдешь никакой. Есь э-э, не знаю, *como así gente grande ya como yo*, и хочешь поговорить чуток по-русски, не понимають тебé.

(It was not very good for our people that girls married Spaniards. This was not good, but they mixed up. Our colony is Russian, when they arrived, it was only Russian language, they didn't speak a word of Spanish. Well, then they started to mix, and already, you will not come across the Russian language. There are, I don't know, people like me, older, and if you want to talk Russian a little bit, they don't understand you.)

In the families of descendants of the Russian migrants the language is no longer transmitted from parents to children. The underlying reason is the language shift towards Spanish, and the lack of interest among the young generation in learning the language which is not even used within the community.

9. **Emel'ian (male, 75 years old):** Дети, не хочуть оны́ учиться по-русскы. Не знаю почему, *qué sé yo* . . . Это моя дочка, а я и хотел научить по-русскы, она: 'Не хóчу'!

(Children do not want to learn Russian, I do not know why. This is my daughter, and I wanted to teach her Russian, but she said, 'I do not want to.)

Even in such metalinguistic utterances, there are Spanish insertions and code switching.

When asked if there is anyone to talk to in Russian, my interlocutors often complained that they could talk only to their peers. The comments on the Russian language use cited below (10–11) were made by Domna, an interviewee from Montevideo, who had moved to the capital from San Javier. Domna comments on the language use in San Javier (10). Her observations correlate with the statements of other interviewees, as well as with my own observations. The Russian language is mainly maintained by representatives of the older generation. Russians may not even be able to speak Russian, even if their given name and the surname are Russian.

10. **Domna (female, 92 years old):** У Сан-Хавьеры теперь больше на испанский язык, потому шо так помешалися, шо соўсем говóрють руссьске имья, а он соўсем, понимать-понимаеть, а не знаеть говорыть.

(In San Javier the Spanish language is now more common, because communities are mixed; they may say a Russian name, they understand, but they do not know how to speak Russian.)

After the mother of Domna's close friend passed away, there were no more spheres of communication in which it was possible to actively use the Russian language. And even when she could still find conversation partners, she admits that they would mix languages. Domna reflects on the processes of attrition in the speech of her own generation due to a lack of practice.

11. **Domna (female, 92 years old):** А, есть ещё старушки ще кой-яки старушки, шо можуть так как я, заикуваться, потому что знаешь, что очень трудно, коуда уода́ отбирають своё, то одно. А друуое, коуда ты не практикуесь, то очень трудно. Ты думаешь, мине́ лёхко уоворыть? Мне очень трудно, не то, шо я не знаю, а не попадёшь слово, потому что, не с кем уоворыть. Я уоворыла с пять э, ну лет сем тому назад, ешо мама када жила мама, моёй подружки. То пойду, у дурака ууляли, ў эти, у *cartas*, у дурака. И мы пели и разуваривали по-русськи, и мешаное! Одно слово по-русськи, а друуое ни по-русски, ни по-испански.

(Ah, there are still old women who can stutter like me, because you know, it's very difficult when the years take their toll, that's the first thing. And the second thing is, when you don't practice, it's very hard to speak. Do you think it's easy for me to speak? It is very difficult for me, and not because I do not know, but because I cannot remember the words, because there is no one to speak to. I spoke five or seven years ago, when my friend's mother was still alive. I went there then, we played the fool, we played cards. And we sang, and spoke Russian, and mixed together. One word in Russian, and another neither in Russian nor in Spanish.)

It is difficult for Domna and for other interviewees to speak Russian. This is a result of both the lack of practice and their age. Their speech is characterised by numerous repetitions, hesitations, syllable stretching, and difficulties in word selection.

Another reason for the decline of the Russian language mentioned in the interviews is the military dictatorship in Uruguay (1973–85), when left-wing organisations were persecuted and Russians were viewed with suspicion (Martínez 2013; Petrov 2010; Seminkina 2009). One of my interlocutors from a Russian family who does not speak Russian says:

> 12. **Arina (female, 51 years old):** We lost our language because of the dictatorship.

The following dialogue discussing the influence of the military regime on the preservation of the language is a good example:

> 13. **Jorge (male, 76 years old):** И нас тута был проблема, *porque dictadura*, ты знал, када тут был *militar-*, русских истрепали *medio, por eso* русские они потом, стали бояться.
>
> **Dem'ian (male, 78 years old):** И русские русских боялись, а-а как русскый – так коммунист! коммунистоў тута боятся, как поруху!
>
> **Jorge:** *Qué sé yo*, а они не знали, чё это коммунизьма, не знали.
>
> (**Jorge:** And we had a problem here, because of the dictatorship. You know, when there was a military dictatorship here. Russians were frayed a bit, because they were Russians, and Russians were then afraid.
>
> **Dem'ian:** The Russians were afraid of the Russians, if you were Russian, you were a communist! They're as afraid of the communists here as they are of gunpowder!
>
> **Jorge:** And they did not know what communism was, they did not know.)]

During this period many members of the Russian community suffered, and the Maxim Gorky Club was closed (Semikina 2009).

LANGUAGE MAINTENANCE IN NEIGHBOURING COLONIES

The participants in the study often compare the language situation in the Russian community of San Javier with the neighbouring German Mennonite colony of Gartental, where the German language is better preserved because there is a German school. This colony was founded later than San Javier, in the early 1950s. Here is one account of the difference between the Germans and the Russians:

14. **Sevast'ian (male, 92 years old):** Мы с первого дня сошлись как надо, но дружбу сделали, а немцы до сих пор *no-o*, ў йих, там ишшо только йихняя. И здесь, и там, это всё только йихнее, и рабочие *sí*! Испанцы, *pero*, ихнее ўсё, школа для йих. (We became friends from the first day [with the Uruguayans], but the Germans still haven't. They have everything there, and it's just theirs. It's all just theirs, and the workers, and yes, there are Spaniards, but they have their own school.)

The interviewees argued there was no assimilation in the German colony, which apparently is due to religious restrictions. The same religious restrictions contribute to the maintenance of the Russian language in another neighbouring colony where the Old Believers live, in Colonia Ofir.

15. **Emel'ian (male, 75 years old):** Это соўсем иначей русскый ихний, чистый, хорошый русскый!

    (Their language is a completely different language; it is pure, good Russian language.)

16. **Sevast'ian (male, 92 years old):** Здесь эти, шо бородачи, шо приехали эти, те чисто по-русски разуоварють.

    (These bearded men here who came [referring to Old Believers],[12] they speak pure Russian.)

Russians from San Javier report that the Old Believers speak Russian almost without the Spanish insertions and loanwords that are common in their own speech. According to my observations made in the colony of Old Believers near Guichón, the Russian language is actively used by children there, and they still do not learn Spanish before they start school. Old Believers live in small villages where Russian is still the main means of communication.

RUSSIAN *SANJAVIERINO*

The residents of San Javier call local Russian *sanjavierino*. From the following narrative we learn about the communicative failures of the Russian consul, who did not understand the Russian speech of the residents of San Javier because of code mixing. He failed to recognise Spanish loanwords intricately intertwined with the local Russian, although he had a good command of Spanish.

17. **Domna (female, 92 years old):** Кадась тут один, один консул русськый поехал, сказал, шо поеду у Сан Хавьер, поехать, шоб не знали русськаи, что он присутствуить: 'А ну что ж они делають тут русськаи?' И ўот вечером идёть и две женщины под ручки разговарюють между собой, а он прыслухуется: 'Щто ж они ѓоворють?' Так ѓоворять: 'А твоя дочка ище *андаре*?' 'Моя дочка *андарыда-андарыла*, а тэпэрь узяла и бросыла!' А он думаить, русськай консул, что ж это такое *андарыла*, потому шо он по-испански очень прыятно понимал.

(The Russian consul went there once. And he said, 'I will go to San Javier.' The Russians will not know that he will be there. 'Let's see what the Russians are doing here.' And then in the evening he goes, and two women go arm in arm and talk to each other. He listens to them, what are they talking about? Here's what they say: 'Does your daughter still go out with someone?' 'My daughter used to go out [*andaryla*], but now she has left him!' And the Russian consul thinks, what is this *andaryla*, because he understood Spanish very well.)

I heard several versions of this story, but the one given here is the most complete. The Russian–Spanish utterance also varies. Instead of *андарыла*, the verb *новьярыла* is sometimes used. In the given excerpt, the adopted verb *андарыти* from the Spanish *andar con alguien* ('to go out with someone') is registered in the speech of Russians. The comic effect is caused by the fact that the consul does not belong to the Russian community, and for him such use of loanwords sounds weird. These verbs are formed in Russian from a Spanish verb stem (*andar, noviar*), followed by vowels *и/ы*, as well as by the infinitive ending *-ть*. Compare the similar way of adopting Spanish verbs in the Ukrainian language of immigrants in Argentina (Ryzvaniuk 1974: 71–6; Pilipenko 2021: 476).

Below I give some examples of mixed speech, with code switching and adopted loanwords:

18. **Jorge (male, 76 years old):** Потом спивають! и по *кажехонах* пьяные, спивають, *ah sí, ¡ellos son muy de cantar!* нравится йим спивать.

(And they sing, drink, in the streets, they like singing.)

19. **Sevast'ian (male, 92 years old):** И я, *dos mil siete-e*, эту коленку меня сделалы, ¡*no*! ¡*dos mil ocho*! Эту коленку

сделали, и *para fin del dos mil ocho* эту сделали, обе, а у́лаза, тоже меня это, *куба́ны*.

(And in 2007 I had an operation on the knee, no! In 2008 there was an operation on this knee, and at the end of 2008, it was an operation on my eye; the Cubans [Cuban doctors] did the operation.)

20. Sevast'ian (male, 92 years old): А пол с урязи оны подымали и набивали, а потом урязью мазали, урязь с этой, с, *con abono de caballo, eso quedaba precioso, bien quedaba*, подметали, только шо низя было́ мыть его, уподмёл его.

(And the floor was made from dirt, they elevated it, filled it, and then smeared it with dirt, with horse manure, it was perfect, they swept it, but they cannot wash it.)

The lexemes *кажехонах* (18) and *кубаны* (19) are adopted according to the models of the Russian language. In (18) the form is derived from the Spanish word *callejón*, which reflects a phonetic feature characteristic of the Spanish variant spoken in the Río de la Plata region: *yeísmo* (the loss of the traditional palatal lateral approximant phoneme [ʎ] and its merging into the phoneme [j]; in addition, in place of [j] a voiced postalveolar, a sibilant is pronounced (see Narumov 2001: 460)). The analysed lexeme in the source language and in the Russian language is a masculine noun ending in a consonant. In this utterance, it is used in the locative plural after the preposition *по* that is a salient dialect feature of Southern Russian dialects. The word *кубаны* (instead of normative *кубинцы*) – 'Cubans' – is also a masculine noun; in (19) it is used in the nominative plural; the word is derived from the Spanish noun *cubano*. One of the most common practices is the borrowing of numerals (cf. I. A. Baudouin de Courtenay's records of Slovenian dialects in the Tera Valley) (Baudouin de Courtenay 1904: 7)). Participants also use code switching, sometimes reiterating Spanish-language fragments in Russian (21) (see Gumperz 1982: 78). Sometimes, especially in the case of communication difficulties (23), translation is not provided (cf. the adaptation of Italian loanwords in Russian (Perotto 2014: 151)).

RUSSIAN DOCUMENTS AND ITEMS

My interviewees showed me various Russian documents that once belonged to their relatives, the first settlers in San Javier. The papers still preserved in their homes as memories of the past are passports, tickets

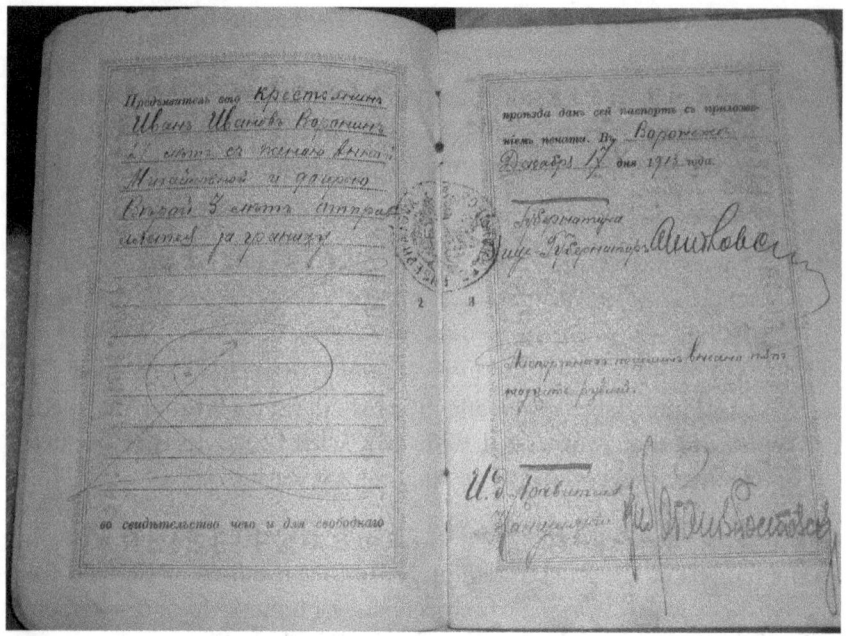

Figure 7.4 Ivan Voronin's passport.

for ships, and advertising brochures of steamship companies, and their routes. Aleksei's archive (male, 75 years old), for example, contains Ivan Voronin's passport, which was kindly lent to the author for scanning (Figure 7.4). This document is valuable as a testimony to the era, as it proves the connection of the Russian community with Russia and also allows us to learn more about the first migrants and their relocation from Russia to Uruguay. The date of the passport issue is the end of 1913, when the first group of immigrants had already settled in Uruguay. The passport was issued in Voronezh for a family of three, Ivan Voronin, his wife and daughter. This documents the South Russian origin of the immigrants and localises their births in the Voronezh region. In addition, here we find important data on the social status of the migrants and their occupations; they were mostly peasants who were illiterate. The departure from the Russian Empire is dated the beginning of 1914 through Libava (Liepāja).

In addition to such documents, some of the interviewees' homes have carefully stored items inherited from their parents and associated with Russian material culture, for example the embroidered towels shown in Figure 7.5. In the house of one interviewee, Pavel (male, 80 years old), these towels frame a large photograph of his parents which hangs on the wall. As objects brought from Russia became shabby or dysfunctional,

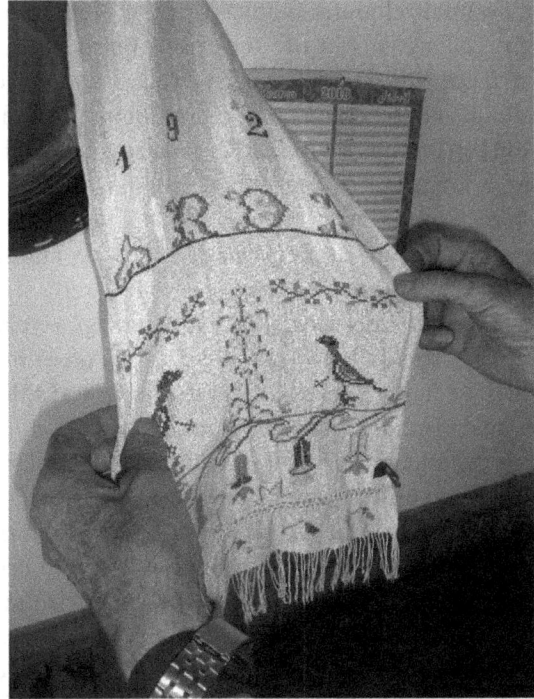

Figure 7.5 Embroidered towel in Pavel's house.

they were thrown out. Like the language, the material culture of the old country has gradually disappeared and only a few pieces have remained as family relics. Such objects are no longer used but have a purely symbolic meaning, serving as a fragile link to the past. The interlocutors are willing to show such things and talk about them, especially to guests from Russia. They are proud that they have preserved them, maintaining a connection with their homeland.

CONCLUSION

To sum up, the Russian language in the Russian community of San Javier is on the cusp of extinction. After migration, Russian was the main language used in the home and with neighbours; it was also mastered by Uruguayans, then later its scope of use was reduced to family, and then there was a decline. Structurally, the Russian language has also undergone changes; numerous loanwords from Spanish are registered, and there are cases of code switching, which is perceived by interlocutors in metalinguistic stories about language mixing. This was facilitated by the loss of the original religious character of the New Israel movement, the involvement of Russians in the social and political life of Uruguay, and mixed marriages with Uruguayans, as well as by the lack of Russian teaching at school. There was also a claim about the influence of the military dictatorship on the loss of the Russian language in the San Javier community. As a language of the home, Russian is still preserved on farms where several older relatives live. This situation is encouraging linguists to investigate the Russian dialect as quickly and thoroughly as possible, as in the near future it may be lost completely.

Traces of the once widely used Russian language remain in the linguistic landscape, in particular on unofficial signs, often made to attract tourists. San Javier retains its Russian character in ways that will not be apparent to an unsuspecting visitor, and much of this is now being commercialised. For instance, San Javier is becoming a popular tourist destination due to its 'Russianness', and this was especially evident during the 2018 FIFA World Cup held in Russia. Tour operators in the Río Negro province actively promoted tourism in San Javier, with organised tours and the watching of football matches in a Russian environment.

In addition to existing cultural organisations in San Javier, it would be desirable to resume teaching of the Russian language, especially for students from Russian families who no longer speak it. However, the presence of a teacher from Russia may negatively affect the preservation of the original dialect of the elderly, who still remember it when it functioned as a home language. Therefore, it is necessary that the teacher does not stigmatise or correct the Russian dialect but, in every way possible, promotes its preservation and popularisation.

NOTES

1   Note the stress transfer in Spanish to the last syllable compared to the stress on the second syllable in the original, and that the voiced Russian *з* is rendered by *s*.
2   Victory in World War II.
3   In the Spanish inscription we find *a* in the first syllable of the word *Valodia*, as a result of akanye, when [o] and [e] are pronounced close to [a] in the unstressed position.
4   Vladimir Roslik (1941–84) was a native of San Javier and a descendant of Russian migrants. He received a medical degree in Moscow, worked as a doctor in San Javier, and was the director of the San Javier Russian cultural centre named after Maxim Gorky. He became a victim of the military dictatorship (Bugaeva 2009).
5   The name *Vladimir* is given in the Russian version. Cf. *Vladimiro* in Spanish.
6   In Montevideo, there is a cultural organisation bearing the same name; many of its members are from San Javier (see Zagorod'ko, Morkovnik and Sanina 2009).
7   In the Spanish speech, we also managed to record the functioning of this word: *la*

sabraña in the feminine gender, which may be a dialect feature of the migrant Russian dialects: the transition of neuter nouns to the class of feminine nouns (Bromlei, Bulatova, Gertsova and Zakharova 2005: 116). The unstressed [o] in the first syllable is pronounced in Spanish as [a] (akanye) (cf. *Valodia*).

8   *Novay* ('new') may reflect the pronunciation of this word in the Russian dialect.
9   The dialect traits of the Russian language spoken in San Javier are not analysed in this chapter. It should be noted only that they belong to the Southern Russian dialects of the Voronezh region (see 9). In the speech of interviewees, we find the fricative [γ] (*горо́д* 'town'), the prosthetic [v] (*вучить* 'to teach'), the sound [ў] (*годоў* 'year.GEN.PL'), assimilative progressive softening of the consonant [k] after paired soft consonants (*маленькяя* 'small'), the absence of alternation of posterior and sibilant consonants in the verb *мочь* (*могём* 'we can'), the verb ending in 3 sg. pl. -*t'* (*понимаеть* 'he/she understands') and specific vocabulary (*дюже* 'very'; *швыдко* 'quick, fast'; *шукать* 'to search') etc. Among the members of the community there were also native speakers of Ukrainian dialects.
10 The narratives are given in Russian orthography with the most characteristic phonetic and morphological features. Unadopted Spanish borrowings are given in Spanish. For the sake of anonymity, I give only the participants' first name and gender.
11 In 2009 the Russian language was being taught in San Javier; classes were conducted by a teacher from Russia who came specifically for this purpose (Roslik 2009: 57). However, during my fieldwork, there was no teacher from Russia working there. Taking into account that San Javier is one of the oldest Russian colonies, it would be advisable to maintain a cultural presence through the teaching of the Russian language and the organisation of programmes aimed at developing children's creativity and strengthening ties with Russia. Supporting the activities of Russian cultural associations would also be beneficial.
12 Code switching is an alternation of languages within a conversation (Matras 2009: 101).
13 Old Believers are called 'bearded' ('бородачи') because men of this religious community do not shave their beards.

REFERENCES

Antonova, N. V. (2011), 'Iz istorii sekty Novyi Izrail' (pervaia tret' XX v.), *Vestnik Moskovskogo universiteta. Seriia 8: Istoriia*, 4, 132–42.

Baudouin de Courtenay, I. A. (1904), *Materialy dlia iuzhnoslavianskoi dialektologii i etnografii. II. Obraztsy iazyka na govorakh Terskikh Slavian severovosnochnoi Italii*, St Petersburg: Imp. Akademii Nauk.

Boiko de Semka, V. (2009), 'Pod inym krestom. Starovery v Urugvae', in S. N. Koshkin (ed.), *Russkie v Urugvae: istoriia i sovremennost*, Montevideo: Mastergraf SRL, pp. 109–30.

Bromlei S. V., L. N. Bulatova, O. G. Gecova and K. F. Zakharova (2005), *Russkaia dialektologiia*, Moscow: Academia.

Bugaeva, V. (2009), 'Vladimir Roslik', in S. N. Koshkin (ed.), *Russkie v Urugvae: istoriia i sovremennost*', Montevideo: Mastergraf SRL, pp. 185–92.

Dubovik, V. (2009), 'Zhyzn' pervykh russkikh poselentsev v Urugvae: vzgliad iznutri',

in S. N. Koshkin (ed.), *Russkie v Urugvae: istoriia i sovremennost'*, Montevideo: Mastergraf SRL, pp. 43–52.
Fernandes Burakova, B. (2009), 'Russkie vo Frai-Bentose', in S. N. Koshkin (ed.), *Russkie v Urugvae: istoriia i sovremennost'*, Montevideo: Mastergraf SRL, pp. 89–108.
Gerasimchuk, A. and E. Gerasimchuk (2009), 'Russkie v Sal'to', in S. N. Koshkin (ed.), *Russkie v Urugvae: istoriia i sovremennost'*, Montevideo: Mastergraf SRL, pp. 79–88.
Gumperz, J. J. (1982), *Discourse Strategies*, Cambridge: Cambridge University Press.
Martínez, V. (2013), *Los rusos de San Javier. Perseguidos por el zar. Perseguidos por la dictadura uruguaya. De Vasili Lubkov a Vladimir Roslik*, Montevideo: Ediciones de la banda oriental S.R.L.
Matras, Y. (2009), *Language Contact*, Cambridge: Cambridge University Press.
Moseikina, M. N. (2003), 'Russkie v stranah Latinskoi Ameriki v 20–30-e gg. XX v.: povsednevnost' kolonizatsii', *Vestnik RUDN. Seriia Istoriia Rossii*, 2, 153–66.
Narumov, B. P. (2001), 'Ispanskii iazyk', in I. I. Chelysheva, O. I. Romanova and B. P. Narumov (eds), *Iazyki mira. Romanskie iazyki*, Moscow: Academia, pp. 411–62.
Perotto, M. (2014), 'Post-Soviet Russian-speaking diaspora in Italy: results of a sociolinguistic survey', in L. Ryazanova-Clarke (ed.), *The Russian Language Outside the Nation*, Edinburgh: Edinburgh University Press, pp. 143–65.
Petrov, S. V. (2010), 'Iuzhnoamerikanskii Izrail': predvaritel'nye rezul'taty polevykh issledovanii v russkoi kolonii San-Khav'er', *Religiovedcheskie issledovaniia*, 3–4, 66–8.
Petrov, S. V. (2019a), ''Novyi Izrail'' i Krasnyi Oktiabr': dvizhenie russkogo religioznogo raznomysliia na perelome epoh', *Gosudarstvo, religiia, tserkov' v Rossii i za rubezhom*, 1–2, 371–95.
Petrov, S. V. (2019b), 'Perepiska mezhdu koopervativnym hoziaistvom novoizrail'tian na Severnom Kavkaze i ih obshchinoi v Urugvae (1917 g.)', *Studia Religiosa Rossica: nauchnyj zhurnal o religii*, 1, 133–49.
Pilipenko G. P. (2017), *Iazykovaia i etnokul'turnaia' situatsiia voevodinskikh vengrov: vzgliad iznutri i izvne*, Moscow: Nestor-Istoriia.
Pilipenko, G. P. (2018a), 'Russkie v Urugvae: polevye zametki', *Slavianski al'manakh*, 3–4, 306–17.
Pilipenko, G. P. (2018b), 'The Ukrainian language in Argentina and Paraguay as an identity marker', *Slověne*, 1, 281–307.
Pilipenko, G. P. (2021), *Iuzhnovolynskii dialekt ukrainskogo iazyka v Argentine (Mis'ones). Dnevnik pereselentsa iz mezhvoennoi Pol'shi Kirilla Vozniuka*, Moscow: Indrik.
Putiatova, E. G. (2008), 'Rossiiskie immigranty v Iuzhoi Amerike: problema sotsiokul'turnoi adaptatsii (konets XIX – nachalo XX veka', *Vestnik Sankt-Peterburgskogo universiteta. Seriia 2*, 1, 265–75.
Roslik, L. (2009), 'San-Khav'er', in S. N. Koshkin (ed.), *Russkie v Urugvae: istoriia i sovremennost'*, Montevideo: Mastergraf SRL, pp. 53–66.
Rovnova, O. G. (2010), 'Poligloty ponevole: iazykovaia situatsiia v staroobriadcheskikh obshchinakh Iuzhnoi Ameriki', in S. Grzybowski and M. Głuszkowski (eds), *Staroobrzędowcy za granicą*, Toruń: Wydawnictwo Naukowe Uniwersytetu Mikołaja Kopernika, pp. 137–57.
Rovnova, O. G. (2011), 'Ekspeditsiia v Braziliiu', *Russkii iazyk v nauchnom osveshchenii*, 1, 298–303.
Rovnova, O. G. (2014a), 'Ekspeditsiia v Boliviiu', *Russkii iazyk v nauchnom osveshchenii*, 2, 300–9.
Rovnova, O. G. (2014b), 'Govor staroobriadtsev Iuzhnoi Ameriki po pis'mennym materialam', *Trudy Instituta russkogo iazyka im. V.V. Vinogradova*, 3, 374–400.

Ryzvaniuk, S. O. (1974), *Ispanizmy v movlenni ukraïns'koï trudovoï migratsiï Argentyny*, Ph.D. dissertation, Kyiv: T. G. Shevchenko State University.

Semikina, A. (2009), 'Kul'turnyj tsentr Maksima Gor'kogo goroda San-Khvav'er', in S. N. Koshkin (ed.), *Russkie v Urugvae: istoriia i sovremennost'*, Montevideo: Mastergraf SRL, pp. 143–51.

Sikimić, B. and M. Nomaći (2016), 'Jezički pejzaž memorijalnog prosotra višejezičkih zajednica: Banatski Bugari / Palćani u Srbiji', *Južnoslovenski filolog*, LXXII, 7–31.

SRNG (2012), 'Slovar' russkih narodnyh govorov', 45, ed. F. P. Sorokoletov and S. A. Myznikov, St Petersburg: Nauka.

Zagorod'ko, I., S. Morkovnik and O. Sanina (2009), 'Kul'turnyi tsentr imeni Maksima Gor'kogo goroda Montevideo', in S. N. Koshkin (ed.), *Russkie v Urugvae: istoriia i sovremennost'*, Montevideo: Mastergraf SRL, pp. 133–42.

CHAPTER 8

The Russian–Israeli Home: A Blend of Cultures

Maria Yelenevskaya

INTRODUCTION

Migration is invariably connected to a voluntary or involuntary loss of home. In the ideology of Israel, the 'Law of Return' guaranteeing every Jew the right to become a citizen is one of the main legal acts of the country.[1] Moreover, providing Jews with a homeland was the main reason for forming the State of Israel (Richmond 1993). So, newcomers are referred to as 'repatriates', people returning to the lost home and 'recalling' the language of their forefathers. Yet, the majority of the people who emigrated from the former Soviet Union (FSU) to Israel in the 1970s, 1990s and in the present century are descendants of families that lived in the Russian Empire and then in the USSR for many generations. Most of them were secular and did not observe Jewish traditions in their countries of origin. Therefore, together with other scholars, I view their coming to Israel as immigration followed by gradual immersion into the culture which was previously either vaguely familiar or completely unknown to them (Al-Haj 2004; Fialkova and Yelenevskaya 2018; Remennick 2007; Ryazantsev et al. 2018). Like migrants everywhere, members of this group have various problems integrating into the host society, both in terms of socio-economic and identity challenges (see, e.g., Fialkova and Yelenevskaya 2013; Remennick 2012; Zbenovich 2016). While many aspects of the immigration experience of Russian-speaking Israelis have been thoroughly researched, so far their material culture – and the culture of homemaking in particular – has seldom been the focus of anthropological, sociological or linguistic research. Among the few exceptions are Lipshitz 1997, Fialkova and Yelenevskaya 2007 and Levin 2014. Yet it is from the interaction with objects in homes that we can learn about their owners' interests, customs, values and language habits; in other words, people's material environment can give us important insights into their everyday practices and inner world.

The project reported in this chapter analyses the perception of home by first-generation immigrants from the FSU. Using the convenience sampling method of finding research participants, I conducted thirteen focus interviews with sixteen people, all of them in Russian.[2] The participants can be divided into two groups. The first group consists of those who arrived in Israel as adults. Three other interviewees, although technically first-generation immigrants, underwent socialisation while already in Israel: one was nine years old upon arrival in Israel, the other two were mere infants. Therefore, from the point of view of acculturation, they can be viewed as second-generation immigrants. The last three interviews were held during the Covid pandemic, so two participants answered my questions in writing, while the third recorded her answers on *WhatsApp*. The other interviews were conducted face-to-face in the participants' homes. The interviews were audio-recorded and transcribed. They were supplemented by photographs taken during my 'tours' of the participants' apartments, and these images illustrate narratives. I asked the participants to tell stories of the objects that had caught my attention, and in some cases the interviewees themselves wanted me to take pictures of the artefacts that were important to them.

Besides the interviews, I studied posts in Russian-Israeli Facebook groups Хайфа HaifaRu.co.il, created in 2009, which has over 26,500 members (facebook.com/groups/228377432160) and *Russkoiazychnyi biznes v Izraile* (Russian-language business in Israel), created in 2013, with a total of over 7,900 members (facebook.com/groups/rusbiz). These groups are very active, and the issues of material culture, identity and home frequently come up in posts and discussions.

My main goal in this project was to find out how living in multilingual and multicultural Israel influences the material culture of the immigrants' homes, what immigrants perceive as a comfortable and cosy home, and whether we can observe any continuity of the Russian/Soviet homemaking tradition or a breaking away from it. The project was organised around the following research questions:

- What features of Soviet dwellings are reproduced in immigrants' homes?
- How do immigrants' dwellings and artefacts reflect perpetuation of and/or changes in homemaking practices?
- What possessions are relevant to the continuity of immigrants' identity?
- How are bi- and multilingualism reflected in immigrants' homes

and what do artefacts tell us about the linguistic biographies of their inhabitants?

Working with the collected data I applied thematic analysis to identify dominant themes and motifs. This method presupposes observation of phenomena presented in the data collected, recognising specific patterns characteristic of these phenomena, and interpreting them (Boyatzis 1998: 4–5). Following Braun and Clarke (2019), I view themes as patterns of shared meaning underpinned or united by a core concept. They result from an analytic and creative process of coding. Notably, they are not just passive entities present in the data but are actively created by the researcher/s at the intersection of data, analytic process and subjectivity (Braun and Clarke 2019: 593–4). Thematic analysis always moves beyond just counting explicit words or phrases and focuses on identifying and describing both explicit and implicit ideas within the data. It seems to be particularly useful in capturing the complexities of meaning within a textual dataset (Guest et al. 2012: 9–10).

Studying the transcripts, I also applied conversation analysis (CA), as interviews in which I did not only ask questions but also shared my own experiences with the interviewees were samples of actual and contextualised talk. The use of actual instances of talk allows for the possibility of an examination of what speakers actually do when speaking, rather than producing an account of what they think they do (Liddicoat 2011). CA is particularly useful in exploring how stories are produced and received and what emotions are expressed by interlocutors. Interaction-based studies of storytelling demonstrate that emotion is communicated through the ways in which tellers launch a story, tell it and bring it to a close, as well as through the ways in which story recipients respond to the tellers and their stories (Prior 2016: 14–15). CA helped me identify the emotions and attitudes of the interviewees to their homes, the artefacts filling them, and the events that are part of the biographies of the objects and their owners. It also enabled me to analyse instances of code mixing and the contexts that triggered it. Finally, I often referred to my ethnographic diary, a simple but effective tool for conducting participant observation.

HOMES BETWEEN MATERIAL AND IMMATERIAL CULTURE

Although artefacts have been studied by anthropologists and archaeologists for more than a century now, some anthropologists – Daniel Miller

(1987 and 2005), Michael Schiffer (1999) and Bjørnar Olsen (2003) among them – have argued that the materiality of social life has been marginalised and even stigmatised in scholarly discourses. Yet in the last three decades there has been a 'material turn' in the humanities and social sciences, and the enquiry and debate have become interdisciplinary. The intellectual points of reference and interest in the objects overlap across such disciplines as anthropology, sociology, cultural and literary studies, and human geography, as well as others (Hicks and Beaudry 2010). I am approaching the material culture of immigrants' homes from the position of cultural and linguistic anthropology. Following Hodder, I believe that material culture should not be viewed as a passive by-product of other areas of life. It is active in that artefacts are produced, so as to transform people materially, socially and ideologically (2012: 174), and, in their turn, people transform objects by putting them to new uses and assigning new meanings and values to them.

Indeed, every realm of human behaviour and communication involves people – artefact interactions – which makes it essential that these interactions, some long-term, others fleeting, should be studied by social and behavioural sciences (Schiffer 1999: 1–10). Focusing on these interactions should help us shed our common-sense opposition between the person and the thing, the animate and inanimate, the subject and the object, which is still perpetuated in the mind of lay people and in scholarly studies (Keane 2003; Miller 2010). In fact, this opposition sometimes disappears in relation to mechanical and electronic objects like cars, computer devices or even such mundane artefacts as glasses, favourite knives or keys. Some people give them names; others 'talk' to them when they are out of order. We anthropomorphise artefacts, for example telling our computer, 'Wake up, please!', when it crashes, or telling our glasses, 'I'm in a hurry, stop hiding from me' (from an ethnographic diary).

Miller posits that humanity constantly returns to vast projects devoted to immateriality, but the paradox undermining these attempts is that immateriality can only be expressed through materiality. So, the more humanity reaches towards the conceptualisation of immateriality and, we may add, in some sense its idealisation, the more important the specific form of its materialisation (Miller 2005: 28). Pervasiveness of the opposition of materiality and immateriality is particularly relevant when we talk about ex-Soviets. Even thirty years of post-Soviet life have not obliterated some of the ambivalences bred by Soviet ideology and way of life. Soviet people were brought up to be 'above' the routines of everyday living and interest in objects. This is what a prominent American scholar and an immigrant herself, Svetlana Boym, wrote about the opposition between *byt* (everyday existence) and *bytie* (spiritual or poetic existence), connecting this dichotomy to the valorisation of heroic sacrifice over both private life and practical accomplishment:

> The border between *bytie* and *byt* seems to parallel the mythical border between Russia and the West. There are radical differences between the representations of the 'American dream' – the dream of the private pursuit of happiness in the family home – and the Russian dream that, according to the philosophers of 'the Russian idea,' consisted of heroic spiritual homelessness and messianic nomadism. (1995: 133)

In a country so often plagued by *defitsit* (shortages), it was important for the rulers to convince the populace that objects were unimportant and consumerism was a vice. The Soviet-speak reflected these attitudes in the pejorative terms *meshchanin* – 'a person driven by property acquisition, a narrow-minded person' – *veshchizm* – 'exaggerated interest in objects and desire to own them at the expense of spiritual interests' – and *veshchepoklonstvo* – 'acquisition of objects as the main goal in life' (Mokienko and Nikitina 1998: 335; 80; 79).[3] But since acquiring those very objects was akin to a victory in a battle, the result was the opposite from what the authorities intended: for numerous people in different strata of society, even such mundane objects as clothes, furniture and household appliances turned into status objects. In the late Soviet period many people, including adolescents, turned into passionate consumers.

Those who emigrated in the early 1990s were exhilarated by the accessibility of consumer goods available at a big range of prices. For some people it was dream fulfilment, what Mikhail Idov neatly defined as *veshchistskoie obzhorstvo* –'object-acquisition gluttony', an unavoidable stage in immigrant life in which some get stuck for the rest of their life (Idov 2018). Let us now see how *byt* and *bytie* interact in the homes of Russian-speaking Israelis.

SELECTING OBJECTS FOR A NEW LIFE IN A NEW COUNTRY

In the early 1990s émigrés tried to send as much luggage as possible to their new home. Although there were weight limits, many people preparing to leave tried to find ways to exceed these limits, even if it meant resorting to bribery. Some managed to send musical instruments, boats and motor bikes in the hope of selling them. Others did not have any

Figure 8.1 In some homes painted wooden spoons and Khokhloma dishes, Gzhel cups and Palekh boxes are on display as decorative objects, but in others they are dismissed as part of the past and hidden away in cupboards.

valuable consumer goods and sent whatever they had at home, including clothes that were too warm for mild Israeli winters, long-used kitchen utensils, soaps, toothpaste and even toilet paper. Some of the luggage sent by sea and containing objects needed in everyday life arrived months later, when immigrants had already acquired replacements. Things like bedclothes, curtains and other mundane objects do not always fit the needs of a different climate, household practices or fashion in a new country. Some things that proved to be superfluous were later given away to the next generation of immigrants who needed them; some others were kept in wardrobes still unused. Even thirty years after migrating, some people have not parted company with sheets and pillowcases that do not fit the size of locally made pillows and blankets, or curtains that are either too long or too short for Israeli windows. From time to time, these objects are taken out and aired, but then put back until the next household refurbishment.

Asked about the principle behind the selection of things to take with them to Israel, those who emigrated as adults clearly divide them into things that were utilitarian and 'necessary in everyday life' and those that were symbolic, things for 'memory'. The 'necessary' was partially determined by what was available. Thus, in the early 1990s, in a time of high inflation and shortages of consumer goods, these were crockery, bedclothes, blankets and even cooking pots. Today, immigrants are much better informed about what is expensive in Israel. They also know that Israelis willingly give away household objects and furniture, which can get a lot of use in the first period of life in a new country. So, today they arrive equipped with electronic and mobile devices and some electric appliances. Here are some excerpts from the interviews illustrating these choices.

1. **Svetlana (from Simferopol, 70-plus):** Clearly, packing was not guided by wisdom or knowledge but simply by greed – I was eager to take as much as possible with me, and everything seemed important: books, crockery, bedwear, clothes, and this is not to mention the things dear to my heart, things that carried memories. As a result, although everything was used, gradually, in the process of moving multiple times from one apartment to another, most of these things got lost and only a small number remained. But because of this you cling to these like to the last link to the previous life.[4]

2. **Interviewer:** You say you came to Israel virtually without any luggage. And yet, when you were packing, what did you decide to take with you?

    Elena (from Moscow, 60-plus): This is really funny. First, we left in 1992, when as you remember, there was nothing [available in the shops]. So, we were dividing things between us. My mother-in-law was dividing things in this way: we have six spoons, so you take three and the other three I'll keep for myself. We have two carpets – so I am giving you one of them. This wasn't perceived as a tragedy, but quite humorously. We had just half a container full. But we sent a lot of books and photographs. And now I think I was really foolhardy to send photographs. What if they had disappeared? I don't remember now what we put into the container. In fact, we were packing as if we were going for a hiking trip. And in the luggage which we took with us to the plane we had bikes. What else did we bring? A guitar. A stroller – they told us it didn't make sense to send this because, by the time it arrived, the child would already have grown up.

3. **Tatiana (from Saint Petersburg, 70-plus):** Lilia [Tatiana's friend who had immigrated earlier] wrote, 'Take everything, absolutely everything, you'll have use for everything.' Now it's funny, but I still have those buttons, and threads and needles – they are still from Leningrad. And also cotton wool which I don't use; well, what they sell here is more pleasant. And also those things from the pharmacy – all those bandages. [. . .] I left some of my vases to friends, but the rest I packed and brought with me, because they were dear to my heart. Here is a clock, which is shown on TV today as a rarity. I guess it is about sixty or seventy years old. The clock, yes, and then I have

a Kasli cast-iron dog,[5] which I got as a gift from a friend when I was twelve. It's bloody heavy, yet still I packed it into a bag.

Mark (from Saint Petersburg, 70-plus): They studied it carefully at customs.

Tatiana: Yes, and they couldn't understand what it was. They said: Are you nuts? Why do you need this extra weight? And I said: Because it is dear to me. There it is, in the middle of the room.

Several interviewees note that their poor choice of what to take and what to leave behind could be partially explained by a lack of information. In the last two decades new arrivals have been much better prepared. Some of them visit Israel as tourists before deciding to emigrate, and others find a lot of information in blogs in which Russian-speaking Israelis share their experience as greenhorns. Stories about the haphazard choice of objects were part of the narrative repertoire of 1990s immigrants and still amuse the narrators and their audiences. Note that in excerpt 3, Tatiana's husband, Mark, makes a remark about customs. Since the couple only met in Israel, he did not witness the scene but knows about it from his wife's stories, and he did not want her to miss a juicy detail. Equally popular are stories about circumventing the rules of the Soviet and post-Soviet customs, in which immigrants emerge as tricksters (Fialkova and Yelenevskaya 2006).

Attachment to objects brought from the old country is more typical of those who have poorly integrated into Israeli society and those who have good memories of their pre-emigration life. It becomes stronger as people age: not only the events of their youth but also objects that remind them of times and people gone by are idealised. For immigrants, probably more than for other ageing people, artefacts help maintain links with the past which help sustain the present. If we view human life as a sequence of settled and unsettled periods, then the upheaval of moving to another country is a highly unsettled condition (Swidler 1986). As Mehta and Belk rightly observe, 'During geographic movement away from the people, places, and things, cities, nations, an increased burden is placed on individual possessions for anchoring identity' (1991: 400). Artefacts act as anchors of stability and security, helping overcome difficulties of rebuilding one's life and adjusting to the new environment. And it is the domestic sphere which serves as an active site for cultural identification (Tolia-Kelly 2004).

At the same time, some immigrants who cannot afford or choose not to buy an apartment of their own move from house to house many times, each time getting rid of or losing objects. Even in my small sample, three of the interviewees have lived in seven different rented apartments, which makes them feel that, because of the objects left by previous tenants or owned by the landlord, their dwellings have been no more than temporary shelters. This has prevented them from expressing their personalities in the arrangement of their homes. One participant has lived in eight different apartments. She said that she has finally come to realise that one does not need to own too many objects in life.

> 4. **Interviewer:** Tell me, when you were leaving, was it difficult or easy to select things? Did you get rid of things easily or did you suffer as you dithered over what to take with you?
>
> **Veronika (from Tiraspol, Moldova, 50-plus):** That depends on a person's nature, right? If a person isn't that hung up about objects [. . .] I came to think that all belongings, all my belongings should fit into the boot of a small car. And so, you have to figure out what is most important and what is less important, so that you can give it up, and leave. It's like when there's a fire: you've got the cat in your right hand, the computer in your left; taking the birth certificate is a must, and also your favourite piece of jewellery.
>
> **Interviewer:** And this is how it was? [Indeed, Veronika had to abandon her house when there was a big fire in the area where she lived.]
>
> **Veronika:** Exactly, and this is how it was. And this is why when I was leaving the USSR I didn't bother, but I brought a lot of books on linguistics, which was important for me. That is, the books were really important. I packed them and didn't care too much about the rest.

All interviewees, irrespective of their age, value symbolic objects more than purely utilitarian things. Photographs, portraits of their family members, their children's drawings and gifts from people they love were on the top of their priority list of artefacts to be carried across continents. Even if these are not on display today, they have a special meaning. Here is what different interviewees said: 'They are dear to my heart', 'I brought a lot of memories', 'Although I am not inclined to nostalgia, this is my life, this is my life.' A motif which comes up several times in my material is the transformation of utilitarian objects into symbolic ones.

One example is a story of a *kazan* – a big iron or copper pot traditionally used in Azerbaijan and Central Asia to cook the dishes of the local cuisine. A friend told me that for her father the *kazan* he uses to cook pilaf is a memorable object because his family brought it from Tashkent, Uzbekistan, where they had been evacuated during the Great Patriotic War (1941–5). From Tashkent the *kazan* travelled to Kyiv and currently continues its service in Israel.[6]

5. **Polina (from Tashkent, 60-plus):** There are some things which you've brought here but you which you don't use. Yet, it's difficult to part from them because they give you some psychological *back-up* [English insertion]. These are things connected to food. They are the last to disappear. It's in the genes of the Soviet personality. Take a meat-mincing machine. I don't think that a single Soviet homemaker who understands that meat shouldn't come to you ready minced but that you should mince it yourself would ever part from her meat-mincing machine. Here it is sitting on my shelf. A mechanical machine. Soon machines like this will be exhibited in museums, but I won't give it up. An electric mincer is right next to it and is hardly used either. But I won't throw it out. Probably, because it is closely connected to food and is engraved in our unconscious.

Interviewer: I have a can opener brought from the Union [frequently used in oral communication instead of the 'Soviet Union']. It cost 27 kopecks then. For some reason, I find the can openers sold here inconvenient. My husband thinks it's an instrument for suicides, and several times he's threatened to throw it out. I leapt to protect it like a tigress, and now I keep hiding it in different places because my husband is always on the hunt to destroy it. And for me it's the best can opener ever.

Polina: Oh, how well I understand you. I also have such a tin opener, and until recently I also had a rolling pin. A wonderful, gorgeous rolling pin. But then Or [Polina's granddaughter] started baking, and several times she put it into a *mediakh* [Hebrew for 'dishwasher']. You can imagine what it looks like after thirty years of use and the *mediakh*. So, I had to buy a new one. I was very, very upset [. . .], how should I say it? Well, that is, I was very upset about this rolling pin. And the tin opener, I cherish it as the apple of my eye. It's even cooler than yours – it cost 17 kopecks. Thirty years of service. Absolutely faultless. Well, we are all tarred with the same brush.

Both narrators are slightly amused by their attachment to gadgets which they don't even use today. Like other participants, they have already got

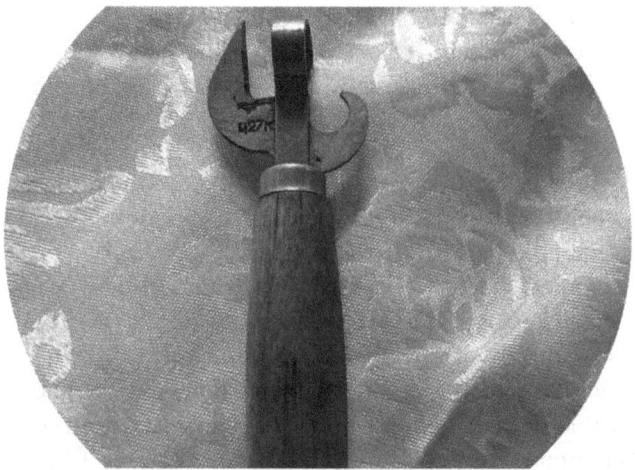

Figure 8.2 A legendary tin opener.

rid of most utilitarian things brought from the old country, replacing them with technically more advanced, more ergonomic or more aesthetic objects, but those that they keep have acquired a symbolic significance. They are elements of what makes a house a home.

> 6. **Interviewer**: You pointed to this saucer and said that it's special. Can you tell me its story?
>
> **Mark**: This saucer ... My father's elder brother, my uncle [...], together with his wife and two daughters, my cousins, they lived in Ukraine. Both he and his wife were porcelain-makers, they worked in porcelain factories. And in 1954 my father, who was an officer, went to the Zhitomir region to visit these relatives during his vacation. So, it was 1954, and my father's brother gave him a tea service for six persons as a gift. And the theme of the service was written in a beautiful way in Ukrainian: *300 rokiv vozedno Ukrainy z Rossiei* [300 years of Ukrainian–Russian unification]. Yes, this is the only saucer that is left today, and it is a memorial saucer now.

The one remaining saucer of a tea service is virtually useless in the household, but it is an important object for Mark, reminding him of his childhood and of his late family members. Moreover, later in the interview he said that the broken cups became a symbol of the broken Russian–Ukrainian unity, but since the last saucer still exists, there is hope that the unity is not lost for ever.

MAKING A HOME AWAY FROM HOME

An important aspect of housing policy in Israel is to provide incentives for young people and new immigrants to buy their own apartments, so as to reduce the chances that they will leave the country. Indeed, some participants in the project said that it was difficult for them 'to live on other people's things', and they could only feel at home after they bought their own apartments. Others, however, tried to lend their rented apartments cosiness and attractiveness, irrespective of how many times they had to move. The most prominent motif of the homemaking narratives, however, was that it was only after immigrating that participants got the opportunity to 'build their own nest'. Six of the interviewees mentioned that, prior to emigration and even after getting married, they continued living with their or their spouse's parents. This limited their freedom to arrange their homes the way they wanted; furthermore, it deprived them of the feeling of having a 'private space':

7. **Frida (from Saint Petersburg, 70-plus)** Only after I divorced and got this apartment did I start to feel I had a home. While living in Leningrad in a communal apartment, and also here when we were together, I didn't have that feeling. Neither did I have it when I lived with my parents. Never! Because I didn't have a nook which was my own. I didn't have my private space. I didn't have it. While here, it is my apartment, it's mine. And it is here that my lifelong dreams have come true. I can have the pets I want. Nobody is giving me orders. I am financially independent, and I don't have to report to anyone.

Note that Frida uses the expression *ne bylo svoego ugla* [literally, 'I didn't have even a corner that was mine']. Due to the shortage of housing in the USSR, some people were made to share a room in a communal apartment with their parents, or in-laws, and sometimes with their landlords, the last referred to as *snimat' ugol* [rent a corner], so that these expressions, though metaphorical, sometimes had a quite literal meaning. At the same time, the crowded living conditions taught people to create their own space even in the rooms divided into sections by curtains or closets (Utekhin 2004: 34–5).

When arranging their first dwellings in Israel, my interviewees, as well as many other new immigrants, made use of what could be obtained from special warehouses for the needy and from what was taken out of the houses and left in the street for others to pick up. My interviewees spoke about the necessity of obtaining objects in this way without inhibitions:

> 8. **Elena:** Serezhka [Elena's husband] is a handyman. So, [in Israel] we made everything with our own hands. Rita's [Elena's daughter] stroller turned out to be very useful. She was already two years old. We lived on the first floor and whenever we found something good on the street we would say: 'Rita, get out of your stroller, we will carry this stuff home.'
>
> 9. **Valeria (from Saint Petersburg, 40-plus):** We arrived and two weeks later we moved into this apartment which was completely empty.
>
> **Interviewer:** Completely empty? No furniture at all?
>
> **Valeria:** Well, there were built-in cupboards in the kitchen, but no electric appliances and just one wardrobe in the sitting room. That's it. All the rest we bought, took from friends or found on scrapheaps. We didn't miss out on doing that.
>
> **Interviewer:** Oh, that's a must!
>
> **Valeria:** As they say, *s vystavki* [from the exhibition]. And I was very proud of our first one – a glass tabletop. We dragged it up here sweating and hiccupping. We hoisted it on top of cardboard boxes, and it became our first coffee table. Later we got rid of it because it took up half of the living room [. . .]. I said it was a monument to my immigration. Am I *olim* [Hebrew for 'immigrants'] or what? Could I resist bringing at least something from a scrapheap?

In the stories about objects acquired for free or almost for free, immigrants again emerge as tricksters. Veronika was amused telling me that her family's first set of furniture was acquired for peanuts. It had had a history of travelling from one immigrant family to another like a 'perpetual trophy'. Note the pun in Valeria's remark about furniture 'from the exhibition': *vystavit'* can mean 'take something out', 'get rid of' or 'exhibit'. Like many immigrant-coined words and expressions, this one makes light of forced circumstances.

Offers to give away used furniture or electric appliances often appear in Facebook groups, and sometimes new arrivals ask whether anyone can provide them with household items they do not have. Here is one of the recent examples in the discussion group *Хайфа HaifaRu.co.il*:

> Hi, everyone! My husband and I are *olim*, we arrived on 25 January and have rented an apartment without furniture. We are looking for a cupboard for shoes, a carpet, curtains, a blanket, and a vacuum

cleaner. Also, for a minimum of crockery and a couple of pots. We only have forks and spoons. We'll be grateful for any help! [smiley and heart emoji]

The message was met with forty-three likes, shared twenty-three times and followed by 110 comments. Some members of the group gave addresses of charity organisations that help new immigrants, and others offered their own household objects or volunteered to deliver the things donated to the new immigrants' home.

Answering a question about what makes a house good, comfortable and cosy, some interviewees mentioned light and warmth, the latter being used not only metaphorically but also literally. One of the participants recalled that as a child she thought that one of the differences between the homes of new immigrants and veteran Israelis was that in the former there was almost no heating and so it was very cold in winter. Indeed, heating in Israel is expensive, and families with limited resources have to economise on it.

Two participants who came from Saint Petersburg expressed special pride in arranging their homes in such a way that reminded them and their guests of typical Saint Petersburg apartments. They feel that this is a sign that their home serves to connect two countries and their own present with the past:

10. **Tatiana:** I really feel that this apartment is home. In the way it is furnished and filled with things, everyone who comes to our place for the first time says that they feel as if they were in Piter [short for Saint Petersburg], not in Israel but in Piter.

The feeling shared by most interviewees is that a good house is one which allows them to host guests. It is considered natural that relatives and friends coming from other towns or from other countries do not stay in hotels. Sometimes these visits last for weeks, yet they are seldom considered to be a burden. Rather, the opportunity to offer hospitality is perceived as a sign of accomplishment and proof that the hosts are properly settled in the new country:

11. **Elena:** We don't get very attached to objects. We bought this furniture, it's already twenty-five years old, but I am not going to change anything, although the cat has torn whatever it could. But I still think it's good. And we are guided by my grandma's principle: if you cannot accommodate five guests, it's a bad apartment.

Interviewer: Oh, this I understand very well.

Elena: So, we have everything adjusted to this [principle]. We have had lots of people staying with us, and I hope to God it won't stop!

GENERATIONAL DIFFERENCES

Project participants whose children have grown up and left the family house compared their homes with those of their children while three of my younger interviewees reflected on the similarities and differences between their parents' and their own homes. The young participants seem to have inherited from their parents an inclination to choose things which are functional and arrange rooms in such a way that they are multifunctional. A bedroom often serves as a study for one of the family members, the living room can be transformed into a guestroom, and the kitchen is still a multipurpose space for cooking, having meals, doing homework and receiving close friends. The young participants like wooden furniture and believe that, while such furniture can be simple, it should be compatible with the other objects in the house. They mention bookcases as an essential component of a cosy home.

Two of my young participants have mixed memories about the rented homes where they spent their childhood. One of them, Larisa, says that she was embarrassed that her family's home was not like the homes of her native Israeli peers.

12. **Larisa (from Saint Petersburg, 30-plus):** I slept in the same room as my parents for many years, and our *salon* [Hebrew for a 'sitting room'] was a separate room, and granny lived with us, which is very typical of a Russian home: *safta be salon* [Hebrew for 'grandmother in the sitting room'], as everyone says jokingly. So, whenever any of my classmates came to see me, I was very concerned, because they had houses in the American style: an open *salon* and a kitchen, the *salon* and the kitchen together and open. And everyone had a room of their own: I never saw anyone sleeping in the same room as their parents. And another thing comes to mind: the carpets. We always had carpets of a very Russian style; sometimes they were put on sofas. I saw this in many Russian houses, and I was always afraid that I was *other*, that I was different. And this is why I always felt more comfortable in Russian houses. Even today, I think, I somehow enjoy visiting families where

everything is familiar to me from childhood more than where it's different.

Intergenerational homes were a usual phenomenon in the Soviet Union, and many new immigrants had to continue this practice after immigration, at least in the first period of life in the new country. This excerpt illustrates the insecurity experienced by child immigrants, who are afraid to be different from their native Israeli peers. Some manage to overcome this feeling as they mature; in others it triggers mimicry and passionate desire to be 'like everybody else'.

While the young participants in my study criticise their parents for stuffing their homes with objects, the parents find their children's apartments too minimalist, attributing this to their immersion in 'the local life':

13. **Tatiana** [about her daughter's house]: They adhere to the principles of minimalism, like everyone here. Everything is put away and hidden – no figurines and no trinkets. Well, they do have some pictures, they have things they like, but everything is very austere. There is a picture here and a picture there, but they are not at all connected to . . . to Piter [Saint Petersburg]. I don't know how an Israeli visiting their house would recognise it as a Russian home.

Besides finding the 'local style' unattractive, the parents find their children's habits not frugal enough. Such criticism of the 'throw-away society' was rather unexpected, as Russian-speaking Israelis, in particular those brought up in the USSR, are not the most ecologically minded of people:

14. **Anna (from Simferopol, Crimea, 60-plus)**: The style . . . theirs is already a local style. We bought things once and for our lifetime, until the very end, furniture and everything. If something broke or was out of order – whether it was an electric fuse or a hook – we used to repair them. Here everything is thrown out without a thought and new things bought. My children, they change things. They have a completely different style. And they speak Hebrew at home. I keep asking them: Why? After all, children have to speak well . . . Well, their children speak Russian with an accent.
Interviewer: But they do speak Russian.
Anna: Yes, but very often [they ask]: What is this? And what is that? They have a very poor vocabulary. And Nadya, my

daughter-in-law, answers, 'You know, Mum, we are already thinking in Hebrew and so it comes naturally; we don't even notice that we're speaking Hebrew.' Sometimes I get offended: we are at the table, they speak Hebrew, and I can hardly understand, not everything. 'Well, we simply think in Hebrew.' They are already locals.

This excerpt brings us to another important aspect of immigrants' home life: language.

SPEAKING FRIDGES

Many artefacts in contemporary households are linguistically defined: books, TV sets, computers, telephones, and various other electronic devices. Medications and foodstuffs are exported and imported, and immigrants visiting their native towns buy familiar medications for themselves and friends in Israel. To suit global customers instruction leaflets and manuals appear in various languages, making it possible for consumers in different countries to use them. Moreover, computer operation systems and teletext can be set up to communicate with the users in their language. Learning how these multilingual objects function in immigrants' homes contributes to our understanding of immigrants' evolving multilingualism and multiculturalism (Aronin 2012; Aronin et al. 2018).

I asked all my interviewees about the place of Hebrew in their homes. Those who were over sixty almost unanimously claimed that their houses were Russian only, but further questions allowed me to find out that everyone often used bilingual dictionaries, to read bills, business letters and medical documents, for example. Where the language used is too sophisticated, they photograph the documents and send them to their children or friends by phone for translation and interpretation. The object that turned out to be most revealing with regard to the use of language turned out to be the refrigerator.

A fridge can tell us a lot about the household. While the contents reflects culinary tastes and to some extent the financial situation of the family, the fridge door can give us a glimpse of the interests, habits and language repertoire of the owners. Since ex-Soviets usually had little opportunity to see the world, they viewed the opening of borders as one of the most important achievements of their post-Soviet life, and some documented their travels by putting magnets on their fridge door. On many fridges in immigrants' homes I saw photographs of the children

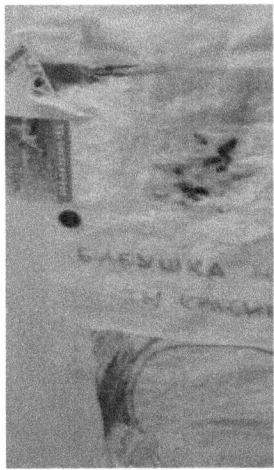  

Figure 8.3 Calendars, notes, photographs of memorable events, children's drawings and telephones of 'husbands for an hour'[7] turn refrigerators into communicative spaces *par excellence*.

taken during school events or trips, pictures of the owners' or their relatives' weddings, to-do lists, recipes, calendars and even selections of maxims. This is what my interviewee Valeria said:

15. **Valeria**: We usually put children's drawings and magnets, which we get from everywhere, on the fridge. Or some . . . here, look at this postcard. Galia [Valeria's daughter] received it from her friend in Russia quite some time ago, and since it is dear to her, the postcard is still here.

There are also the magnetic business cards of various shops and repairmen. Most are bilingual: Hebrew–Russian or Hebrew–English. In one house I saw magnetic letters of the Latin alphabet. These were used to teach the owners' son to read English.

All my interviewees exchange text and voice messages with family members and friends. Some of this correspondence is bilingual. Thus, Tamara (from Kiev, 30-plus) corresponds with her husband in Hebrew, and with her mother and grandparents in Russian. Her husband writes to his parents in Hebrew while they respond in Russian. Dasha (from Simferopol, 30-plus) writes primarily in Hebrew with occasional Russian and English insertions. Larisa's correspondence is even more elaborate: she writes to her parents and family in France in Russian; she corresponds with her nieces in Hebrew; with one of her brothers only in Russian, and with the other in a mixture of Russian and Hebrew.

Figure 8.4 Multilingualism in Russian-speaking Israeli homes starts early. Parents and grandparents read Russian books to the children. Pre-schoolers learn to read in Hebrew, and in the first to fourth grade of the elementary school English is also added to the mix. Most likely, when playing with this *Ivanushka* doll, its owner resorts to translanguaging, imitating everyday communication in the family.

Clearly, even those immigrants who admit that they have not learned enough Hebrew to be fully integrated into Israeli life use it to a different degree and for different purposes in everyday life. In all interviews there were instances of translanguaging.[8] Hebrew insertions unchanged or morphologically adjusted to Russian by the addition of affixes, conjugated verbs and declined nouns and adjectives have become a hallmark of the speech habits of most Russian-speaking Israelis. Members of the one-and-a-half and second-generation immigrants educated in Israel widely use English in the receptive and in the productive mode, in particular if they are employed in white-collar jobs. Moreover, even those who did not learn English as part of their formal education have picked up various words and phrases and included them in their linguistic repertoire. This confirms that for Russian-speaking Israelis the dominant language constellation is Russian-Hebrew and English (Aronin 2020), which is reflected not only in their public but also home communication.

CONCLUSIONS

Most of the interviewees, including those whose apartments are full of objects either brought from their pre-immigration apartments or newly acquired in Israel, claimed that they have little passion for artefacts. Whether explicitly or implicitly they expressed their preference for immaterial values, such as friendships, hospitality and emotional comfort. Among the most valued objects are artefacts connected to memorable events or loved ones, together with photographs. Even the people who have immigrated only recently and were still weighing up whether to return to Russia or re-emigrate considered photographs among their most important belongings. Some of the mundane objects brought from their former home gradually acquire symbolic meanings. Biographies of these artefacts become a part of their owners' narrative repertoire. On the whole, preserving familiar artefacts brought from the homeland has a stabilising effect, in particular in the early stages of post-immigration life. Various artefacts in the participants' apartments testify to multilingual practices in their households, although this aspect of life is not always consciously recognised.

First-generation immigrants brought up in the Soviet Union have preserved the habit of making any room in the apartment multifunctional. Putting up guests from the old country who have come for extended visits in their homes instead of in hotels is common practice. So, the interviewees spoke about the necessity of arranging their dwellings in such a way as to be able to accommodate several guests at a time. Combined with the organisation of sightseeing trips, this type of hospitality is not seen as a burden but as an honour and a pleasant responsibility. Besides the joy of meeting family and old friends, it gives the feeling of satisfaction and serves as proof of their having a comfortable lifestyle in their new home country.

In regard to their attitude to artefacts there is a clear-cut division between generations. Those who immigrated as children or in their teens are deeply grounded in Israeli life. This is manifested in their prevalent use of Hebrew in family communications and in the arrangement and decoration of their dwellings. Their parents are mildly critical of what they call a 'minimalist style' and the ease with which their children part with their possessions. At the same time, the Israeli tradition of sharing household things with newcomers and donating household objects and furniture to the needy has become part and parcel of immigrants' life and is viewed as a moral duty. However, they prefer not to do it through organisations, but to use personal connections when helping their co-ethnics. This was particularly visible in 2014–15 when there was a sizeable increase in immigration from Russia and Ukraine.

As they showed their apartments, all the interviewees said they loved the home they had created in the new place. Moreover, even those who spoke about nostalgia and about the Russian style prevailing in their household patterns affirmed that Israel had become their real home.

Although the elderly admit that they are not involved in the mainstream social life of the country, they have become familiar with Jewish and Israeli festive traditions and practise them, but with some modifications. Children and, in particular, grandchildren serve as facilitators in language and culture learning, which often occurs during big family gatherings on Friday nights and holidays – an indispensable part of Israeli home life.

NOTES

1. See <www.refworld.org/docid/3ae6b4ea1b.html> (last accessed 15 November 2022).
2. I would like to express gratitude to my interviewees for their time, hospitality and willingness to share their thoughts and feelings.
3. Translation of the definitions is mine.
4. I translated excerpts from the interviews without editing them in order to preserve specific features of oral narration and the individual style of each participant. I also preserved instances of code switching: Hebrew, English and Ukrainian insertions are italicised. I have changed the names of the participants to anonymise them.
5. Kasli is a town in the mid-Urals famous for its factory producing cast-iron figures. Many historic iron sculptures displayed in the museums of Moscow and St Petersburg were produced in Kasli.
6. I am grateful to Larisa Fialkova for sharing this story with me.
7. 'A husband for an hour' is a phrase used in small ads placed by handymen. Together with other typed or handwritten ads they are posted on billboards, shop windows, bus stops, streetlamps, etc.
8. An important concept in modern-language pedagogies, translanguaging refers to how bilingual people fluidly use their linguistic resources – without regard to named language categories – to make meaning and communicate (Vogel and Garcia 2017).

REFERENCES

Al-Haj, M. (2004), *Immigration and Ethnic Formation in a Deeply divided Society: The Case of the 1990s Immigrants from the Former Soviet Union in Israel*, Leiden: Brill.

Aronin, L. (2012), 'Material culture of multilingualism and affectivity', *Studies in Second Language Learning and Teaching*, 2:2, 179–91.

Aronin, L. (2020), 'Dominant Language Constellation as an approach for studying multilingual practices', in J. Lo Bianco and L. Aronin (eds), *Dominant Language Constellations: A New Perspective on Multilingualism*, Cham: Springer, pp. 19–33.

Aronin, L., M. Hornsby and G. Kiliańska-Przybyło (eds) (2018), *Material Culture of Multilingualism*, Dordrecht: Springer.

Boyatzis, R. E. (1998), *Transforming Qualitative Information: Thematic Analysis and Code Development*, Thousand Oaks, CA: Sage.

Boym, S. (1995), 'From the Russian soul to post-communist nostalgia', *Representations*, 49, 133–66.

Braun, V. and V. Clarke (2019), 'Reflecting on reflexive thematic analysis', *Qualitative Research in Sport, Exercise and Health*, 11:4, 589–97.
Fialkova, L. and M. Yelenevskaya (2006), 'How to outsmart the system: immigrants' trickster stories', *Studia Mythologica Slavica*, 9, 279–96.
Fialkova, L. and M. Yelenevskaya (2007), *Ex-Soviets in Israel: From Personal Narratives to a Collective Portrait*, Detroit, MI: Wayne State University Press.
Fialkova, L. and M. Yelenevskaya (2013), *In Search of the Self: Reconciling the Past and the Present in Immigrants' Experience*, Tartu: ELM Scholarly Press.
Fialkova, L. and M. Yelenevskaya (2018), 'Evrei iz byvshego Sovetskogo Soiuza za rubezhom', in T. Emelianenko and E. Nosenko (eds), *Evrei. Seriia 'Narody i kul'tury'*, Moscow: Nauka, pp. 611–43.
Guest, G., K. M. MacQueen and E. E. Namey (2012), *Applied Thematic Analysis*, Thousand Oaks, CA: Sage Publications.
Hicks, D. and M. C. Beaudry (2010), 'Material culture studies: a reactionary view', in D. Hicks and M. C. Beaudry (eds), *The Oxford Handbook of Material Culture*, Oxford: Oxford University Press, pp. 1–24.
Hodder, I. (2012), 'The interpretation of documents and material culture', in J. Goodwin (ed.), *Sage Biographical Research. Volume 1, Biographical Research: Starting Points, Debates and Approaches*, Los Angeles: Sage, pp. 171–88.
Idov, M. (2018), 'Chto takoe veshchism i mogut li veshchi sdelat' nas schastlivymi', *GQ*, 17.07, at 1gq.ru/entertainment/hischnye-veschi
Keane, W. (2003), 'Semiotics and the social analysis of material things', *Language & Communication*, 23, 409–25.
Levin, I. (2014), 'Intersectionality in the migrant house: homes of migrants from the former Soviet Union in Metropolitan Tel Aviv, Israel', *Journal of Intercultural Studies*, 35:4, 421–41.
Liddicoat, A. J. (2011), *An Introduction to Conversation Analysis*, 2nd edn, New York: Continuum.
Lipshitz, G. (1997), 'Immigrants from the former Soviet Union in the Israeli housing market: spatial aspects of supply and demand', *Urban Studies*, 34:3, 471–88.
Mehta, R. and R. W. Belk (1991), 'Artifacts, identity and transition: favorite possessions of Indians and Indian immigrants to the United States', *Journal of Consumer Research*, 17:4, 398–411.
Miller, D. (1987), *Material Culture and Mass Consumption*, Oxford: Blackwell.
Miller, D. (2005), 'Materiality: Introduction,', in D. Miller (ed.), *Materiality*, Durham, NC: Duke University Press, pp. 1–50.
Miller, D. (2010), *Stuff*, Cambridge: Polity Press.
Mokienko, V. M. and T. G. Nikitina (1998), *Tolkovyi slovar' yazyka Sovdepii*, Saint Petersburg: Folio.
Olsen, B. (2003), 'Material culture after text', *Norwegian Archeological Review*, 36:2, 87–104.
Prior, M. T. (2016), 'Introduction. Contextualizing emotion in multilingual interaction: theoretical and methodological perspectives', in M. Prior and G. Kasper (eds), *Emotion in Multilingual Interaction*, Amsterdam: Benjamins, pp. 1–28.
Remennick, L. (2007), *Russian Jews on Three Continents: Identity, Integration and Conflict*, New Brunswick: Transaction.
Remennick, L. (ed) (2012), *Russian Israelis: Social Mobility, Politics and Culture*, Abingdon: Routledge.

Richmond, N. C. (1993), 'Israel's Law of Return: analysis of its evolution and present application', *Penn State International Law Review*, 12:1, 95–133.

Ryazantsev, S., Pismennaya, E., Lukyanets, A., Sivoplyasova, S. and Khramova, M. (2018), 'Modern emigration from Russia and formation of Russian-speaking communities abroad', *Mirovaia ekonomika i mezhdunarodnye otnoshenia*, 62:6, 93–107.

Schiffer, M. B. (1999), *The Material Life of Human Beings: Artifacts, Behavior and Communication*, Abingdon and New York: Routledge.

Swidler, A. (1986), 'Culture in action: symbols and strategies', *American Sociological Review*, 51:2, 273–86.

Tolia-Kelly, D. (2004), 'Locating processes of identification: studying the precipitates of re-memory through artifacts in the British Asian home', *Transactions of the Institute of British Geographers*, n.s. 29:3, 314–29.

Utekhin, I. (2004), *Ocherki kommunal'nogo byta*, Moscow: OGI.

Vogel, S. and Garcia, O. (2017), 'Translanguaging', in *Languages and Literacies. Oxford Research Encyclopedia of Education*. DOI: 10.1093/acrefore/9780190264093.013.181, <https://academicworks.cuny.edu/cgi/viewcontent.cgi?article=1448&context=gc_pubs>.

Zbenovich, C. (2016), 'Cross-cultural communication in Russian-speaking families in Israel: language practices of the second generation', *Russian Journal of Linguistics*, 20:3, 103–16.

CHAPTER 9

Russian-speaking Immigrant Women in Turkey: Histories of Moving 'Homes' and 'Homelands'

Liaisan Şahin

INTRODUCTION

Russian-speaking ex-Soviet immigrants constitute one of the most numerous immigrant communities in Turkey. According to the Turkish Statistical Institute, in 2019 the total number of foreign citizens living in Turkey with a residence permit was 1,531,180, and 258,588 out of this number were foreigners from the former Soviet countries (TÜİK 2019).[1] These numbers do not include foreigners having Turkish citizenship. According to TÜİK's Place of Birth Statistics, 531,430 citizens of the Turkish Republic were born in former Soviet countries (TÜİK 2020b).[2] Therefore, according to official statistics, the total number of Russian-speaking ex-Soviet immigrants in Turkey amounts to 790,018. It can be considered among the largest Russian-speaking immigrant communities in the world.

The most important feature of this community is the predominance of women. Turkey's case is a good illustration of the observed fact that migration movements have feminised with the intensification of globalisation processes. In Turkey, Russian-speaking immigration definitely has a female face. This has been mostly related to the so-called 'marriage migration', which remains the most important reason for Russian-speaking women's immigration to Turkey.

There is a long tradition of identifying the woman/mother with the house/home. Women are seen as the 'pivots of home' (Chapman 1999), as those who are responsible for its construction and representation. It is not simply the house itself which is coded as feminine, but also the realm of tradition, culture, community and nation are often understood as women's business (Morley 2000 in Bozkurt 2009: 69). Women are seen as 'ethnic actors' (Anthias 2000) who are responsible for preserving values, guarding traditions, transmitting the language to the young, and retaining/communicating nationhood and belongingness (Yuval-Davis 1997 in Bozkurt 2009: 69). However, conventional understandings of 'home' as a stable and fixed location have long been problematised. People's relationship with places has changed with growing mobility. Unfixed, plural and multi-referential understandings of home have emerged, especially in the context of migration and everyday practices of homemaking abroad (Bozkurt 2009: 31).

How do migrant women and in particular those who migrate because of marriage with a foreigner make their homes in an unfamiliar environment and how do they find their way between two value systems and between two different ethnic/cultural 'homes'? Do communication technologies help or hinder the onset of immigrants' feeling at home in the new country? This chapter attempts to deepen our understanding of migrant women's perceptions of 'home' and 'homeland' using Turkey as an example.

POST-SOVIET RUSSIAN-SPEAKING MIGRANTS TO TURKEY

The formation of the post-Soviet Russian-speaking immigrant community in Turkey began in the 1990s as a consequence of elimination of the Iron Curtain and the end of the Cold War, followed by the collapse of the USSR and the Eastern Bloc, and the concomitant globalisation processes in the world. Until the 1980s Turkey's experience of international migration was limited to Muslim refugees who arrived in Turkey from the Balkans, non-Muslim minorities leaving Turkey for other countries, and Turkish guest-workers in Europe. Relations with the countries of the Eastern Bloc were very limited (Erder 2000).

Since the early 1980s Turkey's position and role in international migration has changed dramatically. The Iranian Revolution, political turmoil in the Middle East, the end of the Cold War, the Gulf War, and Turkey's geographical location between the West and the rest have all resulted in flows of migrants to Turkey. The arrival of various migrant groups, such as refugees, asylum seekers, shuttle traders, and circular and transit migrants was an unexpected and challenging phenomenon for Turkish policymakers and researchers as well as for Turkish society as a whole (Erder and Kaşka 2012: 116; İçduygu and Keyman 2000).

The most striking change was the growth in the number of newcomers from the former Eastern Bloc countries. Relations between these countries and Turkey had been interrupted as a result of World War II. In the 1990s the situation changed drastically. The collapse of the existing socio-economic and political regimes in these countries was followed by a rapid transition to a market economy accompanied by unemployment and poverty which were major drivers of migration. Rigid migration regulations introduced by the EU countries made people look for other places where they could find jobs. Turkey with its liberal visa regime and a large informal labour market became a centre of attraction (Toksöz and Ünlütürk 2012: 85–6). More than five million arrivals from the former Soviet countries were reported in 2009, compared to only 4,500 in 1988 (Erder and Kaşka, 2012: 117).

The majority of the migrants from former Soviet countries were women seeking economic opportunities. They wanted to provide for their family and, most importantly, ensure the wellbeing of their children, covering their education costs. Most of these women found informal employment in the domestic and care services, the textile industry, and the trade and tourism sectors (Toksöz and Ünlütürk 2012). The so-called 'suitcase/luggage trade' was a very important aspect of the informal trade activities carried out by migrants from the former Eastern Bloc countries. It provided a significant foreign currency inflow to the Turkish economy throughout the 1990s and early 2000s. Later it lost its importance as the former socialist countries integrated into the world economy (Erder 2007: 49–55; Yükseker 2003).

Some migrant women from the ex-Soviet countries became engaged in the entertainment and commercial sex sectors which thrived in Turkey's large informal economy. Among these women were victims of human trafficking deceived by promises of employment in other sectors. Though the majority of migrant women were employed in other sectors, the entertainment and commercial sex industry attracted wider media coverage and drew public attention in Turkey's conservative, male-dominated society in which sexuality was a taboo. The sensational way in which the media publicised these women's lives and public interest in these issues led to the rise of prejudice. Women from the former Soviet countries were pervasively labelled as sex workers and stigmatised as 'Natashas' (Erder 2015: 266–7; Erder and Kaşka 2003; Gülcür and İlkkaracan 2002: 288–9). However, as time went on, Turkish society became less biased against migrant women from the ex-Soviet countries (Deniz and Özgür 2013).

In connection with this, it is important to consider the issue of mixed marriages. The difficulties as well as new opportunities of the transition period of the 1990s gave rise to 'marriage migration'. For many ex-Soviet women, marriage with a foreigner gave hope of a better life. Sociologists explained such marriages in terms of the economic, social and demographic difficulties as well as cultural characteristics of post-Soviet societies. They were identified as a new model of adaptation of the female population of the former Soviet countries to the changed conditions (Anashkina and Pogodina 2003).

Marriages between Turkish and ex-Soviet citizens have been on the increase since 1995. Apart from the growth in trade and other economic activities between Turkey and post-Soviet countries, there has been also a significant increase in tourist movements. Turkey, and particularly the city of Antalya, became a major destination for ex-Soviet tourists after the fall of the USSR. Travels and short-term work in the tourism sector eventually result in marriage for some women. Others meet their future husbands in their own countries, as many Turkish businessmen establish contacts and stay for extended periods in the former Soviet countries. Moreover, there have been other channels for international contacts resulting in mixed marriages, such as studying abroad, scientific exchange trips, international cultural events, and so on. Judging by the number of mixed marriages in Turkey, from a rarity they are turning into a cultural tradition and are gaining social acceptance.[3] An important sociological aspect of these mixed marriages is that the children experience a dual lifestyle from birth. When they reach adulthood, they are likely to influence Turkish social and cultural life significantly just as their mothers have influenced it so far (Deniz and Özgür 2012).

RESEARCH ON RUSSIAN-SPEAKING MIGRANTS IN TURKEY

The literature on post-Soviet migration to Turkey mostly focuses on 'irregular' migrants. Many studies cover ex-Soviet migrant women employed in domestic and care services and provide detailed information as to their social and working conditions (Erder and Kaşka 2012; Toksöz and Ünlütürk 2012). Studies on irregular migrants are mostly limited to Istanbul.

Migrants with a legal permission to stay and/or work in Turkey make up a small part of all migrants and can be defined as a 'special' group. Studies on Russian-speaking immigrants permanently residing in Turkey are few. So far, most research projects have concentrated on citizens of the Russian Federation, especially ethnic Russians, and on Antalya as the dynamically developing centre of the Russian-speaking community (see, e.g., Deniz and Özgür 2010, 2013 and 2020). A study by Antonova-Ünlü et al. (2015) deals with the language attitudes of Russian immigrants. The study reveals that Russian immigrants are well integrated into the Turkish culture and at the same time retain Russian cultural characteristics. They are bilinguals who use Russian and Turkish languages depending on the communication context. In a recent study, Uçar-İlbuğa (2020) briefly discusses the linguistic situation, professional and social life, reasons for migration, and prospects for the future of Russian-speaking women of various ethnic origins in Antalya.

Further research and more qualitative and comparative studies on the Russian-speaking immigrant community in Turkey are needed. In particular, its ethnic/cultural diversity and implications of this diversity have not been yet adequately addressed. With its mosaic but predominantly Muslim and Turkic culture, and somewhat suspended position between Eastern and Western civilisations, Turkey is a rather peculiar host country for ex-Soviet – and mostly female – immigrants. Since the early 1990s Turkey has been an important centre of attraction especially for migrants of Turkic origins and/or Muslim faith. As my own long immigration experience in Turkey and observations during the past years have convinced me, the ethnic factor plays a very important role in cultural adaptation processes in Turkey. Although different ex-Soviet immigrant groups share the same socio-psychological background and show many important similarities in their mindset and behavioural patterns, there are also many issues in respect of which immigrants of different ethnic origins assume quite different attitudes. There are dissimilarities in adaptation patterns and strategies not only between ethnic Russians versus non-Russians but also between different Turkic people (e.g. Tatar versus Azerbaijani). Immigrants from the same country can feel and behave very differently due to the peculiarities of their native languages and ethnic cultures and the degree of closeness of their languages and compatibility of cultures to the host Turkish language and culture.

RESEARCH METHODS AND CHARACTERISTICS OF RESPONDENTS

This chapter is based on initial findings of my ongoing research on the intercultural adaptation experience of Russian-speaking immigrant women of various ethnic origins who have come to Turkey from various ex-Soviet countries, mostly because of marriage with Turkish men or for some other reasons (educational or labour migration).[4]

To collect initial data, I used a questionnaire. I distributed it among my close immigrant friends and asked them to direct me to their own friends who might want to participate in my project. This questionnaire provided me with additional information on my respondents and on the history of their immigration. This made it possible to compare different cases; moreover, it helped me create an interview guide for in-depth interviews which allowed my respondents to talk freely and offer their interpretation of events (Kümbetoğlu 2017; Marsh and Stoker 2002).

Twelve women were interviewed: five Russians, five Kazan Tatars and two Azerbaijanis. All interviews were held via Zoom in December 2020 and January 2021. The interviews were recorded and transcribed. The interviewees were free to choose their preferred language: Tatar, Russian or Turkish. During the conversation we frequently switched from language to language and sometimes translanguaged.[5]

Eight participants live in Istanbul, the rest in various cities of Anatolia; 75 per cent of the participants have Turkish citizenship; 75 per cent are employed. Eight women are married (two with co-nationals), three are divorced and one woman is widowed. Eight women have one child, two have two children and two have no children. The mean age of participants is 47; 50 per cent of the interviewees are aged between 51 and 55. The mean age of arrival in Turkey is 30, and the average length of permanent residence is 16 years. All participants have university BA or graduate degrees. The majority of the participants (75 per cent) defined their knowledge of the Turkish language as either 'excellent' or 'good'.

POSITIVELY AND NEGATIVELY ASSESSED ASPECTS OF LIFE IN TURKEY: THROUGH IMMIGRANT EYES

The majority of my respondents expressed high level of satisfaction with their life in Turkey: 'everything is perfect' (four women), 'in general, I am content' (five women). Two stated that their conditions could be better, and only one woman with the shortest immigration experience (six years) expressed her desire to move to another country. On closer examination, I could see, as might be expected, that those women who did not speak Turkish well had no job and no close Turkish friends. They rated their satisfaction with life much more lowly than the women who had jobs, a good command of the language, and an active social life in interaction with a wide circle of Turkish friends and acquaintances.

Among the factors that negatively affect the quality of life in Turkey, the respondents most often named deficiencies in the Turkish educational and cultural infrastructure. For example, the interviewees complained of the low educational level of the majority of the population and the scarcity of sports and cultural leisure opportunities, compared to what they were accustomed to in their native countries.

Among the positive aspects of life in Turkey the respondents name such factors as the natural beauty, good weather, rich cultural environment, better economic opportunities and high job satisfaction. But the most important positive factor, which was mentioned by all respondents without exception, was the friendliness of the Turkish people. The well-being of migrants strongly depends on the socio-psychological atmosphere of the host country and on the attitude of the natives towards foreigners. All my respondents described socio-psychological conditions in Turkey as quite favourable in this regard. Even those interviewees who were not very happy with their life in Turkey agreed that in general the Turkish people have been exceptionally friendly and helpful. Two respondents noted that, even if sometimes they were treated unfairly, it happened rarely and was usually limited to attempts to cheat them as customers.

One of the respondents made special emphasis on the positive atmosphere at her workplace:

1. **Revana (from Baku, Azerbaijan, 50-plus):** I am comfortable here. I'm on good terms with everyone and everyone treats me in the same way. At any moment I can ask for assistance, and everyone will help me. And that's why I feel like a human being in the workplace, you know. I didn't feel that in my country. Every minute the bosses could come and humiliate you.[6]

Another respondent says that she is treated in the same way as native Turks by Turkish government institutions, even if public servants are aware that she is a foreigner and even if she does not speak Turkish well:

2. **Inna (from Krasnodar, 40-plus):** I don't like government institutions, the bureaucratic machine. When I go there, I'm afraid to speak Russian, let alone Turkish. But here [in Turkey], even if you falter, they [public servants] are okay with it. It sometimes happens that they behave horribly. But it has nothing to do with you: they treat everyone like that. Mostly they are helpful, and you feel as though you are a citizen [Inna does not have Turkish citizenship]. They are always accessible. They explain everything to you. If you don't understand, they explain it to you one more time. In principle, it makes no difference to them whether you are a [Turkish] citizen or not, especially if you know a little Turkish and can make yourself understood.

Respondents note that Turkish people treat their nationality with respect: 'Russians are respected. They consider us smart'; 'They know about famous Tatar personalities and speak about them with respect'; 'When they find out that I am Azerbaijani, they treat me with special warmth, and try to help and take care of me.' It emerged in the interviews that immigrants of Turkic origins feel themselves more favoured by Turkish people compared to people of other ethnicities. Azerbaijani respondents, in particular, emphasised the special welcome Turkish people give them due to the linguistic and cultural similarities between them. Here are some excerpts illustrating these attitudes:

3. **Interviewer:** You say you feel comfortable in Turkey.

   Revana (from Baku, 50-plus): I feel comfortable because, first of all, there is no language problem. Azerbaijani Turkish and Turkey's Turkish are 80 per cent the same. Just some of the words that we use are not used in Turkey. But they know these words and can understand us. They know immediately that we are Azerbaijani. They ask right away: You are *Azeri* [Turkish for 'Azerbaijani']? When they find out that we are from Azerbaijan, joy appears on their faces. We feel mutual friendliness, you know, pleasant feelings. [. . .] For me, there is no difference between Turks from Turkey and Turks from Azerbaijan. We are one nation and two countries.

4. **Tuba (from Baku, 50-plus):** I never felt like a stranger [in Turkey]. Well, never. Maybe because there was no language barrier. [. . .] I lived in Russia for a long time. When I arrived in Turkey I remembered that it was much more difficult for me in Russia, because Azerbaijani and Turkish mentalities, they are very similar. And the Russian mentality is unusual for us. It is not traditional for us. If you do not take into account the regions where Turkic-speaking peoples live [. . .] I immediately got used to life in Turkey. All [Turkish] traditions are very similar to Azerbaijani ones.

Ten out of the twelve respondents answered the question whether they felt themselves to be full members of Turkish society in the affirmative. Notably one of those was a woman who does not have Turkish citizenship. She said that, despite the lack of the right to participate in the political life of the country, she feels she is a true member of society, because she has an opportunity to express her will and actively participate in the niche where her life unfolds (*vozmozhnost' na voleiz"iavlenie i aktivnoe uchastie v iacheike zhizni*).

5. **Marina (from Moscow, 40-plus):** Well, I found some ways to pursue my interests, to somehow participate, not just stay at home. I already feel that I can, yes. [I] can cooperate. For example, I arranged things with Kadıköy Belediyesi Çocuk Sanat Merkezi [Kadıköy City Hall Children's Art Center]. We had a musical group. In general, I realised that I could function. [I] carry out some kinds of activity.

    Interviewer: You interact with Turkish government organisations, and you feel like a member of this society through this interaction?

    Marina: Yes, yes.

FEELINGS AND THOUGHTS ABOUT 'HOME' AND 'HOMELAND'

For the majority of respondents, the concept of 'home' is, above all, associated with family, especially with children, and in a broader sense with relationships with loved ones. For some, their family circle includes not only relatives but also close friends, and even pets.

6. **Sofia (from Bishkek, Kyrgyzstan, 40-plus):** My 'home' is where my family is! Before moving to Turkey, it was my parents' home. For the last twenty years, my 'home' has been my family: my son and my husband.

7. **Tuba:** For a house to become a real home for me, there must be animals there. When I got a dog, I realised that everything was OK; this is my home.

The second most frequently mentioned dimension of the concept of 'home' is that it is a place of residence. Respondents expressed this in such phrases as 'my apartment', 'a place where my family lives', 'a place where your family resides and where you are always welcome', 'a place where there are things that I have chosen and bought' and 'my personal space'.

Some respondents – especially those who do not feel completely satisfied with life in Turkey and used to miss their homeland badly – indicated that the spatial dimension of their 'home' changed after their moving to Turkey and became at once narrower and wider. This change also has temporal connotations and is strongly related to the perception of and feelings towards the homeland.

8. **Rasima (from Kazan, Tatarstan, 50-plus):** Before moving to Turkey, 'home' for me meant only my apartment. After moving abroad, its meaning expanded. It now includes my home village in Tatarstan, the city of Kazan, where I lived for twenty years, and my friends and relatives. 'Home' in the homeland includes my childhood near parents, my youth, my student years, my ten years of work at the university, theatres, museums, and my friends with whom I sat at the same table at feasts. Most of these values are irretrievably lost, left in the past. I remember them with longing. 'Home' in Turkey includes my family, my child, my work, my students and my son's future, that is, my present and my dreams and plans for the future. Images of 'home' in both countries are equally dear to me.

9. **Leila (from Kazan, Tatarstan, 50-plus):** My 'home' here is the space of my apartment. Before moving to Turkey, the 'home' was much larger. It included my relatives, my city, my school, my classmates, my teachers. [. . .] There in Kazan you are at home probably when . . . when you are around your mum, when you remember that you were once a little girl . . . Old memories are what 'being at home' is all about. In Tatarstan, the past is 'being at home'. And here [in Turkey] we have the present.

Respondents have different feelings about their homelands. For some, their 'abandoned' homelands are certainly dearer than the country of residence, and their remoteness from the homeland is still acutely felt. This motif emerges when they talk about spaces beyond their apartments or houses:

10. **Marina:** It feels completely different in Moscow: ['Home' is] the familiar streets of the old city, the fragrance of spring, the smell of the subway, museums, parks, relatives and friends.

11. **Rasima:** The Internet is not sufficient to relieve homesickness. Completely insufficient, because you can't breathe the air of [your homeland] or do other things. When the plane lands at the airport in Kazan and I go outside . . . It's always cool there . . . You breathe in the air and it's different, yes.

Other respondents speak about their countries of origin with calm or even indifference:

12. **Inna:** To say that Russia is my home... Well, I don't know. It is more my historic home.

13. **Tuba:** Azerbaijan falls outside this concept. It's my birthland, but it's not my 'home'.

Some respondents deliberately avoid using 'homeland' when talking about the country where they were born but apply it when talking about the country of their ethnic belonging:

14. **Revana:** I do not consider Armenia my homeland, although I was born and lived there until the age of eighteen. They ask me [about my homeland], but I don't want to name Armenia. My roots are very mixed, but of course I call Azerbaijan [my homeland].

15. **Sofia:** Since I was born in Bishkek, I have never had Russian citizenship. I used to have Kyrgyz citizenship and now I have Turkish. And for me, every trip to Russia is just a mockery of me, an ethnic Russian, because each time I need to get a visa. [...] For me, Russia is really not an empty word and I always think of it as my homeland. Bishkek does not evoke such feelings. Well, yes, I was born there. My mother is there. But I have never considered it an option to go back to Bishkek. But I would probably consider Russia as an option.

On closer examination, it becomes clear that attitudes towards the homeland and Turkey depend on many factors such as satisfaction with a job, patterns of daily life, family wellbeing, social relations, one's husband's support, life experience in the homeland, features of ethnic culture, proficiency level in Turkish and some other factors. As can be expected, the higher the respondents' level of satisfaction with themselves and their lives, and the closer their ties with Turkish society, the more they feel comfortable in relation to both their homeland and Turkey, and the less they suffer from nostalgia.

Some respondents indicated that over time they had become emotionally distant from the country of origin. The death of their parents or their parents' moving to take up permanent residence in Turkey, dissatisfaction with developments in the country of origin, ageing, and increasing adaptation to Turkey were mentioned most often. The growing up of children, conversion to Islam and growing interest in Turkish culture and art were also mentioned among factors that spiritually alienate immigrants from their country of origin.

16. Leila: Oddly enough, I feel more 'at home' in Turkey, despite some limitation in the concept of 'my home' here. I don't feel 'at home' in Russia. Time and a different way of life have alienated me. [. . .] I feel like a tourist or something there. As if I am a guest of some kind. I don't belong there . . . Sometimes you feel disappointed. Not with the country, but because you are already a stranger there.

A sense of distance and alienation from the homeland is felt differently by respondents and produces different reactions. Those respondents who experience this feeling without an acute sense of nostalgia and show more satisfaction with their life in Turkey tend to feel either equally 'at home' in both countries or become more attached to Turkey:

17. Albina (from Kazan, Tatarstan/Russian Federation, 40-plus): I fully associate myself with Turkey.

18. Jamila (from Archa, Tatarstan/Russian Federation 50-plus): I have no plans to move somewhere, to leave this country, because I have already transferred the concept of the homeland to Turkey.

19. Elena (from Mytishchi, Moscow Region, 50-plus): I feel 'at home' both in Turkey and in Russia. There is no difference at all.

20. Inna: Home is where you feel comfortable. As long as I am comfortable in Turkey, my home is here.

For those who are not sure about their future, estrangement from their homeland and getting used to Turkey have created an unpleasant feeling of being in limbo:

21. Pavlina (from Saratov, 20-plus): I have very complex feelings of being 'somewhere in between'.

22. Leila: Our situation is very interesting. We are not Turks here. But even at home we are already strangers. This is an uncertain state.

Those respondents who have experienced strong nostalgia over many years find comfort in the thought that after retirement they will live alternately in the two countries. For some of them, these plans are also accompanied by a desire to be buried in their homeland, namely in the cemetery of their home village, near the graves of their parents and ancestors. This desire can be interpreted as longing for an opportunity to eventually return home to the family of their childhood time, at least after death:

> 23. Leila: Still, the roots are there [in Tatarstan]. When my mother and I go to the cemetery, we walk among the graves; we remember those who lie there. If you lie there, someone will remember you. And here [in Turkey] you will be . . . Well, just a fence. A stone. The children will only remember. And how often?

The following discursive features of the interviews are worth mentioning. Speaking about their ties with their homeland, trips to their homeland, and communication with loved ones living in the homeland, many respondents used the words *ėnergiia* (energy), *pishcha* (food), *ruchi azyk* (Tatar: spiritual food), and the expressions *pitat'sia informatsiei* (to feed on information), *dukhovno napitat'sia* (to spiritually nourish oneself), *vpikhivat' v detei informatsiiu o kul'ture* (to stuff children with cultural information), *vziat' ėnergetiku* (to draw energy), *ėnergeticheski pobyt' s rodstvennikami* (to share energy with relatives), *üzeñne kabattan tugan iak ėnergiiäse belän tutyru* (Tatar: to recharge oneself with the energy of the homeland). Judging by these statements, the homeland, co-ethnics and native culture are viewed as an important source of spiritual energy and strength for my respondents.

COMMENTS ON ONLINE COMMUNICATION

All respondents noted with appreciation that communication technologies have greatly facilitated contacts with people in their homelands, and that these contacts have become very close. Those respondents, who had moved to Turkey before the advent of the Internet and new communication technologies, emphasised that staying in touch had become inexpensive. These daily contacts have contributed to their adaptation process and emotional wellbeing:

> 24. Elena: I remember we installed the antenna and when I began to watch Russian channels, it seemed that [the nostalgia]

somehow began to ease. Now we are constantly on Skype. So now you don't feel it at all. As if there were no borders. [...] It has become easier to communicate and identify with both Turkey and Russia.

25. **Marina:** I cannot even imagine how we lived without it. Without a telephone, and now video is here too. The feeling you are having breakfast with your family is quite real. You switch it on and here is tea, and here is coffee. And you are having breakfast. And it's like you had breakfast with your relatives. Only you cannot hug.

The immediacy of communication, the flow of daily information about their loved ones and the opportunity to see them on screen brings homeland and loved ones closer to the interviewees ('no boundaries', 'no sense of distance'). Some participants even said that the communication technologies had made it unnecessary for them to travel to their home countries frequently. However, some respondents emphasised that online communication is by no means a substitute for live communication: 'You can't breathe the air of [your homeland]', 'There is no exchange of energy.' In their opinion, online communication differs greatly from old modes. Even though one participant spoke about online contacts in a positive light ('Communication has moved to the plane of the spiritual, and it has become more concentrated'), others stressed shortcomings ('No deep meaning is invested; it comes down to a daily exchange of routine greetings').

26. **Marina:** My mum and dad cannot spend time with their grandchildren and pass on their experience. I would very much like their knowledge and experience to be passed on [to my children] in close proximity, on a daily basis. When this is done via online communication, just 'Mum, hi! What's up?'... It is very different from being together and doing something together.

Considering this, we cannot conclude that communication technologies have unequivocally improved the psychological wellbeing of migrants. On the contrary, sometimes such technologies can aggravate homesickness, making them feel even more strongly that they remain outside the life of their homeland:

27. **Rasima:** Holidays, events in Tatarstan are transmitted via Instagram. I can't take part in those events. They slip away

before my eyes and I cannot take part in them. And my child misses them too. It upsets me. I want my child to grow up participating in these activities. My mom had her eightieth birthday. Our relatives came and congratulated her. That feeling that I was not there . . .

28. **Anisa (from Chally, Tatarstan/Russian Federation, 50-plus):** You know, you're kind of robotising yourself. A neighbour from our [home] village sends me photos and videos of our village every day. I then want to walk through our village. [. . .] You try to stop these feelings. Of course, you miss [your homeland], but you control yourself, putting up some kind of a wall, because if you don't put it up . . . You have to live.

PERCEPTIONS OF DOMESTIC SPACE AND MEANINGS OF 'BEING AT HOME'

When I focused on my interviewees' perceptions of their domestic space, I noticed that, to call a space their 'home', it was important for all my respondents to feel completely free and active in transforming it. Some expressed it indirectly, but others were more explicit:

29. **Jamila:** Everything in my house should please me and be a reflection of myself.

30. **Pavlina:** Home for me is a place where there are things that I have chosen and bought, a place where I put my energy, arranging dishes, laying out pillows, etc. If I move into an apartment that someone else has furnished, I won't feel at home there. It's important for me to do it myself . . . I can say it this way: for me, the house is not the walls, but the pictures on these walls.

31. **Elena:** To be 'at home'? Well, it is to feel satisfaction and peace. [It is to be inside] home walls. [It also means] you can do whatever you like in the house.

Note how one respondent emphasised the active attitude as the most important element of the concept of 'being at home':

32. **Leila:** Now we know everything here [in Turkey]. We are active and in the frame [*v dele*], and we are really at home here.

Figure 9.1 Ethnic items used in kitchens for practical and decorative purposes.

According to their active attitude to the home space, some women emphasise minimalism and practicality and seek to reduce their possessions, while others attach importance to the material elements of their home such as indoor plants, books and paintings. As for items with ethnic and cultural content, it turns out that, although most of my interviewees have such artefacts, they attach different meanings to them. Some artefacts are valued for their practicality, for example kitchen gadgets. Two interviewees – teachers – like to use cultural souvenirs as visual aids in the classroom. Some cultural objects are valuable only as gifts from other people. One respondent put it with humour:

33. Sofia: I have matryoshka dolls, spoons and . . . I didn't even buy them myself, they are gifts. Apparently, they [those who gave them] thought that I was like . . . Russian in a foreign land and I could not do without matryoshkas here.

Figure 9.2 Some cultural artefacts are used purely for decoration (amber panel pictures, painted trays, etc.). Some are used as visual aids in teaching Russian or Tatar languages (matryoshkas, souvenir dolls and other ethnic items). A photograph of the owner's home village is an object endowed with an emotional meaning.

Only a few participants attach particular emotional significance to ethnic or cultural souvenirs and use them to emphasise their ethnic and cultural identity. This function is carried out by flags, albums, books, magazines, photographs, paintings, calendars, ethnic handicrafts, decorative dishes, figurines, dolls, tea sets and refrigerator magnets. Small souvenirs brought from the homeland as gifts for friends are meant to be tokens of appreciation but also serve as ethnic self-representation:

34. **Leila:** I gave these Tatar embroidered boots [magnets] to everyone here. This [object] seems to represent me. I am a representative of Tatarstan, a Tatar woman, I brought you

Figure 9.3 Items displayed in the workplace and at home for the purpose of ethnic representation: flags, albums, books, magazines, paintings, photographs, decorative dishes, ethnic handicrafts and tea sets.

this. I tell them a little about us, what kind of embroidery we have, and what kind of sweets. Well, along with the gift, you also give them some information.

There are also ethnic accessories used in everyday life such as earrings, shawls, brooches and bags. It is interesting to note that the respondent who spoke ironically about matryoshka dolls was quite enthusiastic about ethnic accessories, that is items that one can wear.

35. Sofia: I have a few Pavlovo Posad shawls. These are my pride. That is, they are not only a beautiful accessory. When I wear such a shawl, I just feel like . . . I carry it with pride. I have a pair of brooches, Khokhloma, etc. This is such an element

for me . . . It is meant to let me stand out from the crowd and show that I'm Russian. That is, for me, these accessories are meaningful. I proudly carry my Russianness.

Two respondents stated that it was not as important for them to decorate their apartments or themselves with artefacts from home as to 'keep in touch with the homeland through actions': cooking ethnic dishes, celebrating traditional holidays, familiarising children with important events and dates, and so on.

As we see, respondents' definitions of the concept of 'home' and 'homeland', and their attitudes towards these concepts, strikingly differ from one another. Immigrants' interaction with both the material and immaterial worlds around them reflects the differences of their personalities, the nature of their connection with their homeland, their past and present. It is also important to emphasise that the ability to freely and independently transform one's life and surroundings emerges as the most important element of the concept of 'being at home'.

CONCLUSION

Researchers of international migration and cultural diasporas have long paid attention to the considerable heterogeneity found in the personality of each migrant and refugee, let alone within any diasporic group. Back in the early 2000s a group of researchers emphasised that:

> it is not only transnational fields and practices, but also particular living conditions before and after migration in the country of origin and residence, which impact on migrants' articulations of 'home'. Moreover, 'homes' are gendered spaces, inhabited by people of various social classes, different generations and political orientations. People with diverse experiences of previous and current homes and the movements between them identify with their homes in different ways. Accordingly, conceptions of home tend to vary even within one specific group of refugees or migrants at any given point of time. (Al-Ali and Koser 2002: 6)

I think my findings support these words. The group of women I have studied is a circle of my close friends and acquaintances, and it may be said that this is a fairly homogeneous group in terms of educational level, mindset and professional characteristics, but even in such a group of people, a wide range of opinions on all issues can be observed. Each woman has her own unique experience of migration and her own unique emotional and intellectual reaction to it. Moreover, as we can see, each individual and his/her ideas about himself/herself and the world also change over time. Therefore, all of us are constantly engaged in 'the acts of imagining, creating, unmaking, changing, losing and moving "homes"' (Al-Ali and Koser 2002: 6). It is important to understand the meaning of 'home' in the context of a given person's life, in a complex network of interacting factors and through a person's desire and ability to actively transform his/her life and surroundings.

NOTES

1 68,515 are from Azerbaijan, 44,906 from Uzbekistan, 40,201 from the Russian Federation, 23,541 from Kyrgyzstan, 22,096 from Georgia, 21,151 from Kazakhstan, 20,228 from Ukraine, 8,070 from Moldova, 4,652 from Tajikistan, 2,501 from Belarus, 1,760 from Armenia, 545 from Lithuania, 251 from Latvia and 171 from Estonia.
2 136,881 were born in Turkmenistan, 97,847 in Azerbaijan, 77,968 in Uzbekistan, 56,974 in the Russian Federation, 36,216 in Kazakhstan, 32,689 in Kyrgyzstan, 29,793 in Ukraine, 29,285 in Georgia, 14,860 in Moldova, 5,514 in Tajikistan, 4,294 in the USSR, 4203 in Belarus, 3,495 in Armenia, 702 in Lithuania, 443 in Latvia and 266 in Estonia.
3 According to the Turkish Statistical Institute, in 2019 the total number of international marriages between Turkish men and foreign brides was 23,744. Marriages with brides from the former Soviet countries constituted nearly half of this number (10,114) (TÜİK 2020a).
4 In my study, I intend to consider various aspects of the women's experience: migration histories, language issues, ethnic identity perceptions, family life, children's upbringing, educational life, professional life, social life, etc. I am very grateful to researchers of the Department of Sociology of Marmara University in Istanbul for their continued methodological support and guidance. All shortcomings of this study are mine.
5 I have noticed that some Turkish researchers have pointed out language difficulties in their contacts with Russian-speaking women. These researchers talked to the women in Turkish or through intermediaries. They noted that, although the women defined their knowledge of Turkish as good, they had difficulties in expressing themselves in Turkish (Uçar-İlbuğa 2020). In this regard, I would like to note that my knowledge of all languages spoken by my respondents eliminated any difficulties of the linguistic nature and allowed my respondents to freely express their thoughts and feelings, switching from language to language if necessary. Moreover, because I am an immigrant myself and their fellow countrywoman, and for some of them also a fellow national, the interviews were conducted in an atmosphere of mutual understanding, which facilitated our conversation and helped my interviewees feel at ease.
6 The names of participants have been changed.

REFERENCES

Al-Ali, N. and K. Koser (2002), *New Approaches to Migration? Transnational Communities and the Transformation of Home*, London and New York: Routledge.
Anashkina, G. and S. Pogodina (2003), 'Brak s inostrantsem kak novaia model' adaptatsii rossiiskikh zhenshchin v usloviyakh perekhodnogo perioda', *Etnozhurnal*, available at: <ethnonet.ru/etnografiya/brak-s-inostrancem-kak-novaja-model-adaptacii/> (last accessed 15 November 2022).
Anthias, F. (2000), 'Metaphors of home: gendering new migrations to southern Europe', in F. Anthias and G. Lazaridis (eds), *Gender and Migration in Southern Europe: Women on the Move*, Oxford: Berg, pp. 15–47.
Antonova-Ünlü, E., Ç. Sağin-Şimşek, E. Ateşman and A. Lozovska (2015), 'Russian immigrant diaspora in Turkey: language use, preference and attitudes', *Turkish Studies*, 16:3, 391–410.
Bozkurt, E. (2009), *Conceptualizing 'Home': The Question of Belonging among Turkish Families in Germany*, Chicago: University of Chicago Press.
Chapman, T. (1999), 'Spoiled home identities: the experience of Burglary', in T. Chapman and J. Hockey (eds), *Ideal Homes? Social Change and Domestic Life*, London and New York: Routledge, pp. 133–46.
Deniz, A. and E. M. Özgür (2010), 'Rusya'dan Türkiye'ye Ulusaşırı Göç: Antalya'daki Rus Göçmenler', *Ege Coğrafya Dergisi*, 19:1, 13–30.
Deniz, A. and E. M. Özgür (2013), 'Antalya'daki Rus Gelinler: Göçten Evliliğe, Evlilikten Göçe', *Sosyoloji Dergisi*, 2:27, 151–75.
Deniz, A. and E. M. Özgür (2020), 'Mixed marriage and transnational marriage migration in the grip of political economy: Russian–Turkish case', *Turkish Studies*, 22:3, 437–61.
Erder, S. (2000), 'Uluslararası Göçte Yeni Eğilimler: Türkiye Göç Alan Ülke Mi?', in F. Atacan, F. Ercan, H. Kurtuluş and M. Türkay (eds), *Mübeccel Kıray İçin Yazılar*, Istanbul: Bağlam, pp. 235–59.
Erder, S. (2007), 'Yabancısız Kurgulanan Ülkenin Yabancıları', in A. Arı (ed.), *Türkiye'de Yabancı İşçi*, Istanbul: Derin Yayınları, pp. 49–55.
Erder, S. (2015), *İstanbul bir Kervansaray (mı?)*, Istanbul: İstanbul Bilgi Üniversitesi Yayınları.
Erder, S. and S. Kaşka (2003), *Irregular Migration and Trafficking in Women: The Case of Turkey*, Geneva: IOM.
Erder, S. and S. Kaşka (2012), 'Turkey in the new migration era: migrants between regularity and irregularity', in S. Paçacı Elitok and T. Straubhaar (eds), *Turkey, Migration and the EU: Potentials, Challenges and Opportunities*, Hamburg: Hamburg University Press, pp. 113–32.
Gülçür, L. and P. İlkkaracan (2002), 'The "Natasha" experience: migrant sex workers from the former Soviet Union and Eastern Europe in Turkey', *Women's Studies International Forum*, 25:4, 411–21.
İçduygu, A. and E. F. Keyman (2000), 'Globalization, security, and migration: the case of Turkey', *Global Governance*, 6, 383–98.
Kümbetoğlu, B. (2017), *Sosyolojide ve Antropolojide Niteliksel Yöntem ve Araştırma*, Istanbul: Bağlam.
Marsh, D. and G. Stoker (eds) (2002), *Theory and Methods in Political Science*, New York: Palgrave Macmillan.
Toksöz, G., and Ç. Ünlütürk Ulutaş (2012), 'Is migration feminized? A gender

and ethnicity based review of the literature on irregular migration to Turkey', in T. Straubhaar and S. Elitok (eds), *Turkey, Migration and the EU: Potential, Challenges and Opportunities*, Hamburg: Hamburg University Press, pp. 85–112.

TÜİK (2019), 'Türkiye'de İkamet Etmeye Başladığı Yıla, Cinsiyete ve Vatandaşlık Ülkesine göre Yabancı Uyruklu Nüfus, 2019', available at: <data.tuik.gov.tr/Kategori/GetKategori?p=nufus-ve-demografi-109&dil=1> (last accessed 15 November 2022).

TÜİK (2020a), 'Erkek ve Kadının Uyruğuna Göre Evlenmeler, 2009–2020', available at <data.tuik.gov.tr/Kategori/GetKategori?p=nufus-ve-demografi-109&dil=1> (last accessed 15 November 2022).

TÜİK (2020b), 'Yurtdışında Doğanların Doğum Yeri ve Cinsiyete Göre Dağılımı, 2014–2020', at <data.tuik.gov.tr/Kategori/GetKategori?p=nufus-ve-demografi-109&dil=1> (last accessed 15 November 2022).

Uçar-İlbuğa, E. (2020), 'Antalya'da Göçün Dişil Yüzü ve Göçmenlik Halleri', in Y. Ahi, M. N. Gültekin and M. Açıkgöz (eds), *Göç ve Kent: Etkileşimler*, Ankara: Nika.

Yükseker, D. (2003), *Laleli Moskova Mekiği*, Istanbul: İletişim Yayınları.

CHAPTER 10

A Journey to a New Home: Language, Identity and Material Culture

Larissa Aronin

INTRODUCTION

The contemporary meaning of 'home' implies a mixture of connotations that together make it a particularly multi-layered concept. 'Home' embraces the ideas of privacy, stability, safety, solid materiality and personal distinctiveness as well as group belonging linked to ethnicity and nationality. It also subtly implies the physical, mental and emotional journey that one undertakes to obtain home or to claim a cosmopolitan stance. No wonder that home has been studied from a variety of angles and by a range of disciplines. As a tangible physical thing, a building or an apartment with its particular configuration and arrangement of material contents, home usually complies with the conceptions of a particular society and period of time as to what is good and proper for a home. From such a perspective, home embodies the previous and the current values held by its dwellers reified through material things. From another perspective, home is treated as a unique spacetime where traditions can be kept no matter how far in time and space their origins are. A place where one 'feels at home' denotes, among other things, a territory where one is able to act in correspondence with one's feelings, ideas and beliefs. In the context of emigration such an opportunity becomes vital. These conceptualisations do not exhaust all the aspects from which home is investigated and viewed.

The 'diversification of diversity' is defined by the sociologist Steven Vertovec as a phenomenon that 'has not just occurred in terms of movements of people reflecting more ethnicities, languages and countries of origin, but also with respect to a multiplication of significant variables that affect where, how and with whom people live' (2014: 86–7). The current patterns of mobility that allow either for settling in another place permanently or commuting between places, together with technological advances, have caused significant transformation of language practices across the globe (Aronin 2019b). Global transformations have changed our possibilities and our thinking about what a proper home should be. Such changes in real life have led to an interdisciplinarity of research fuelled by the interconnectedness of various aspects of human life. 'Mind and matter no longer appear to belong to two separate categories, but can be seen as representing two complementary aspects of the phenomenon of life – process and structure' (Capra 2015: 246).

This chapter emphasises the superdiversity and interconnectedness of all the aspects of home, and, most importantly, materialities and language. It is only in the interrelation of many factors that we can identify the trends, tendencies and patterns of homemaking of Russian-speaking immigrants. In this chapter I ask the following questions:

1. How does the material culture of home differ from the materialities in public spaces?
2. What are the particularities, if any, of homemaking for Russian-speaking immigrants?

To this end, in this chapter, I briefly review the theoretical underpinnings of the current concept of home. Then I present the material culture of the multilingualism approach as that which best fits the contemporary complex concept of 'home' and propose it as a distinct branch of the multilingual materialities of home (MMH). Two further sections of this chapter identify the main characteristics of the multilingual material culture of home and the MMH of the Russian-speaking immigrants as described in the contributions to this volume.

THEORETICAL UNDERPINNINGS OF THE CURRENT CONCEPT OF HOME

The contributions to this volume adopt a multi-focal perspective of home relying on semiotics, social analysis, ethnography and cultural geography as well as cultural and linguistic anthropology. The view of the contemporary human condition as formed by social and behavioural sciences is crucial for understanding home, homemaking and homecoming. This section is devoted to an overview of some recent multidisciplinary theoretical frameworks that enhance the understanding of home as a multimodal and superdiverse phenomenon. These are (1) the active externalism perspective; (2) the notion/view of co-dependency between mind, action and matter; and (3) the Dominant Language Constellations (DLC) framework.

Active externalism

The perspective known in philosophy as active externalism holds that our environment has an active role in driving cognitive processes. In their article titled 'Where does the mind stop, and the rest of the world begin?' Clark and Chalmers (1998: 11) pointed to 'the general tendency of human reasoners to lean heavily on environmental supports' and argued that the 'human organism is linked with an external entity in a two-way interaction, creating a coupled system that can be seen as a cognitive system in its own right'. Under 'external entities' we list communities, milieu and places, material culture and, definitely, a home with its material contents as a meeting point of materialities, bodies and personalities.

Extended cognition, like cognition in general, embraces language, thinking, imagination, perception and memory as well as actions which allow people to interact with the world and engage in planning, decision-making, and problem-solving. It is these higher-level functions of the brain that underlie immigrants' activities related to home. Due to the coupling of an organism with external cultural factors, the active external features, home and its inward and outward elements have a direct impact on the people and their behaviour. Thus, home may be thought of as our external entity that houses memories of past events and images of the proper home fitting one's personality and defining our behaviour, thoughts and lifestyles in certain ways. The theory of extended cognition brings us closer to the interaction of the bodily, cognitive and material.

Interrelation of language, cognition and material culture

The close interrelation of language, cognition and material culture has been investigated in the emerging fields of cultural neuroscience, neurophilosophy and neuroarchaeology (Boivin 2010; Malafouris 2010a and 2019; Neidich 2014; Varela et al. 1991; Wolfe 2014). Grounding philosophical inferences in the synthesis of archaeology and neuroscience, researchers have proposed new concepts and theories – among them, the notion of the brain–artefact interface that relates to the point of intersection between cognition and material culture (Malafouris 2010b) and the Material Engagement Theory in which Lambros Malafouris (2013) underscores the inseparability of thought, action and material things. The neurobiologist Antonio Damasio (2010) has demonstrated the involvement of emotions in decision-making, memory and communication.

Seconding the role of emotions in human daily life, Alan Jasanoff, in his 2018 book, *The Biological Mind: How Brain, Body, and Environment Collaborate to Make Us Who We Are*, claims that emotions, as much as our brains, mediate how we perceive and interact with the world.

The works investigating co-dependency between mind, action, feelings and matter represent new research trends and resonate with a variety of issues connected with home, immigration and other social aspects of human life. The intricate interactions between multiple languages and the cultures associated with them, as well as migration trajectories, goals, time and reasons for immigration, produce utterly complex outcomes in terms of recreating and managing a home. Importantly, homemaking, the creation and management of a home, is of utmost importance for keeping a language for future generations of immigrants in multilingual settings (see the chapters by Kaluyga, Yelenevskaya, Protassova and Reznik, and Pilipenko in this volume).

The expansion of the margins of identity from brain and 'soul' to the body and the environment of an individual has implications that spill into day-to-day life, and especially so with regard to immigrants. Taking into consideration the multiplicity of interacting factors for immigrants in their homemaking, describing and investigating these processes is a challenging task. It is only in interrelation between many factors that we can identify the trends, tendencies and patterns of homemaking of Russian-speaking migrants. A framework that would contain and organise the complex reality of immigrant homecoming into manageable patterns is needed.

The Dominant Language Constellations (DLC) framework

The multiple languages with their accompanying cultures, changing settings and incessant new experiences and needs – everything that produces the reality of immigrants' life and homemaking – are better described if placed within a clear structure. This dynamicity and changing roles of languages may be captured by Dominant Language Constellations (Aronin and Vetter 2021; Lo Bianco and Aronin 2020). The DLC framework turns the multiple social and linguistic factors into a concise workable form. The DLC approach puts languages first, as the term indicates, but here 'language' is understood not just as a linguistic phenomenon but rather as one indivisible from and inseparably connected with the cognitive, psychological, cultural and physical aspects by which it operates in real life.

What is a DLC? Today's reality of superdiverse societies and their linguistic contexts have resulted in global transformations in the use of languages. It is *a set of languages* rather than a single language that operates as a unit of 'linguistic currency'. DLCs are clusters of key languages that individuals adopt to serve their immediate needs in their social environment. The famous words by Nabokov, 'My head says English, my heart, Russian, my ear, French', was the answer to an interviewer's question 'Which of the languages you speak do you consider the most beautiful?' This also points to his DLC (Nabokov 1964). The languages of a DLC function *as a unit* deployed according to the exigencies of practical life in a variety of domains in multilingual settings (Aronin 2019a and 2019b; Lo Bianco 2020).[1]

Unlike a linguistic repertoire, which embraces all skills and registers of all the acquired languages, the DLC includes only the most relevant languages for a given person at a particular time and space. For immigrants, the group of their most important languages normally includes the language of their origin, an official language of the host country and one or two other languages that are important to them. For example, DLCs of refugees to Norway, according to a study by Krulatz and Dahl (2021), variously consist of Norwegian Bokmål / English / Polish; Norwegian Bokmål / English / Lithuanian or others.

The DLC quality of being always context-bound (Aronin 2019a: 18) is definitive for immigrants. It is not only that linguistic behaviour acquires different qualities in different multilingual environments, but DLC also reflects social rhythms and timing and, therefore, is immediately indicative of any changes occurring to individuals and communities. Immigration and settling in another country always involve meaningful changes. Immigrants' linguistic and social transformations do not occur overnight; rather language and cultural practices change progressively, through constant fluctuations and adaptations to input from a wider society and then accommodation and negotiation of a new with the existing identity. A particular context and other contiguous languages present in certain settings influence DLC's dynamics based on inner interactions (between the languages of a DLC) and external interactions (input from a new host society). This can be associated with what Capra (2005: 33–4) calls 'the breath of life'. Such a 'metabolism' of a DLC unit, resulting from an interplay of multiple agents and factors of the change of context (immigration) and continual flow of modifications when accommodating previous languages, cultures, assumptions and mentalities within a new setting, produces the evolving immigrant's DLCs in a variety of diverse contexts and times.

With immigration and a consequent change in a linguistic and social environment and personal circumstances, some languages of a DLC may become less relevant to an individual while others become more expedient, and new languages may enter the DLC. A recent study by Anna Krulatz and Jennifer Duggan (2021) pointed out that, whereas some immigrants link their identities to one or several languages in their DLCs, others accept multilingualism as the core of their identity.

This volume provides evidence that the DLC of Russian-speaking immigrants is affected by both transnational and cosmopolitan discourses, as well as by adherence to particular cultures – Russian and that of the host country. As mentioned earlier, 'the DLC concept similarly places the focus of interest in academic analysis and description on *speakers' practices* as they are situated in social spaces, and therefore moves attention away from languages *per se*' (Lo Bianco 2021: 7). Thus, materialities can also be seen as following the DLC pattern. Language-associated contacts between cultures and lifestyles as well as other dimensions of human identity – emotional, cognitive and physiological – are condensed and tightly interconnected within each DLC (Aronin 2020: 24). Consider the example of a multimodal DLC – Russian/Hebrew/English – as described by Maria Yelenevskaya in this volume.

This wealth of aspects defines a DLC as a *multimodal entity*, that is, as a unit characterised by several different modes of activity or occurrence and as such applied to social and ethnological research. Cultures, traditions, lifestyles and world representations merge or coexist in a unit of DLC, reflecting a unique identity configuration of an individual and their home. The place-identity (Proshansky et al. 1983) and lifestyles of Russian speakers transpire through DLC patterns. The next section looks into immigrants' materially grounded transformations in their interconnectedness with languages. This accounts for the interrelations between language-materialities discussed in this volume. To this end, the notion of the *material culture of multilingualism* is put forward.

THE MATERIAL CULTURE OF MULTILINGUALISM

Materialities possess features that make them express social reality and social change with tangible clarity: solidity and concreteness; temporal tenacity and dynamicity in time, space, form and value, as well as three-dimensional indexicality (Aronin 2018). It should be clear from the interconnectedness of cognition, language, bodies and materialities discussed above that the field of investigation referred to here is not 'material culture' in general, or *just* places and materialities. The addition of 'of multilingualism' to the phrase 'the material culture of multilingualism' is meaningful. It outlines the field as specifically referring to the contemporaneous multilingual human condition whose aspects are variously indicated in literature as globalisation, the post-human era, superdiversity, new linguistic dispensation and current multilingualism. The main thrust of the material culture of multilingualism (MCM) that distinguishes it from otherwise-focused interest in materialities in ethnography or history is that the MCM is a fusion between materialities, cultures and languages.

So, what is the MCM? The term is used in two ways. First of all, the MCM is an assortment of material things and artefacts, places and events that are found in real life in the current multilingual world. Material culture includes physical objects encompassing an array of everyday objects, such as goods and products, food and utensils, furniture and pieces of art, medications and medical appliances, books and clay tablets of the past, pens and carpentry tools, roads, monuments and buildings. There are also technological objects that today constitute a large and important part of the global multilingual material culture. Technological artefacts such as computers, digital devices and the Internet, ATMs, fMRI machines, progressively more sophisticated prosthetic extensions and aids such as cochlear implants and artificial limbs, smartphones, or wearable computers such as smartwatches – all represent a particular category of language-defined objects and events. The realm of material culture also embraces various spaces, such as offices, factories and schools. Some scholars include intangible phenomena in the 'list' of items of material culture, such as sound waves and smells, rituals, events as well as organisations' decisions and procedures. The MCM is defined as 'a specific blend of materialities, originating from many cultures which constitute a multilingual society' (Aronin and Ó Laoire 2013: 228).

The second meaning of the term 'MCM' is *a theoretical framework* that reflects the reality of global materialities. This perspective merges several domains of knowledge, including but not exhausted by semiotics, pragmatics, globalisation studies, ethnography, migration studies, multilingualism and material culture. In a broad understanding, material culture is *a discourse* of a particular kind which expresses values, assumptions and ideas through material items (Aronin 2018: 34). Materialities 'talk', merging their 'voice', or rather 'touch', complementing and supporting verbal communication. In this, their function of merging with languages, the MCM is especially relevant to immigrants' homemaking. What kinds of material culture can we come across in immigrants' homes?

Objects of material culture relevant to studies in multilingualism are categorised as 'language-defined objects'. This term denotes 'a meaningful wholeness of material and verbal components considered as a representation of its user or users, or sociolinguistic environment' (Aronin and Ó Laoire 2012: 311). Normally, these are objects bearing inscriptions, decorative script, carvings or engravings or technological objects which contain language(s) 'inside' (in the software) and on them. The distinctive feature of language-defined objects is that *they exist as such only in the unity of their material and language constituents.* The physical component provides 'thingness', through its material properties such as size, form, smell, material and even physical availability, or distance, as in the case of monumental art; they are directed for a particular purpose (e.g., a cap for wearing on one's head, or a stone for commemoration having a particular shape and size). The verbal part enhances, modifies, specifies, marks or labels the physical component of an artefact through language or languages in various forms. Thus, language-defined objects represent the blend of 'thing' and linguistic properties out of which a meaningful wholeness and functional unity emerge and make things what they are. Banknotes of any currency would be a noteworthy example. To fulfil their particular function of circulation and exchange, banknotes are produced on special paper and have inscriptions that show their denomination (e.g. 500 roubles, 5 euros, 50 dollars). It is clear that neither the material quality of the banknote alone nor the inscription '100 euros' printed using the best possible font or colour on everyday paper would enable you to use it for purchasing goods or services. According to the degree of language presence in or on an object – that is, whether an inscription uses the letters of one, two or more languages, or of any language at all – language-defined objects can be divided into at least three types:

1. *Objects of material culture with inscriptions in several languages.* This category, besides all kinds of printed matter and billboards, includes containers, boxes, T-shirts, handkerchiefs, pens, vessels, cars, memorabilia, and even human bodies with tattoos and piercings (see, e.g., Roux, Peck and Banda 2019). Naturally, dwellings belong to this group of objects as today they normally contain inscriptions in multiple languages. These can be artefacts with texts, sentences, letters, hieroglyphs and various characters inscribed, engraved or carved, or images incorporating text.

    Technological objects may deserve special categorisation within this type of language-defined objects due to *a different kind of interplay between their material and verbal parts.* Although, like conventional non-electronic objects, digital devices bear inscriptions indicating their name and series, the name of the producer and other details, the major verbal content is 'inside'. Electronic objects also differ from non-digital material objects in the way they transcend space and time.
2. When contemplating the MCM, we should not only consider objects

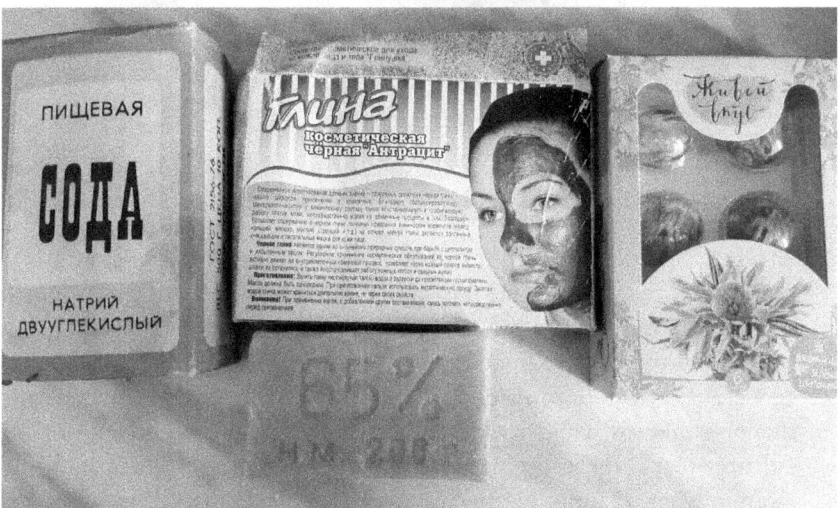

Figures 10.1a and 10.1b Language-defined objects with various languages maintained in one home (image courtesy of Ekaterina Protassova).

themselves in isolation, but how they are situated in a wider context. An object can be considered trilingual when the inscriptions are in two languages, and the settings include an additional one. Alternatively, the inscription on an object might be in one language, and the settings may include two additional ones (see Figures 10.1a and 10.1b).

Figure 10.2 The traditional Russian pastry *vatrushka* (image courtesy of Maria Yelenevskaya).

3. Artefacts and objects without an obvious linguistic component are also relevant to the MCM and play a big role in immigrant multilingual homes (see the examples in this volume). Such material objects bear features of the culture linked to a certain language, evoke associations and emotions, add knowledge, or stimulate behaviour, thus making the presence of a particular language or languages and culture or cultures real and meaningful. It often happens that such things found in an immigrant's home are emotionally charged for their owner. An example of such an object is a traditional Russian pastry, *vatrushka* (see Figure 10.2).

Consider matryoshka (nesting) dolls, metal trays from Zhostovo, delftware from Gzhel, samovars, Pavlovo Posad shawls, wall units (popular in the 1960s), and the crystal chandeliers found in many homes of Russian speakers. In folklore studies, such items are commonly referred to as 'ethnic objects' (see the contribution by Protassova and Reznik in this volume).

Jessner et al. (2018) add a fourth type of language-defined objects: paradoxically, the absence of a physical object. It is based on the quality of things to be emotionally charged even in their physical absence. Such situations are not rare for immigrants. The researchers explain:

> Memories and associations might be triggered by an object with no obvious deeper meaning for an outsider; a sound or smell of an object, for example, might trigger memories in an individual – in other words, the memories, connotations, associations and mental representations of a material existence. Objects or the absence of a concrete object are highly tied to people's individual perceptions and the meaning and interpretation one gives these phenomena. (Jessner et al. 2018: 118)

All the types of material objects described above display the unity of material and language constituents as they are in a mutual interrelationship with a wider physical environment and social arrangements. These are, for example, a range of objects described in the contributions by Protassova and Reznik, and Pechurina – in Russian homes in Finland and in the UK, respectively. The latter two types of language-defined objects remind us that two individuals with different background might not share the same perception of materialities and testify to a highly individual mode of manipulating with them. While virtually all the surroundings in the physical world contain linguistically defined and linguistically marked objects and events, one's ability and possibility to use objects and change their appearance, their location and their shape are superdiverse.

Along with objects and artefacts, the MCM takes into consideration actions, activities, emotions and reflections which together provide a unique insight into a particular important domain of human life – home. The next section is devoted to the multilingual materialities of home – first in general terms and then in reference to the homes and homemaking of Russian-speaking immigrants.

THE MULTILINGUAL MATERIALITIES OF HOME

To distinguish the general field of the MCM from its branch related to one domain of human life – home – we introduce the term 'multilingual materialities of home' (MMH). MMH include things, artefacts and places, as well as events in the framework of home life and its surrounding territory, and places that are purposed to have a homely atmosphere such as historic Russian restaurants in Los Angeles, as described by

Sasha Razor in this volume. MMH constitute a distinctive part of the MCM. The features and functions of the material culture of multilingualism described above acquire particular modifications in the home environment or in places that are prearranged with at least some functions of home.

Why is home so special a domain of human life?

It is hard to disagree with Edward Relph that home is 'the central reference point of human existence' (1976: 20). The sociologist John Urry examined the concept of *dwelling* in relation to Heidegger's writings (2000: 131–2) to uncover the engrained bond of an individual and a dwelling. Dwellings are opposed to other kinds of buildings, such as railway stations and bridges. A dwelling, according to this view, always involves staying with things, and a home is not separated from the people who live there. Urry further points out that the emergence of new mobilities rendered the modes of dwelling 'enormously more complex' and the patterns described by the sociologists of the twentieth century 'require extensive reconceptualisation' (Urry 2000: 136). Theoretical developments heavily linked home with identity, individual's emotions, memories and activities.

Home and identity

When considering the close connection between a home and the person who dwells in it, it is worth referring to the works of the environmental psychologists investigating identity in the 1970s–90s. They were keen to distinguish *place identity* as an important element of 'self-identity' (Proshansky et al. 1983). According to this line of research, place identity consists of knowledge and feelings developed through everyday experiences of physical spaces. This view resonates with the extended cognition perspective discussed in this chapter and connects home and its dwellers in one phenomenon as its internal and external elements. The present volume offers abundant evidence of the past – and memories, values and preferences – of Russian-speaking immigrants. In the contributions by Yelenevskaya, Protassova and Reznik, and Pechurina, we see how immigrants' dwellings and the artefacts belonging to them reflect their emotional and material past and perpetuation and/or changes in homemaking practices.

Notably, Proshansky et al. (1983: 62) stress that 'the cognitions or percepts preserved in memory are both highly selective and stylized'. The original memories, images and other cognitions recorded during childhood often change, especially if the individual is no longer part of that physical setting (ibid.). Such a change/stylisation is exactly what Nabokov did not wish to happen with his 'environmental past' when he answered the following question from an interviewer in 1964:

> *You spent 20 years in America, and yet you never owned a home or had a really settled establishment there. Your friends report that you camped impermanently in motels, cabins, furnished apartments and the rented homes of professors away on leave. Did you feel so restless or so alien that the idea of settling down anywhere disturbed you?*
>
> The main reason, the background reason, is, I suppose, that nothing short of a replica of my childhood surroundings would have satisfied me. I would never manage to match my memories correctly – so why trouble with hopeless approximations?

In this volume, the various modifications of past perceptions of home and memories are traced in Şahin's chapter devoted to Russian-speaking women immigrants to Turkey. For some of them the past spatial image of home 'expanded' from just their apartment to their whole village or city, as well as friends and relatives. And also 'home' in the previous homeland came to include their childhood and later life experiences.

Inside a home there can be things that acquire special significance in connection with self-identity, memories and family history over time. Feelings towards the 'old' and 'new' homes may be explained with the help of what social psychologist Irwin Altman and anthropologist Setha Low called *place attachment* – the bonding of people to place (1992). Researchers addressed the effects of such bonds in identity development, place-making, perception and practice, defining the ways in which people connect to various places. Low (1992) presented six types of overlapping cultural place attachments: (1) genealogical – links to family and places of origin; (2) narrative – links created through storytelling and place naming, loss and destruction; (3) links forged through disasters or migration; (4) economic – owning property or workplaces; (5) celebratory cultural events – links formed through participation in cultural events like concerts, religious ceremony or sports, and (6) cosmological – links formed through religious pilgrimage or connection to sacred religious sites. Later, in development of this concept, Jennifer Cross (2015: 501) proposed a framework of seven distinct interactional processes through which people create meaning and affective bonds with places: (1) sensory, (2) narrative, (3) historical, (4) spiritual, (5) ideological, (6) commodifying and (7) material dependence. Most of them proved relevant to the Russian-speaking immigrants described in this volume.

The perceptions and memories of home, whether exact or becoming imprecise after migration and the above processes of place attachment, are possible largely due to a special sensory knowledge that is derivable from material culture (Schlereth 1985: 12). Physical data provides us with a certain type of knowing, 'an affectivity mode of apprehension', as Jules Prown (1980: 280) put it. Emotions and feelings associated with home, homecoming and homemaking may be positive, indifferent or negative, but the feature of 'affective mode of apprehension' applies to many things in homes.

Home, emotions and activities

Importantly, place-identity, or the sense of belonging, does not depend solely on emotions and feelings, but largely on the degree to which *the activities important to a person's life* are centred in and around the home (Buttimer 1980; Proshansky et al. 1983). Activeness and influence can be exerted by a physical structure of home and specific things that allow for an activity. Let us consider several examples.

The autobiography (1960) by the famed prima ballerina of the Saint Petersburg Imperial Theatres, Matilda Kshesinskaya (1872–1971), holds evidence of an activity-directed attitude to her multiple dwellings and homes. It follows from Kshesinskaya's story that her first and foremost requirement for a dwelling, in addition to convenience and aesthetic value, was the capability to support her professional and social activities. Truly attached to Russia but having a cosmopolitan lifestyle, Matilda Kshesinskaya resided in numerous houses and domiciles in Europe and Russia, including an imperial salon-wagon lent for her tour across Russia to Kyiv, Baku and Tiflis by Prince Sergey Mikhailovich (1960: 247). She selected her apartments in such a way as to have ample space to accommodate guests, visitors and service people – her favourite housekeeper, Margo, her valet Arnold, and her son's tutors – as well as family members and social acquaintances. Perhaps, due to this 'set of conditions' consisting of space, things, people and activities, Kshesinskaya felt content irrespective of whether she was in Russia or in the estate she built on the French Riviera (1960: 232–7). Things changed when the ballerina arrived at the same house in Cap-d'Ail as an immigrant from Russia. She wrote:

> So, on 12/25 March 1920, on Thursday, after a six-year absence I came back again to my favourite villa 'Yallam' to start a new life of an immigrant. Naturally, I was happy to be in my home again where a lot of small things dear to my heart had been preserved.

And yet, the pain of my loss lingered on in my soul. I was pleased to see Margo, the cook, and Arnold who managed to take out photographs and albums reminding me of the wonderful past that was gone forever. (Kshesinskaya 1960: 321)

Later, when her financial situation worsened, Kshesinskaya faced the need to open a ballet studio in Paris in order to earn her living. And again, the main requirement for her new home concerned professional activities: '. . . to find a flat where we can live and which can also serve as a ballet studio' (1960: 352).

A home may be the activities and emotions expressed in domestic collections of things (Ros i Solé 2020), possessions of sentimental and personal meanings, such as a travel iron, tea towels or a dish for jellied meat (Kalyuga, this volume), or symbolic objects that are more than purely utilitarian (Yelenevskaya, this volume).

The role of technology objects for home

A comparatively new kind of activity that pervades contemporary homes is carried out with the help of computers, gadgets, smartphones and other technological items. Technological objects have become a manifest type of the MCM that can be found in almost any home. An example from day-to-day life is a trilingual keyboard with an opportunity to use various scripts, with Hebrew, Roman and Cyrillic characters on each key (Figure 10.3).

Technological objects transcend physical distance and often serve as a shortcut to feeling at home. For some Russian speakers, even having

Figure 10.3 Keyboard used to write in Hebrew, English and Russian.

other languages in their DLC – the screen and the programs set in Russian, and not in English or other languages – becomes an important feature that eases the first months of being far from their original home (see, e.g., Şahin in this volume). The digitalisation and *internetisation* of experiences of home and migration among women from Russia living in Japan are explicated by Golovina (this volume) through Maya's story (pp. 67–9). Maya has retained what is by today's standards an oversized satellite dish which reflects her initial emotional state when she first came to Japan and felt isolated.

Specific features of the multilingual materialities of home (MMH)

The scholarship on the topic and findings of this volume warrant singling out the following features of the multilingual materialities of home:

1. The MMH is a unique space when public, social and individual come together. Public and social considerations and personal preferences all work together and exert mutual influence.
2. Although the MMH is dependent on societal discourse and trends, it is to a great extent personal.
3. The material and spatial characteristics of home, on the one hand, and its dwellers and their traits, on the other hand, are mutually dependent and impact each other.
4. Despite the very practical purpose of a home, quite a portion of a home's interior are symbolic for its owner, displaying or hiding meanings, emotions, and the dwellers' attitudes to their past and present life.
5. The material culture of home plays at least two roles: first, it helps migrants to adapt themselves to a new environment and new stage of their life; and second, it allows those outside the Russian-speaking world to decode, understand and deal with Russian-speaking immigrants. Both possibilities of intercultural cognition via home and homemaking are precious for research and for the practical life in multilingual multicultural environments.
6. MMH is roughly delineated by a DLC of its owner. The dynamicity of languages and cultures are captured by the Dominant Language Constellations concept.
7. MMH is indexical in that it points to a stage in the development of one's identity. Arranging one's home and filling it with particular items is a material manifestation of the vital inner needs of one's identity. Constant negotiations between the social and the personal lead to fluctuations of identity.

8. Technological items have become inherent elements of the home, often especially useful for immigrants in terms of emotions, information and audio-visual connection with relatives and friends.
9. As in other areas of contemporary human life, superdiversity with regard to home and trajectories towards it is an attribute of immigrants' homes. The markers of diversity include time, space, the country's political and ethnic make-up, the individual's financial and emotional situation, family members, education, languages involved and previous lifestyles.

For research, the home culture and language associated with it provide both tangible and intangible data on immigrants, a remarkable cohort of people moving across the continents and countries, then staying put and rooted, or moving around relentlessly, and actively changing the world. The MMH should take its own place in research and aim at identifying tendencies, patterns and meaningful benchmarks in addition to established interpretive stances.

Some features of the homes of Russian-speaking immigrants

The MMH of Russian-speaking immigrants shares the general characteristics discussed earlier. With that, the present volume reveals some more specific features common to the immigrants whose DLC includes Russian. The features of superdiversity and technological objects becoming an indivisible part of 'home' are applicable to homemaking by Russian speakers and bearers of a Russian culture. Other features presented below arise only from the contributions of this volume and need to be further researched to be confirmed.

The variety in time periods, causes and circumstances of Russian-speaking immigrants and their personal journeys to their new homes presented in contributions to this volume is striking. The diversity the contributions reveal exists on a number of scales. The most visible is a wide variety of countries and times: interwar Russian refugees and the post-Soviet migrants in Greece (Kaurinkoski); the Russian community in San Javier, Uruguay (Pilipenko); women from Russia living in Japan (Golovina); the homes of Russian speakers in Finland (Protassova and Reznik); immigrants from Russia and Ukraine to Australia between 1980 and the 2000s (Kalyuga); Russian-speaking migrants in the UK (Pechurina); and first-generation immigrants to Israel from the FSU (Yelenevskaya). Other scales of diversity are the range of stances, from the cosmopolitan (compare Krulatz and Dahl's 2021 findings on the cosmopolitan stances of immigrants in Norway, described earlier in this chapter) to adherence to ethnic groups.

The contributions of this volume show that migrants negotiate other-than-Russian locations and cultures of their pre-immigration life such as Armenian, Azerbaijani, Bulgarian, Tatar and Kyrgyz (Şahin) and that the loyalties, memories and experiences related to these cultures are not to be ignored.

The functions of the home as seen by the Russians constructing new homes change after settling in another country. Immigrants differ in the ways they display Russianness (whatever one might mean by this) or belonging to Russian culture. They differ in the ways they present their affinities to the world and to the self in the process of building a new home and negotiating their identity. These differences are rooted in the manner of manifesting belonging in their country of origin. Moving to other geographical and social realities, in which other languages and cultures dominate, emigrants face the need to express their Russianness or absence of it in some way: home and homemaking are exactly the place and the time to stage such a manifestation. It appears that for a substantial part of Russian-speaking people from various backgrounds and different waves of immigration to different continents, activities linked to culture, arts and literature seem to be an important element of home.

The Russian language has a varied standing in the DLCs of Russian speakers. Proficiency levels of Russian and co-occurring languages, such as English, Finnish, German, Greek or Japanese, also differ. With that, the DLCs of Russian-speaking immigrants are categorisable into the group 'DLC-with-Russian'. It makes sense to collect DLC maps or DLC models with Russian to provide a pool and basis for further research and identification of DLC patterns. These would be useful for immigration studies, linguistic anthropology, education and political studies.

CONCLUSIONS

The theme of home for Russian speakers in diaspora – their language and material culture – is interdisciplinary. This chapter has emphasised the close interrelation of language, cognition and material world. The Dominant Language Constellations outline the cultural, material and linguistic life of multilinguals. The DLCs of Russian-speaking immigrants constitute a special category with its own particular features that is in need of further study. As a unit fusing language skills, emotions and materialities, each personal DLC is as unique as a fingerprint, though similar in their general pattern. As an extension of an individual, home embraces all the repercussions of the life of Russian-speaking immigrants whatever their origins, life trajectories, worldviews and activities in the past, present and future.

Like other immigrants in the world, Russian-speaking immigrants tell stories that are made striking by the variety of contexts in which they left their country of origin and in which they find themselves after migration. From their narratives we learn about their intentions, ambitions, life trajectories, memorable events and homes. The world of Russian-speaking immigrants and their homemaking, as shown in this volume, are superdiverse. The material culture of multilingualism (MCM) is a theoretical framework that brings together multiple aspects related to home, materialities, identity, and ethnic and national traditions. Most importantly, MCM treats language as an ineluctable part of multiple processes that converge in the concept and actualities of 'home'. The subdivision of the material culture of multilingualism that concerns home – the multilingual materialities of home (MMH) – displays distinctive characteristics.

The findings of this volume warrant further interdisciplinary studies of the historical and new realities of Russian-speaking migrants and their homemaking in search of their own identity. Accepting superdiversity and individual variation, along with looking for trends and patterns, seems to be the approach to follow.

NOTE

1 Domains, according to Fishman (1965: 94), are specific settings, a 'cluster of social situations typically constrained by a common set of behaviour rules' and as a 'social nexus which brings people together for a cluster of purposes' (1965: 75; 1965: 94). Fishman identified five domains: 'family', 'education', 'employment', 'friendship', 'government and administration'. Each domain is associated with a specific field of experience and the roles of participants, appropriate to its language variety and language behaviour.

REFERENCES

Altman, I., and Low, S. M. (eds) (1992), *Place Attachment*, New York: Plenum Press.
Aronin, L. (2018), 'Theoretical underpinnings of the material culture of multilingualism', in Aronin, Hornsby and Kiliańska-Przybyło (eds), pp. 21–45.
Aronin, L. (2019a), 'Dominant Language Constellation as a method of research', in E. Vetter and U. Jessner (eds), *International Research on Multilingualism: Breaking with the Monolingual Perspective*, Cham: Springer, pp. 13–26.
Aronin, L. (2019b), 'What is multilingualism?' in D. Singleton and L. Aronin (eds), *Twelve Lectures in Multilingualism*, Bristol: Multilingual Matters, pp. 3–34.

Aronin, L. (2020), 'Dominant language constellations as an approach for studying multilingual practices', in Lo Bianco and Aronin (eds), pp. 19–33.
Aronin, L. and M. Hornsby (2018), 'Introduction', in Aronin, Hornsby and Kiliańska-Przybyło (eds), pp. 1–17.
Aronin, L., M. Hornsby and G. Kiliańska-Przybyło (eds) (2018), *The Material Culture of Multilingualism*, Berlin: Springer.
Aronin, L. and M. Ó Laoire (2013), 'The material culture of multilingualism: moving beyond the linguistic landscape', *International Journal of Multilingualism*, 10:3, 225–35.
Aronin, L. and D. Singleton (2010), 'Affordances and the diversity of multilingualism', in L. Aronin, and D. Singleton (eds), *The Diversity of Multilingualism*, special issue of *International Journal of the Sociology of Language*, 205, 105–29.
Aronin, L. and E. Vetter (eds) (2021), *Dominant Language Constellations in Education and Language Acquisition*, Berlin: Springer.
Attfield, J. (2020), *Wild Things: The Material Culture of Everyday Life*, London: Bloomsbury.
Baudrillard, J. (1996/2005), *The System of Objects*, London: Verso.
Boivin, N. (2010), *Material Cultures, Material Minds: The Impact of Things on Human Thought, Society, and Evolution*, Cambridge: Cambridge University Press.
Capra, F. (2005), 'Complexity and life', *Theory, Culture and Society*, 22:5, 33–44.
Capra, F. (2015), 'The systems view of life: a unifying conception of mind, matter, and life', *Cosmos and History: The Journal of Natural and Social Philosophy*, 11:2, 242–9.
Clark, A. and D. J. Chalmers (1998), 'The extended mind', *Analysis*, 58, 7–19.
Cross, J. E. (2015), 'Processes of place attachment: an interactional framework', *Symbolic Interaction*, 38:4, 493–520.
Damasio, A. (2010), *Self Comes to Mind: Constructing the Conscious Brain*, New York: Pantheon Books.
Fishman, J. A. (1965), 'Who speaks what language to whom and when?,' *La Linguistique*, 2, 67–88.
Heidegger, M. (1993), *Basic Writings*, London: Routledge.
Jasanoff, A. (2018), *The Biological Mind: How Brain, Body, and Environment Collaborate to Make Us Who We Are*, New York: Basic Books.
Jessner, U., D. Unterthiner, S. Topf and M. Megens (2018), 'Multilingual awareness in Tyrolean material culture', in Aronin, Hornsby and Kiliańska-Przybyło (eds), pp. 113–30.
Krulatz, A. and A. Dahl (2021), 'Educational and career opportunities for refugee-background adults in Norway: a DLC perspective', in Aronin and Vetter (eds), pp. 109–28.
Krulatz, A. and J. Duggan (2021), 'Exploring identities and life stories of multilingual transnational couples through the lens of multilinguality and dominant language constellations', in Aronin and Vetter (eds), pp. 173–201.
Kshesinakaya, M. (1960/1998), *Memories*, Smolensk: Rusich.
Lo Bianco, J. (2020), 'A meeting of concepts and praxis: multilingualism, language policy and the Dominant Language Constellation', in Lo Bianco and Aronin (eds), pp. 35–56.
Lo Bianco, J. and L. Aronin (eds) (2020), *Dominant Language Constellations: A New Perspective on Multilingualism*, Dordrecht: Springer.
Low, S. M. (1992), 'Processes of place attachment', in Altman and Low (eds), pp. 87–112.
Malafouris, L. (2009), 'Neuroarchaeology: exploring the links between neural and cultural plasticity', *Progress in Brain Research*, 178: 251–9.

Malafouris, L. (2010a), 'Metaplasticity and the human becoming: principles of neuro-archaeology', *Journal of Anthropological Sciences*, 88, 49–72.
Malafouris, L. (2010b), 'The brain–artefact interface (BAI): a challenge for archaeology and cultural neuroscience', *Social Cognitive and Affective Neuroscience*, 5: 2–3, 264–73.
Malafouris, L. (2013), *How Things Shape the Mind*, Boston, MA: MIT Press.
Nabokov, V. (1964), Interview given to *Playboy*, available at <nabokov-lit.ru/nabokov/intervyu/playboy-1964.htm> (last accessed 16 November 2022).
Neidich, W. (2014), 'The mind's eye in the age of cognitive capitalism', in Wolfe (ed.), pp. 264–86.
Proshansky, H. M., A. K. Fabian and R. Kaminoff (1983), 'Place-identity: physical world socialization of the self', *Journal of Environmental Psychology*, 3:1, 57–83.
Prown, D. J. (1980), 'Style as evidence', *Winterthur Portfolio*, 15: 197–210.
Relph, E. (1976), *Place and Placelessness*, London: Pion.
Ros i Solé, C. (2020), 'Lived languages: ordinary collections and multilingual repertoires', *International Journal of Multilingualism*, DOI: 10.1080/14790718.2020.1797047
Roux, S., A. Peck and F. Banda (2019), 'Playful female skinscapes: body narrations of multilingual tattoos', *International Journal of Multilingualism*, 16:1, 25–41.
Schlereth, T. J. (1985), 'Material culture and cultural research', in T. J. Schlereth (ed.), *Material Culture: A Research Guide*, Lawrence, KS: University Press of Kansas, pp. 1–34.
Urry, J. (2000), *Sociology beyond Societies: Mobilities for the Twenty-First Century*, London: Routledge.
Varela, F. J., E. Thompson and E. Rosch (1991), *The Embodied Mind: Cognitive Science and Human Experience*. Boston, MA: MIT Press.
Vertovec, S. (2014), 'Reading "super-diversity"', in B. Anderson and M. Keith (eds), *Migration: A COMPAS Anthology*, Oxford: COMPAS, pp. 86–7.
Wolfe, C. T. (ed.) (2014), *Brain Theory: Essays in Critical Neurophilosophy*, Basingstoke: Palgrave Macmillan.

Index

action, 3, 205, 211–12, 219
adaptation, 15, 92, 97, 115, 130, 143, 157, 190–1, 198–9, 213
agency, 6, 35
agent, 3, 92, 213
alien, 7
alienate, 12, 198
alienation, 21, 198
ancestor, 2, 15, 199
anthropological, 78, 99, 164
anthropologist, 8, 78, 166, 221
anthropology, 1, 15, 167, 210, 226
artefact, 1–3, 11, 13, 68, 87, 98, 110, 115, 120, 165–7, 171–2, 180, 183, 202–3, 205, 211, 215–16, 218–20
association, 10, 49, 58, 66, 78, 93, 107, 218
attraction, 143, 189, 191
autobiographical, 46
autobiography, 222

background, 45–6, 55, 64, 110, 191, 219, 221, 226
bedclothes, 169
biographical, 45, 81
biographic object, 4
biography, 3, 14, 46, 48–9, 58, 120, 128, 141, 147, 166, 183

clock, 86, 170
cloth, 8, 86, 92, 101, 103–4, 168–9
clothing, 115, 141
co-ethnic, 7, 31, 199

collection, 12, 29, 33, 48, 52, 67, 83, 85–6, 88, 91, 99, 112, 119–20, 223
commodification, 119
communication, 2–6, 31, 56, 66, 68, 81, 148–51, 153, 155, 157, 167, 173, 182–3, 188, 191, 199–200, 211
consumer, 1, 12–13, 85, 107, 115, 168–9, 180
consumerism, 11, 168
consumption, 11–13, 44
contact, 6, 9, 12–13, 36, 121, 148, 150, 190, 199–200, 214
conversation, 8, 53, 67, 91, 146, 150–1, 153, 192
conversation analysis (CA), 166
country of origin, 7, 31, 87, 100, 105, 107, 197–8, 205, 226–7
craft, 49, 52, 67, 92, 105, 110
cross-border, 63
cross-linguistically, 7
cross-referencing, 64, 68
cultural identity, 43, 45, 203

decor, 46, 50, 64, 121–2, 133
decorate, 86, 90–1, 110, 122, 205
decoration, 8, 11, 79, 83, 89–91, 115, 120, 123, 183, 203
diaspora, 8, 21, 30, 37, 54, 79, 98, 115, 150, 205, 226
diasporan, 2, 6, 21
discourse, 3, 5, 21, 35, 71–2, 78, 119, 167, 214–15, 224

critical discourse analysis, 5
discourse analysis, 5
discursive, 8, 13, 15, 199
discursively, 31, 65
order of discourse, 5
disintegration, 33
display, 8–9, 11, 13, 44, 49–50, 52, 58, 83, 89–90, 101, 112, 169, 172, 204, 219, 226–7
dissatisfaction, 197
diversity, 45, 191, 209, 225
doll, 47, 49, 52–3, 83, 89, 93, 110, 143, 145, 182, 202–4, 218
domestic, 11, 31, 44–6, 48, 57, 72, 171, 189–90, 201, 223
domestically, 72
domesticity, 98–9
Dominant Language Constellation (DLC), 11, 211–14, 224–6

economic, 7, 14, 30, 37, 71–2, 81, 92, 114, 119, 189–90, 193, 221
economical, 115
economise, 177
economy, 8, 189
elite, 13, 29, 36
emigration, 3, 9, 14, 25, 37, 92, 120
emotion, 3, 7, 14, 49, 51, 56–8, 63–4, 69, 166, 211–12, 218–20, 222–4
emotion-loaded, 6
emotional, 3, 14, 21, 43–4, 51, 55, 57, 69, 73, 122, 183, 199, 203, 206, 209, 214, 220, 224
emotionally, 20, 197, 218–19
ethnic, 15, 111, 114–15, 202–3
  ethnic accessory, 204
  ethnic actor, 187
  ethnic belonging, 98, 197
  ethnic culture, 191, 197
  ethnic dish, 205
  ethnic diversity, 191
  ethnic enclave, 121
  ethnic factor, 191
  ethnic Finn/Finnish, 30, 90
  ethnic food, 44
  ethnic German, 30
  ethnic Greek, 22–3, 29–31, 33–4, 36
  ethnic group, 225
  ethnic handicraft, 203–4
  ethnic home, 188
  ethnic identity, 37, 110, 146, 203
  ethnic item, 50, 202–3
  ethnic Jewish, 30
  ethnic make-up, 225
  ethnic marker, 133
  ethnic meaning, 98, 112, 114
  ethnic object, 49, 83, 92, 209
  ethnic origin, 23–4, 37, 191
  ethnic (self-)representation, 203–4
  ethnic restaurant, 122, 136
  ethnic Russian, 12, 136, 190, 197
  ethnic souvenir, 203
  ethnic tradition, 227
ethnically, 22, 29, 194
ethnicity, 46, 209
ethnographic, 4, 166
ethnography, 5, 99, 210, 215
ethnocultural, 87, 110
ethnolinguist, 15
ethnolinguistic, 146
ethnological, 214
exhibition, 34, 119–20, 176
exile, 9, 21, 25–7, 121, 123, 135–7

feeling, 6–7, 21, 51, 54, 56, 58, 71, 81, 98, 107, 110, 123, 134, 175, 177, 179, 183, 194–8, 200–1, 209, 212, 221–2
  feeling of being at home, 37
  feeling of belonging, 34, 45
  feeling at home, 21, 46, 56, 188, 223
  feeling of home, 58, 64
feminine, 187
feminise, 187
former Soviet country, 70, 187, 189–90
former Soviet republic, 37
former Soviet Union (FSU), 12, 22–3, 29–31, 33–5, 89, 106, 164–5, 225
fraction, 27
furnish, 8, 57, 78, 137, 177, 201, 221
furniture, 6, 8, 31, 44, 82–3, 85, 88–9, 98, 121, 168–9, 176, 178, 183, 215
fusion, 6, 136, 215

gadget, 6, 11, 115, 173, 202, 223
gender, 36, 66, 100
gender role, 85
gendered division, 85
gendered role, 3

gendered space, 205
generation, 6, 12–13, 78, 84–6, 134, 136, 141, 149, 152–3, 164–5, 169, 182–3, 205, 212, 225
generational, 45, 178
gift, 48, 50–3, 84, 87, 89, 171–2, 174, 202–4
globalisation, 187–8, 215
Gzhel, 83, 110, 169, 218

handicraft, 98, 121, 203–4
heritage, 54, 136, 143
historian, 112
historic, 119, 121, 197
historical, 24–5, 48, 73, 80, 88, 111, 136
history, 3–4, 33–4, 48, 50, 79, 93, 120–1, 135, 137, 141, 176, 187, 192, 215, 221
home life, 5–6, 10, 184, 219
homecoming, 210, 212, 222
homemaker, 1, 173
homemaking (making home), xv, 6–7, 9, 13, 15, 21, 43–5, 49, 137, 164–5, 175, 188, 210, 212, 215, 219–20, 222, 224–7
hospitality, 10, 22, 177, 183
host society, 8, 10, 12, 21, 29, 34, 54, 81, 164, 213
household, 4, 9, 11–12, 63, 67, 69, 85, 89, 97–101, 105, 110, 112, 148, 168–9, 174, 176–7, 180, 183
householder, 8
human–object relations, 1
hybrid, 6, 31, 36, 82, 92, 131
hybridisation, 5
hybridise, 45
hybridity, 5, 15, 33

icon, 49–51, 80, 86, 89, 92, 111
iconic, 82
immateriality, 167
immigration, 10–1, 14, 44–5, 54–5, 97, 110, 125, 132, 134, 148, 164, 179, 183, 187, 191–2, 212–13, 226
    immigration experience, 164, 191–2
    post-immigration, 183
    pre-immigration, 79, 106, 110, 171, 182, 226
inscription, 68–9, 143–6, 216–17

integration, 7–8, 15, 29, 35–6, 56, 81
interaction, 4, 29, 31, 37, 65, 164, 166–7, 192, 195, 205, 211–13
interactional, 221
interdiscursivity, 5
interethnic, 141, 151
intergenerational, 71, 148, 179

Khokhloma, 83, 87, 110–11, 169, 204

lifestyle, 10, 11–15, 79, 92, 103, 110, 183, 190, 211, 214, 222, 225
lingua franca, 31, 37
local, 8, 11, 26, 29, 35–7, 56, 68–9, 81, 85, 88, 90, 93, 101, 103, 107, 115, 120, 128, 130, 142, 148, 151, 155, 172, 179–80
localise, 158
locality, 20, 30, 69
locally, 8, 101, 169
location, 20

material culture, 2–3, 11, 12, 14, 31, 35, 44–5, 57, 158–9, 164–5, 167, 210–11, 214–16, 220, 222, 224, 226–7
material culture of multilingualism (MCM), 215–16, 218–20, 223, 227
Material Engagement Theory, 211
material object, 43, 45, 57, 64, 69, 72, 78, 97, 216, 218–19
materiality, 11, 14, 43, 167, 209
matryoshka, 47, 49, 52–3, 83, 89, 93, 110, 143, 145, 202–4, 218
medical, 29, 67, 180, 215
medication, 11, 106–7, 180, 215
memorabilia, 13, 89, 98, 216
memorable, 173, 181, 183, 227
metaphor, 10, 69, 79
metaphorical, 79, 175
metaphorically, 120, 177
metonymic, 107
metonymically, 120
metropolis, 13, 66, 80, 143
migration, 9–12, 15, 21–2, 29–31, 33–7, 43–6, 49–50, 52–5, 57, 63, 65–6, 69, 71–2, 74, 78, 80, 85, 92, 97–8, 105, 107, 111, 114, 141, 144, 159, 164, 187, 189–91, 205–6, 209, 212, 215, 221–2, 224, 227

circular migration, 31, 188
educational migration, 191
international migration, 188, 205
labour migration, 191
marriage migration, 187, 189
migration experience, 44, 53–4
post-migration, 115
primary migration, 140
secondary migration, 140
mobility, 6, 20, 24, 36, 44, 64, 96, 188, 209, 220
multidimensional, 15, 43, 57
multilingual materialities of home, (MMH), 210, 219–20, 224–5, 227
multimodal, 210, 214
multimodality, 4

national food, 79
national home, 10, 79
national identity, 23, 37, 79
national tradition, 82
nostalgia, 10, 20–1, 26, 33–5, 37, 56, 69, 81, 92, 107, 109, 112, 121–2, 172, 183, 197–9
nostalgic, 7, 33, 35

painting, 8, 82–3, 86, 88–9, 92, 113, 121–3, 202–4
paraphernalia, 89, 119
pattern, 2, 5–6, 11–13, 69, 81, 110, 166, 183, 191, 197, 209–10, 212, 214, 220, 225–7
patterning, 3
possession, 3–4, 45, 49–50, 58, 84, 97–103, 105, 107, 110–14, 165, 171, 183, 202, 223
practice, 1–3, 6, 12–5, 44–6, 48–51, 58, 64, 90, 140, 153, 157, 165, 169, 179, 183, 188, 205, 210, 213–14, 220–1
pragmalinguistic analysis, 5

reaction, 21, 34, 198, 206
redecorate, 127
refrigerator (fridge), 89, 92, 180–1, 203
root, 20, 34, 36, 54, 79, 87, 90, 197, 199, 225–6
rootedness, 7, 31
rooting, 6
rootlessness, 30

routine, 12, 167, 200
Russian culture, 6, 31, 45, 79, 111, 225–6
Russianness, 6, 46, 55–6, 58, 64, 80, 83, 87, 89, 92–3, 98, 110, 120, 123, 160, 205, 226

samovar, 11, 48, 51, 83, 89, 110–11, 121, 218
satisfaction, 105, 183, 192–3, 197–8, 201
semiotic, 4, 5, 8, 67
semiotics, 4, 93, 99, 210, 215
smartwatch, 215
social media, 5, 81
socio-economic, 46, 71, 164, 189
sociolinguistic, 8, 215
sociolinguistics, 1, 4, 15
space and time, 64, 216
    spacetime, 209
    spatiotemporal, 66, 74
    spatiotemporality, 65
    time and space, 46, 68, 71, 74, 209, 213
stereotype, 55, 78, 89, 135
stereotypical, 52, 58, 98, 144
stereotypically, 52
story, xv, 4, 10, 25, 44–5, 48, 50, 57–8, 63–5, 67–9, 71–4, 84, 86, 130, 141, 149–50, 156, 159, 165–6, 171–2, 174, 176, 222, 224, 227
storytelling, 166, 221
style, 8, 12–13, 83, 89–90, 101–4, 110, 115, 127, 130, 178–9, 183
    cabaret-style, 121
    German-style, 131
    oriental-style, 135
    Russian-style, 90, 110
    Soviet-style, 47
stylisation, 221
stylish, 103
stylistically, 87
stylize, 134, 220
suitcase, 54, 90–1, 112, 189
superdiversity, 6, 210, 215, 225, 227
symbol, 2, 8, 10, 50, 74, 78, 82, 84, 90, 110, 114, 145, 174
symbolic, 3, 7–8, 10, 26, 54, 67, 83, 98, 110, 114–15, 145–6, 159, 169, 172, 174, 183, 223–4
symbolically, 64, 79

symbolise, 87, 98, 100
symbolism, 2, 9, 49, 68, 98, 114

taste, 8, 12, 44, 57, 85–7, 93, 100, 106, 110–11, 120, 180
technological, 111, 210, 215–16, 223, 225
technology, 6, 10, 98, 111, 188, 199, 200, 223
thematic analysis, 5, 166
toy, 11, 53
tradition, 7, 11, 15, 21, 37, 44, 78–80, 82, 90, 136, 140–1, 143, 164–5, 183–4, 187–8, 190, 194, 209, 214, 227
traditional, 49, 78–9, 85, 89–91, 105, 110, 127, 157, 194, 205, 218
traditionally, 106, 172
trajectory, 127–8, 135, 212, 225, 227
transform, 74, 93, 113, 167, 178, 205–6
transformation, 3, 69, 74, 93, 122, 144, 172, 210, 212–14
transformative, 50
transforming, 36, 201

translanguage, 192
translanguaging, 5, 182
tray, 11, 48, 83, 203, 218

uproot, 43, 97
uprooted, 33
uprootedness, 98
uprooting, 43, 55
utensil, 11, 169, 215
utilitarian, 3, 146, 169, 172, 174, 223
utility, 8, 53

value, 7, 11–12, 15, 21, 29, 37, 46, 48, 51, 54, 78, 84–6, 92–3, 98, 101, 103–4, 107, 110–11, 115, 164, 167, 172, 183, 187–8, 196, 214–15, 220, 222
value-loaded, 6
vase, 87–8, 101, 106, 170

watch, 88
wave, 14–15, 22, 34–5, 79, 97, 120–1, 134–5, 137, 226

EU representative:
Easy Access System Europe
Mustamäe tee 50, 10621 Tallinn, Estonia
Gpsr.requests@easproject.com

www.ingramcontent.com/pod-product-compliance
Lightning Source LLC
Chambersburg PA
CBHW071707160426
43195CB00012B/1607